the **BUILDING** in the text

# the **BUILDING** in the text

*Alberti to Shakespeare and Milton*

**ROY ERIKSEN**

The Pennsylvania State University Press
University Park, Pennsylvania

*Publication of this book has been aided by a grant from the Norwegian Research Council.*

Library of Congress Cataloging-in-Publication Data

Eriksen, Roy T.
The building in the text: Alberti
to Shakespeare and Milton / Roy Eriksen.
p.     cm.
Includes bibliographical references and index.
**ISBN 978-0-2710-2-7838**
1. Architecture and literature.
2. English literature—Early modern,
1500–1700—History and criticism.
3. Italian literature—16th century—
History and criticism.
I. Title.
PN56.A73 E42 2001
809'.93357—dc21
99–055273
CIP

Published by
The Pennsylvania State University Press,
University Park, PA 16802-1003

*for* **BERIT**

# CONTENTS

Although often a lonely task, writing this book has also been a collaborative effort in that colleagues, friends, and family have patiently shared their time and expertise with me during the years this book was in the making. My first thanks go to my wife, Berit, and our children, Erik and Frida.

At Castello di Vincigliata, Sunniva and Gidon Graetz provided us with what became our second home. Walter Kaiser generously invited me into the wondrous world of Harvard's Villa I Tatti, where Fellows and Staff provided a congenial atmosphere for productive work during my various stays from 1990 to 1996. I would particularly like to thank colleagues who patiently put up with my many questions and unfailingly offered valuable advice: Kathryn Bosi, Salvatore Camporeale, Paul Davies, Sabine Eiche, Amanda George, Mary Hollingsworth, Julian Kliemann, Thomas P. Roche Jr., Ingrid Rowland, and Patricia Rubin. I am indebted most to Paul Barolsky, Naso redivivus, to whom, for his friendship, wit, and wisdom, I owe more than I can express. Ever since I first met Ruth and Paul Barolsky in 1991, they have been a fixed point of reference, and I particularly look back with fond memories to stimulating encounters in Florence and Rome.

Across the seas in the United States, S. K. Heninger Jr., Jerry Leath Mills, Ellen Rosand, John Shawcross, and William E. Wallace have taken an interest in my work and given welcome encouragement.

In Rome, Magne Malmanger of the Norwegian Institute provided stimulating opposition, and in Frascati, Laura Visconti and Mario Fierli offered good companionship.

In Oslo, I am particularly indebted to Maren-Sofie Røstvig, who generously read and commented on the typescript, and to Olav Lausund, who inspired me to work on topics that later resurfaced in the present book. In Tromsø, Dag T. Andersson and Rolf Gaasland have shared my research interests and objectives.

Last but not least, my research was made possible by generous travel grants from the Norwegian Research Council for the Humanities (NFR) and the Humanities Faculty in the University of Tromsø.

Rome, June 1999

[I]magine that *Jerusalem Delivered* were a building of not too large dimensions, but well conceived with the measures and proportions of architecture; and suitably adorned with real friezes and colors.

—Camillo Pellegrino (1584)

This book explores the surprisingly understudied relationship between architecture and literature, how such essential expressions of Renaissance culture as writing and building draw on the same compositional ideals to produce what Walter Pater termed a "literary architecture." The notion of a close affinity between a building and a well-crafted poem seen in Pellegrino's comment on Tasso is firmly rooted in classical periodic rhetoric. The relationship was succinctly formulated by the first-century rhetorician Demetrius, who wrote: "The members in a periodic style may, in fact, be compared to the stones which support and hold together a vaulted dome."[1] It is clear that Renaissance humanists and poets zealously studied the classical art of composing periodic sentences. In *Giotto and the Orators* Baxandall observes that "the periodic sentence is the basic art form of the early humanists" (p. 21). Indeed, in the Renaissance "the analytical vocabulary of rhetoric and art is one entity,"[2] and the formal properties of the period furnish artists and poets with a miniature model for shaping a larger compositions. These properties are embodied not only in the syntactic structure of periods but also in the rhetorical figures deployed to mark the balanced and cyclical form of periodic sentences.[3] Thus words were repeated to indicate the beginning, middle, and end of a composed whole, in order to make the sentence formally analogous to the vaulted dome described by Demetrius.

Such thinking may seem strange to modern readers, but let us consider how this analogy was applied in practice. Take, for example, a sentence in Augustine's "Enarratio in psalmum CXXIX," where the father of Christian rhetoric argues that man should be in accord with the word of God:[4]

Est enim Dei adversarius tuus, quamdiu *cum* illo non *concordas.*
*Concordas* autem, *cum* coeperit te delectare facere quod dicit *sermo.*

[For *the Word of God* is thine adversary, as long as *thou dost not agree* with it. *But thou agreest,* when it has begun to be thy delight to do what *God's Word* commandeth.] (Italics added)

Augustine articulates in the sentence's antithetical structure the very idea of unity with the Word of God by qualifying the initial statement with the phrase "[b]ut thou agreest" and by balancing his own words: *sermo . . . cum . . . concordas / concordas . . . cum . . . sermo.* His sentence structure thus makes the meaning visible on the page, as it were. If we imagine that these repetitions occupy positions on a curve, that curve could be said to be formally analogous to the section of "a vaulted dome," to borrow Demetrius's phrase, or again it may be seen as a triangle or a pyramid (see diagram).

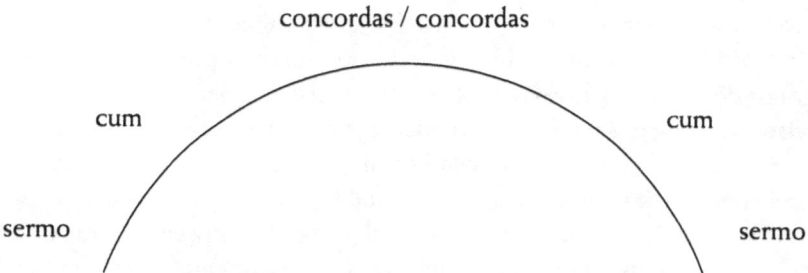

concordas / concordas

cum          cum

sermo          sermo

In a comment on such well-crafted writing in Dante, the Florentine humanist Cristoforo Landino praises precisely the harmony that arises from the use of such repetitions: "And this is wonderous; the way in which the colors [of elocution] combine with form so that the effect of both is doubled, because one takes ornament from the other."[5] Augustine's practice and Landino's comment illustrate the vital role of rhetorical ornament in composition, a role reflected in Brian Vickers's caveat that "modern disapproval of stylistic rhetoric is wholly unhistorical."[6]

The analytical method that examines the distribution of rhetorical markers to clarify the structure and plot of a text I have termed *topomorphology.*[7] The method entails studying the design and distribution of topoi (that is, "places" and "themes") within the structure (*morphē*) of a text—hence *topomorphology.* In other words, in the analysis of written compositions topomorphology considers the spatial relationships and the shape of segments within a text as an aid to interpretation, while in the arts it considers the integration and distribution of parts on a pictorial plane, or within the plan for an edifice.[8] Topomorphology is not a modern invention, because Aristotle's definition of the period in *The Rhetoric* presupposes precise visibility and distribution in space: it is "a portion of speech that has in itself a beginning and an end, being at the same time not too big to be taken in at a glance."[9] In this respect his definition implies *enargia*, the light or the visual effect produced by rhetorical ornament, a fact confirmed by his own use of cyclical repetitional patterns in his definition of long periods.[10]

To introduce the reader to the broad theme of this study, I present a few examples that illustrate how to read topomorphically. The first example is the opening stanza of an English philosophical poem, *A Treatise of Humane Learning*, by the humanist, poet, and politician Fulke Greville:

> *The Mind of Man* is this *worlds* true dimension;
> And *Knowledge* is the measure of the mind:
> And as the minde, in her vast *comprehension*,
> Combines more *worlds* than all *the world* can finde:
> So *Knowledge* doth itselfe farre more extend,
> Than all *the minds of Men* can comprehend.[11]

As Torquato Tasso reminds us, the first stanza of poems was often a place for a certain artifice: "[it] should be full of grandeur, magnificence and splendor, like the facade of palaces."[12] That is the case here too. Greville has created a form of verbal harmony that unites the stanza and articulates the beginning, middle, and end of the stanza in accord with the Aristotelian formula for wholeness.[13]

Notable is the chiasmus (inverted repetition) that frames the entire stanza by verbally linking lines 1 and 2 ("the Mind of Man," "Knowledge") to lines 5 and 6 ("Knowledge," "the minds of Men"). In addition Greville creates a double verbal link between the beginning and the middle ("worlds" versus "world"), and the middle and the end ("comprehension" versus "comprehend"). These highly visual interlocking configurations serve to unify and to emphasize the argument that although the mind of man is the measure of the world, it cannot grasp the "vast comprehension" of Knowledge itself. Accordingly, the final, emphatic position is reserved for recognition of what man cannot "comprehend." Thus the stanza spatially encapsulates the theme of the whole poem in the way that the frontispiece of, for example, Vincenzo Scamozzi's *L'idea dell'architettura universale* does for that work (Fig. 1).

FIG. 1
Architectural frontispiece, Vincenzo Scamozzi, *L'idea dell' archittetura universale*
(Vinegia, 1615)

Greville's stanza is an example of special artifice, functioning as the lavishly decorated doorway into the work. Of course, such art does not regulate all levels of written composition in the Renaissance, but the rules of periodic rhetoric were often put to good use to provide emphasis. An example is the sonnet, a short form of lyric that is antithetical and circular in terms of its argumentative structure and religious subtext. This fact is seen most strikingly in the codified division of the Italian sonnet into eight plus six verses in accordance with an accompanying change in the argument (the *volta*) after the octave.[14]

If we turn to the elocutionary pattern of an early sonnet, Giacomo da Lentini's "M'aggio posto in core il mio Signor servire" ("I have set my heart on serving God"), we note that the poet repeats words to delineate the sonnet's main division, inverting two words from the final line of the octave (*"estando da la mia donna diviso"*; "being separated from my lady") in the last of the sestet (*"veggendo la mia donna in ghiora stare"*; "beholding my lady standing in glory"). We see literally on the page how the inversion of similar words serves to mark the poet's positive reinterpretation of his separation from his lady, for at the end of the sonnet he is consoled by that fact that she now resides in glory. The passage from mundane grief to celestial celebration has been accomplished and made visible.

The practice of marking the structural and thematic divisions of a sonnet visually becomes a salient trait in several of Petrarch's sonnets,[15] a particularly full example being *Il Canzoniere 140*, "Amor, che nel penser mio *vive* e regna"; ("Love, who lives and reigns in my thoughts"). The sonnet displays clear verbal linkages between the first lines of the octave and the first and last lines of the sestet.[16] The relations thus established between the main phases in a sonnet's argument became an integral part of sonneteering. It therefore comes as no surprise to find that Michelangelo, in the sonnet "Non vider gli occhi miei cosa mortale," shapes his poetry in the same manner when describing how the external beauties of his lady serve as a ladder to the vision of celestial beauty:

> Non vider gli occhi miei cosa *mortale*
> Allor che ne' bei vostri intera pace
> Trovai, ma dentro, ov'ogni mal dispiace,
> Che *d'amor l'alma* a sé simil m'assale;
> E se creata a Dio non fusse eguale,
> Altro ch 'l bel di fuor, c'agli occhi piace,

Più che vorria; ma perch'è sì fallace,
Trascende nella forma universale.
  Io dico c'a chi *vive* quel che *muore*
Quetar non può disir; né par s'aspetti
L'eterno al tempo, ove altri cangia il pelo.
  Voglia sfrenata el senso è, *non amore,*
*Che l'alma* uccide; e 'l nostro fa perfetti
Gli amici qui, ma più per *morte* in cielo.[17]

[Verbal repetitions are italicized]

My eyes did not see any mortal object
When I found complete peace in your beautiful eyes,
But saw within them where every evil's despised,
Him that invests [afflicts] my soul, so like him, with love.
For if my soul weren't created equal to God,
It would wish for nothing more than outward beauty,
Which pleases the eyes; but since that's so deceptive,
It rises beyond that, to the universal form.
I say that, for one who lives, whatever dies
cannot appease desire; nor can the eternal
Be sought in time, where human flesh still alters.
Unbridled desire is merely the senses, not love,
And slays the soul; our love makes us perfect friends
down here, but even more, through death, in heaven.

Michelangelo marks off the borders of the sonnet's principal divisions with repeated words—"mortale" (1), "muore" (9), and "morte" (14)—in accord with the techniques practiced by da Lentini and Petrarch. In addition, he introduces a chiastic structure to underline how his eyes find beauty not in the outward vision but solely in the inward vision prompted by his lady's eyes. This mirroring structure (*occhi . . . bei . . . ma dentro* versus *bel di fuor . . . occhi*) also helps to unify the two parts of the octave, thus reinforcing its enclosing rhyme structure. Possibly to counteract this centripetal effect within the octave, Michelangelo not only unites the first quatrain together with the last tercet by means of the verbal link of *mortale-muore* (1; 14), but also repeats the words "love" and "soul" from line 4 ("chi *d'amor l'alma* a sé simil m'assale") in lines 13–14 ("non *amore,* / che *l'alma* uccide"). When he joins his sonnet together in this fashion, Michelangelo reveals himself to be a master with words, demonstrating a capacity to fortify with pen on paper or to draw outlines ("d'intornare") with rhetorical figures. Such figures may not be impressive, but they clearly ensure cohesion and—to stay within the theme of the sonnet—serve as visible steps to the interpretation of the text. Then too, as Renaissance poets elaborated on the sonnet form, they developed this technique to become an art in itself.

Ideally, the sonnet functions just like Aristotle's period as a whole, to be surveyed in its entirety more or less at once—Michelangelo's rhythmically distributed repetitions being a case in point. This process is akin to how one looks at a figure poem, a mosaic, or a plan for a building, but it requires greater active participation because most patterns (with the exception of rhymes and anaphoras [repetition in initial position]) are embedded in the body of the text. With this in view let us consider the mannered playfulness of one final example, Shakespeare's Sonnet 129:

1    Th' expense of spirit in a waste of shame
        Is *lust* in *action*, and till *action*, *lust*
        *Is* perjured, murd'rous, bloody full of blame,
        Savage, *extreme*, rude, cruel, not to trust,
5    *Enjoyed* no sooner but despised straight,
        *Past reason* hunted, and no sooner *had*
        *Past reason* hated as a swallowed bait,
        On purpose laid to make the taker *mad*.
        *Mad* in pursuit and in possession so,
10   *Had*, having, and in quest, to have *extreme*,
        A bliss in proof and proved, a very woe,
        Before a *joy* proposed behind a dream.
          All this the world *well knows* yet *knows* not *well*,
14     To shun the heaven that leads men to this hell.

[Verbal repetitions are italicized]

The rhyme-scheme identifies the poem as an English sonnet of twelve lines with cross rhyme plus a couplet. The various extrasyntactic structures—chiastic patterns, antitheses, parallelisms, and other minor repetitions—are the visual result of deliberate aesthetic choices of a more personal nature, examples of individual poesis. They may be explained in two ways: to the eye of a trained reader, the repetitions will be immediately evident, whereas for a reader not trained to spot them they would function as manipulations grasped on a subliminal level. In both cases, though, the repetitions unquestionably produce a pattern that strengthens the sense of unity in the poem, at the same time that its circularity reinforces the vicious circle of sexual passion that grips the persona. In terms of style, the sonnet can therefore be said to exemplify the artifice of what has been called literary mannerism.[18]

Equally evident in the sonnet is Shakespeare's playful attitude toward the underlying formal subtext of the Italian sonnet, particularly the traditional division into a sequence of eight plus six verses. The Italian style is recognized by the placement of a rhetorically marked *volta* after the octave, and in the puns on spirit, heaven, and hell in the opening and concluding verses. The octave thus exhibits two "embedded" quatrains identified by the use of *anaphora* in verses two and three *("Is* lust . . ."; *"Is* perjured . . .") and six and seven *("Past reason* hunted . . ."; *"Past reason* hated . . ."), which produces a striking typographical effect. Sorting out these anaphoric repetitions, we see that the other repetitions create a pattern centering on the iteration of the thematically significant word "mad" in verses eight and nine. The figure used is *climax*, that is, the final word of the second quatrain ("mad") is repeated as the first word of the third quatrain. The pattern is as follows:

> spirit . . . shame   (antithesis)
> lust . . . action . . . action . . . lust   (chiasmus)
>
> well . . . knows . . . knows . . . well   (chiasmus)
> heaven . . . hell   (antithesis)

The various types of carefully plotted repetitions in the poem emphasize the traditional break that occurs after eight verses in the Italian sonnet. The effect is therefore one of almost perfect mirror symmetry.[19] In Shakespeare's sonnet, however, the effect is not accompanied by a new direction in the argument. Instead we have repetition without development around a visually framed center, when the poet continues with the word "Mad" at the beginning of verse nine. In terms of theme, therefore, this emphasizes the strife between lust and reason that is basic to *The Sonnets* as a whole.[20]

These compositional procedures are inevitably tied to the concept of design as practiced in the arts, and architecture and painting in particular. As an exploration of the tectonics of literary and artistic texts and its relation to architectural theory, this study has no intention of discovering laws. It aims instead at a description of actual practice, which makes it necessary to speak of an architecture of the text.[21]

I therefore argue that Renaissance aesthetic theory and practice reveal an impulse to control the various systems of signification that reproduce and communicate the artist's initial idea. This urge to control form emerges as a will to impose order in an act of composition that will make "discordance appear concordant."[22] On the other hand, it may appear as a deliberate play with or dramatization of the borderline between coherence and incoherence.

This book concentrates primarily on how writers designed their writings, weaving them together visually both on a micro-level and on a macro-level. My approach is interdisciplinary: in addition to studying traditional literary genres, I also analyze treatises on art. In other words, this book pursues the interplay between aesthetic concepts and compositional practice in both poetry and architecture. The texts analyzed are mainly written between the first half of the fifteenth century and the end of sixteenth. However, for the sake of comparison and to provide perspective, examples dating from antiquity, the Middle Ages, and the seventeenth century have been included, but without any pretense about being a comprehensive history.[23] The book will also show how Renaissance writing and artistic theory share a common ground in a small body of formal devices ultimately originating in periodic rhetoric.[24]

Although the architectural design in Renaissance writing often occurs without accompanying architectural metaphors or technical terms, many of the works examined in this book have been chosen with a view to illustrating how often architectural metaphors are essential to Renaissance notions of artistic creation—a surprisingly understudied phenomenon in Renaissance studies. Modern readers are not apt to readily recognize the compositional practices that were applied, possibly because those practices may be all too visible.[25] By focusing on elocution as a clue to form, this book therefore addresses the intriguing nexus between ornament and inner structure and the shared aesthetic ideas that allowed Renaissance artists, theoreticians, and poets to use rhetorical terms to describe buildings in the language of writing, and poetry as a form of architecture.

## Architecture and the Art of Plotting

> These are the Arkes the Trophies I erect,
> That fortifie thy name against old age,
>
> —Samuel Daniel, *Delia* 46.9–10

What are the formal implications for Renaissance writers of their poems as buildings or paintings? Does the metaphorical thinking reflected in a title like *The Temple* point to something crucial in Renaissance aesthetics and composition, or does it merely point to pleasant but unproductive embellishment? This study tries to answer these questions by outlining some of the ways in which architectural metaphors and principles of composition function in Renaissance literature and writings on art. Let us begin by considering a practical example. A speech in Shakespeare's 2 *Henry IV* brings sharply into focus the alignment between notions of textual and architectural plotting. The speaker is Lord Bardolph and the scene is one of conspiracy, the other noblemen present being Lord Hastings and Lord Scroop. They are in the process of plotting high treason, calculating the risks involved when trying to overthrow King Henry:

36    Yes, if this present quality of war—
       Indeed the instant action, a cause on foot—
       Lives so in hope, as in an early spring
       We see th'appearing buds; which to prove fruit

40      Hope gives not so much warrant, as despair
         That frosts will bite them. When we mean to build,
         We first survey the plot, then draw the model,
         And when we see the figure of the house—
         Then must we rate the cost of the erection,
45      Which if we find outweighs ability,
         What do we then but draw anew the model
         In fewer offices, or at last desist
         To build at all? Much more, in this great work—
         Which is almost to pluck a kingdom down
50      And set another up)—should we survey
         The plot of situation and the model,
         Consent upon a sure foundation,
         Question surveyors, know our own estate,
         How able such a work to undergo,
55      To weigh against his opposite; or else
         We fortify in paper and in figures,
         Using the names of men instead of men:
         Like one that draws the model of an house
         Beyond his power to build it; who, half through,
60      Gives o'er, and leaves his part-created cost
         A naked subject to the weeping clouds,
62      And waste for churlish winter's tyranny.

(I.iii.35–62)

Lord Bardolph here outlines the very real dangers involved in such an enterprise. The speech mixes a number of suggestive images drawn from economy and architecture, but I want to concentrate on those relating to the building of a house: "plot of situation," "figure of the house," "erection," "survey," "model," "offices," "foundation."[1] Today "plot" most frequently denotes literary structure, but here the term has other connotations as the speech progresses; in fact, it suggests all four meanings listed by Peter Brooks in *Reading for the Plot*:

    1. (a) A small piece of ground, generally used for a specific purpose.
       (b) A measured area of land; a lot.
    2. A ground plan, as for a building; chart; diagram.

3. The series of events consisting of an outline of the action of a narrative or drama.
4. A secret plan to accomplish a hostile or illegal purpose; scheme.[2]

Surprisingly, Brooks half dismisses the view that there may be a connection between these various and heterogeneous senses, except for a certain "subterranean logic." I believe, however, that the logic involved is concretely "terranean" in its strong insistence on place, as in the phrase "plot of situation."

In the speech, we witness the preparations for a coup d'état; plot as used by Shakespeare here also assumes the sense of a plan for later action, as in the French *complot*, current already in the 1590s.[3] Moreover, because Lord Bardolph's speech discusses a line of action that coincides with the ensuing dramatic action, "this great work—to pluck a kingdom down," "plot" here would also denote the "outline of the action of a . . . drama" as in (3) above. Hence the structure of the speech may tell us something about how a work was planned and put together in an architectural sense of the word.[4] Let us begin by investigating how the patterns on the page reflect and embody the artist's initial idea and its realization as *dispositio cum* rhetorical ornament. The purpose, therefore, is severely practical.

Although I do not offer an analysis of 2 *Henry IV,* the emphasis on form in the speech may possibly tell us something of Shakespeare's emplotment of the rebels' abortive plot. The rebellion against King Henry may briefly be said to complete the triangular rise-fall pattern found in tragedy in general, ending with the rebels' defeat later in the play. Examining the imagery and rhetorical structure of Bardolph's speech, we discover a similar rise-fall pattern, which virtually turns the speech into an example of proleptic anticipation. The speech centers on what might result if the rebels should fail to prepare a viable plan and raise the required resources, a theme expressed in terms of a reworked biblical metaphor.[5] Thus in Luke 14:28–30, we read about the dangers of improvident building:

28    which of you minding to buylde a towre, fitteth not downe before, and counteth the cost, whether he haue sufficient to performe it,

29    Lest that he after he hathe laid the foundation, and is not able to performe it, all that beholde it, beginne to mocke him,

30 Saying, This man began to buylde, and was not able to make an end?

The topos of a roofless house is an apt vehicle for a potential failure, particularly when the aim is to establish a new royal "house." Shakespeare strengthens this metaphorical thread considerably by adding images of change. In fact, the seasonal symbolism here approximates that of Northrop Frye's "mythos of tragedy" in its movement from the initial mention of "early spring" and "buds" bearing the prospect of "fruit," to the concluding emphasis on "weeping clouds," "waste," and "churlish winter's tyranny" (61–62). This movement is also underscored by the stress on hope in line 38 and abandonment in line 60 ("gives o'er"), indicating the transition from optimism to despair so typical of tragedy. In terms of the distribution of topoi within the speech, we observe that the references to seasonal change enclose the main body of the speech, where architectural metaphors are dominant (41–59). The two strands of metaphor merge, however, in the expression "to pluck a kingdom down" in the central line 49, in which the verb "to pluck" harks back to "fruit" in line 39. The two strands are also woven together in the segment's concluding lines (58–62). In this sense the speech emerges as a unified structure in which verbal and conceptual recurrences link its beginning, middle, and end.

 We furthermore note within the main body of the speech how the lines drawing on architectural metaphor fall into two sections. In an initial long period comprising lines 41–48, building proper is described, whereas the building metaphor is directly linked with the planning and implementing of the rebellion in the ensuing nine lines (48–57). If we outline the main topoi of the speech in terms of imagery, we discover the following symmetrical distribution:

| | |
|---|---|
| Seasonal imagery ("early spring") | lines 36–41 |
| Images of building proper | lines 41–48 |
| Images of building applied to the rebellion | lines 48–60 |
| Seasonal imagery ("Winter's tyranny") | lines 61–62 |

In terms of planning, we register that the desired change from one royal house to another ("to pluck a kingdom down / And set another up") is situated in line 14 at the exact numerical center of the twenty-seven-line speech.[6] It would therefore be appropriate to see this as the speech's peripety and as a kind of miniature version of the function of plot reversal in the play as a whole.

It is obvious that Shakespeare chose the biblical metaphor to undermine the legitimacy of the rebels' cause and to plot their final defeat, because the relevant verses in Luke stress the necessity of building on the word of God. The passage communicates an obvious moral lesson, which combines the need for prudent planning and the moral aspects of architecture as *aedificatio* in humanist thought.[7] The rebels are bound to fail in their attempt, their failure being implicit in the very speech in which they begin to plot. The New Testament offers a source for Lord Bardolph's building metaphor, but the biblical passage also embodies a simple chiastic structure similar to the balanced pattern of topoi in Lord Bardolph's speech. The structure is created when two verbs are repeated in a chiastic pattern ("to buylde," "to performe" [v. 28] versus "to performe" [v. 29], "to buylde" [v. 30]), providing a rudimentary pattern for Shakespeare to develop. We discover that this pattern is based on scriptural authority when we consult the Vulgate text of these verses (14.28–30):

28     Quis enim ex vobis volens turrem aedificare
       non prius sedens conputat sumptus
       qui necessari suntsi habet ad perficiendum

29     ne posteaquam posuerit fundamentum
       et non potuerit perficere
       omnes qui vident incipiant inludere ei

30     dicentes quia hic homo coepit aedificare
       et non potuit consummare.

Here we note a similar antithetical structure. Although the four repeated verb forms *aedificare, perficiendum, perficere,* and *aedificare* form an inverted pattern, the Latin version is overtly more rhetorical in its greater reliance on alliteration and parallelismus.[8] Antithetic parallelism, it has been said, "points beyond itself, linking the particular and the individual to the eternal and the infinite."[9] Shakespeare reproduces a similar pattern in the second period of Bardolph's speech, where the phrases "mean to build," "draw the model," "draw anew the model," and "desist to build" closely follow the New Testament pattern. Bardolph's speech functions in a way not unrelated to Jasper's description of the figure: it points beyond itself to the "great task" in hand as well as to its biblical origin and superstructure. In this referential dichotomy resides the very irony of the speech.

The New Testament passage cannot be said to account fully for Shakespeare's emplotment of Lord Bardolph's speech, despite its importance for Renaissance authors. Not only is Bardolph's speech far longer than its scriptural source, it is also metaphorically far richer. Indeed, the ideas in it also suggest a relationship with such influential poetic manuals as Geoffrey de Vinsauf's *Poetria nova* (c. 1207–16), which was to remain a popular text for more than three centuries.[10] De Vinsauf is particularly important for an understanding of literary structure and architecture because he specifically relates architectural planning to poetic creation. In the section on "The Invention of Matter and of Expression" he writes:

Siquis habet fundare domum, non currit ad actum
Impetosa manus: intrinseca linea cordis
Praemetitur opus, seriemque sub ordine certo
Inferior praescribit homo, totamque figurat
Ante manus cordis quam corporis; et status ejus
Est prius archetypus quam sensilis. Ipsa poesis
Spectet in hoc speculo quae lex sit danda poetis.

(43–49)

[If anyone is to lay the foundation of a house,
his impetuous hand does not leap into action:
the inner design of the heart measures out the work before,
the inner man determines the stages ahead of time in a certain order;
and the hand of the heart, rather than the bodily hand,
forms the whole in advance, so that the work exists first
as a mental model rather than as a tangible thing.
In this mirror let poetry itself see what law must be given to poets.]

(17)

Following immediately upon de Vinsauf's prefatory address to Innocent III, this passage introduces the treatise proper. Thus it offers an important statement stressing the ethical function of poetry; the poem is seen both as spiritual edification and as verbal artifice. Then too the devotional and moral aim is made evident in the poetic samples included, some of which will be dealt with in Chapter 2. The lesson taught in Luke 14:28–30 has been internalized, as it were, in de Vinsauf's passage. But the Bible is not the only source or point of reference. Equally striking are the visible signs of a structural aesthetics couched in architectural terms in the commentary on creation written by Philo Judaeus.[11] As we saw in Shakespeare's speech, de Vinsauf uses verbal patterning to reinforce what the words convey. He concludes his remarks on abstract planning by claiming that it constitutes a mirror for poets to imitate: "Ipsa *poesis* / *Spectet* in hoc *speculo* quae lex sit danda *poetis*" (48–49, italics added).

"In this mirror let poetry itself see what law must be given to poets." The phrase invites the reader to perceive its balanced structure a-b-b-a (*poesis* / *spectet* / *speculo* / *poetis*). The structure reflects a compositional practice according to which "the inner line of the heart" ("intrinseca linea cordis") "figures forth the whole" ("totamque figurat"), to use de Vinsauf's own words. These are terms that will reappear in such Renaissance writers as Alberti, Vasari, Tasso, Sidney, and Shakespeare, frequently accompanied by similar textual patterns. In de Vinsauf there is nothing that shows a direct knowledge of, for example, Vitruvius, and there are no references to physical buildings, whereas in Shakespeare's speech the high incidence of technical architectural and poetic terms alone points to a more specialized context.[12] Then too, this impression is strengthened by the highly intricate architectural pattern formed by these terms.

Contemporary Renaissance theories of artistic creation provide a context that can help explain the insistent focus on the idea of working from an abstract pattern or "model." In fact, when Shakespeare uses the term "model" four times (lines 42, 46, 51, 58)—for example, "the plot of situation and the model"—he reveals an interest in the crucial concept of "disegno" or "disegno interno" that was so popular in Late Renaissance aesthetic theory, where "modello" is an alternative term.[13] But then too the art that went into the fashioning of the speech tells us that the dramatist is not just paying lip-service to a fashionable continental ideal, but is recreating the relevant designs in his own poetry. Indeed, his emphasis on what one of his contemporaries had referred to as a "figure, and symmetry mentall" and the "immaterialitie of perfect Architecture"[14] emerges clearly in the "model" formed by the following underscored repetitions:

41      When we mean *to build*,
We first survey the plot, then *draw the model*,

And when we see the *figure* of the house,
Then must we rate the cost of the erection,
45    Which if we find *outweighs ability*,
What do we then, but draw anew *the model*
In fewer offices, or at least desist
*To build* at all? Much more, in this great work
(Which is almost to pluck a kingdom down
50    And set another up) should we survey
The plot of situation and *the model*,
Consent upon a sure foundation,
Question surveyors, know our own estate,
How *able* such a work to undergo,
55    *To weigh against* his opposite; or else
We fortify in paper and in *figures*,
Using the names of men instead of men:
Like one that *draws the model* of an house
59    Beyond his power *to build* it; . . .

The system behind these tangible repetitions appears clearly if we extract the repeated words from the flow of blank verse (see diagram).

| | | | | | | | | | |
|---|---|---|---|---|---|---|---|---|---|
| | | | | a | to build | (48) | | | |
| | | | f | model | | model | f | | |
| | | e | ability | | | able | e | | |
| | d | outweighs | | | | weigh against | d | | |
| | c | figure | | | | | figures | c | |
| b | model | | | | | | | model | b |
| a | to build | (41) | | | | | to build | a | (59) |

The recessed structure of repetitions results when Shakespeare "doubles" and expands the limited chiastic structure drawn from Luke, coordinating the two halves of the enlarged structure by introducing three new repetitions that stress the basic idea of working from a "disegno interno."[15] The final product is an unusually well developed example of rhetorical construction. The careful positioning and use of multiple inversions is exact even down to the way the verb "outweighs," and it is balanced by its counterpart "weigh against." The principle of composing by rhetorical *opposita* or *antitheta* is echoed in the emphasis on the need to weigh everything "against his opposite," thus making the phrase self-referential. Equally striking is the way in which this pattern strengthens the balanced structure of topoi pointed out above. The verb "to build" is made to mark the beginning, middle, and end of the verbal web. Repetitions surround and single out the central lines, where we witness the switch from architecture to politics, from erecting a house to establishing a royal house. We also find that the mention of the planned coup, "this great work— / Which is almost to pluck a kingdom down / And set another up—" harks back to the opening line of the speech ("this present quality of war"). Again the origins of such a tripartite structure are not necessarily found only in Aristotle's *Poetics* and his *cinquecento* commentators; they may also be seen in poetic practices current since the *Poetria nova*.[16]

Everything is carefully plotted and situated within the antithetical "frame" of seasonal references enclosing the main body of a speech dominated by architectural metaphors. Still, the verbal artifice does not end here; the speeches by Hastings that precede and follow upon Lord Bardolph's speech are part of the overall pattern of balance. In his speech Hastings makes the following comment:

> But, by your leave, it never yet did hurt
> To lay down *likelihoods* and forms of *hope.*

The words italicized there are echoed in Hastings' response to Lord Bardolph's speech:

> Grant that our *hopes*—yet *likely* of fair birth—
> Should be still-born, . . .

Again we see how iterated words—*likelihood* and *hope*, versus *hopes* and *likely*—form a chiastic frame around the speech itself, thus contributing further elements to its structure.[17]

Lord Bardolph's speech is a remarkably rich and detailed illustration of how Renaissance poets, starting from an inner design that emerges in the text as a configuration of embedded structural markers, could plan and execute their works. Such a pattern is the visible imprint of the writer's shaping, or *formal intention*. The important role of verbal repetitions for the establishment of such structures suggests one way of developing a method for approaching what Mark Rose termed "Shakespearean Design" in his 1972 study by that name. In that book Rose presented a number of analyses showing how the dramatist arranged individual scenes, groups of scenes, or entire plays in balanced, symmetrical, or contrasting patterns by analogy with groupings in the visual arts of the Renaissance. The two basic patterns of Shakespearean composition, he argued, are "the framing pattern" and "the diptych pattern," and he offered analyses of individual plays to prove his point. It is interesting that he saw Shakespearean design as similar to the use of proportion in Renaissance art and architecture, and even suggested that "[r]hetorical terminology . . . could provide us with a precise language for describing many aspects of Shakespearean dramaturgy."[18] Despite his insistent focus on *dispositio* in the arrangement of individual speeches and scenes, Rose did not consider the important role of *elocutio* and ornamentation in this process. Therefore he did not propose analytical tools appropriate for describing the constituent elements in the texts he studied, tools that would have facilitated an understanding of their relationship more specifically to important Renaissance theories of artistic creation. My topomorphical analysis of Lord Bardolph's speech suggests that an investigation of the pattern of rhetorical repetitions in a text provides a clue to the inner workings of Renaissance *poesis*.

Shakespeare is far from the first Elizabethan author to exhibit this interest in architecture. In fact, Elizabethan poets and thinkers were keenly interested in the principles of moral and textual edification expressed in humanist architectural treatises and their classical sources. The work of one man in particular caught their interest, the Florentine architectural theorist Leon Battista Alberti (1404–72), whose "gift for conceptual abstraction"[19] appears to have appealed directly to the Elizabethan version of Protestant humanism. Although English architects might have been familiar with the treatises of Alberti, Serlio, Philander, and others, the relative paucity of architecture executed in Italian Renaissance style in sixteenth-century England is conspicuous.[20] Longleat—an architectural sport, which tells us that Renaissance architecture on English soil was predominantly decorative, at least before Inigo Jones—is one extant example. Consequently, the study of the influence of Renaissance architecture on Elizabethan culture must focus on the dissemination of ideas through texts, reporting what Elizabethans saw when in Italy.

The Renaissance idea of the analogy of the arts is rooted in the notion of a shared universal harmony informing all artistic expressions.[21] Plato's powerful description of God as architect and the world as architecture,[22] in the *Timaeus*, added status and philosophical depth to the profession and its theory, and central in this image is the notion of working from a model. In a key passage in the tradition, we read that God works like the artificer who uses a model. Plato poses the question about the origins of the universe—"after which of the models did its Architect construct it?"[23]—and explains that it is composed of numbers and of musical proportions, thus providing concepts that were to become central in Renaissance aesthetics.[24]

As a prominent exponent of early humanism, Alberti was fully aware of Plato's powerful metaphor and embraced the concepts of *innata ratio* and the necessity of working from an idea or model. In so doing he followed the example of Vitruvius, and though undoubtedly a greater intellect than his Roman predecessor, Alberti too kept a predominantly practical profile in his monumental work *De re aedificatoria*.[25] Nevertheless, his greater understanding of the problems at hand, and the fact that he favored investigation and experiment, turns the treatise into a proto-scientific work.[26] Although partly inspired by Platonic ideas, his is a rational, if not scientific, brand of Platonism, with less emphasis on the contemplative aspects. His relations to Platonism are complex, and his faith in the human will and his doctrine of following nature depend more on early humanist thought and less on the contemplative mysticism of the kind later found in Ficino and Pico.[27] In this respect he reveals the civic spirit that informed and dominated the merchant city of Firenze before the Medici takeover. He believed in the ideal of the active life, and he thought that the citizen should contribute to the good of the city.[28] The interest in a rational and scientific approach to architecture and art appears clearly in *De re aedificatoria* and *De pictura*. In the first books of both works Alberti emphasizes the links with mathematics and artistic composition, thus laying down a firm and rational basis for his theories of beauty and utility. The laws of beauty, he avows, are given to man as a language "innate in our minds" ("animis innata quaedam ratio").[29] In the Italian Renaissance rendering, the logocentricity of his theory appears clearly, where "ratio" is rendered as "uno discorso, & . . . una ragione" (IX.v.337) in keeping with the common alignment between *ratio* and *oratio*.[30] The earliest translation into English ("a secret Argument and Discourse") demonstrates the same connection.[31] When Alberti therefore advocates *concinnitas*, it is an expanded and Christianized version of the Ciceronian rhetorical concept.[32] A tangible example of the rhetorical coherence of his theory of architecture is found in his definition of design or *lineamenta*:

Haec cum ita sint erit ergo lineamentum certa constansque prescriptio concepta animo, facta lineis et angulis perfectaque animo et ingenio erudito. (*De re aedificatoria* I.i.2)

[(W)e shall call the Design *a form and graceful pre-ordering of the Lines and Angles conceived in the Mind,* and contrived by an ingenious Artist.] (Italics added)

The passage represents an advance on de Vinsauf, but we cannot avoid noticing the similarity between this precise formula and the more metaphorical expression in de Vinsauf's influential treatise: "the inner design of the heart," which "the inner man determines . . . ahead of time in a certain order." The resemblance hardly becomes less suggestive when Alberti explains the function of design in relation to building:

> Atqui est quidem lineamenti munus et officio praescribere aedificiis et partibus aedificiorum aptum locum et certum numerum dignumque modum et gratum ordinem, ut iam tota aedificii forma et figura ipsis in lineamentis conquiescat. (I.i.19)

> [Thus the purpose and function of the design is to bestow on buildings and their parts, an appropriate placing, an exact proportion, a suitable disposition, and a harmonious order, so as to make the whole form and figure of the composition reside entirely in the design itself.] (My translation)

The terms Alberti uses to define design (*lineamenta*)—"tota aedificii forma et figura" ("the whole form and figure of the composition")—stem from the *De finibus* and the *De oratione* by Cicero,[33] which surely explains why almost the same phrases occur in de Vinsauf's definition of preconceived, abstract design.[34] This dependence on Cicero is understandable in view of Alberti's appreciation of a precise style and his frequent irritation with Vitrivius's obscure Latin (6.5). His balanced period structure throughout reveals a familiarity with the Roman author.

Rudolf Wittkower, in *Architecture in the Age of Humanism*, has demonstrated that rhetoric is precisely the discipline that informs the various arts, that it was by applying the rules of rhetoric to the theory of architecture and painting that Renaissance art was developed to such perfection. The impact of Cicero, for example, on the language of the *De re aedificatoria* illustrates this point. Strangely enough, the reverse argument concerning the impact of architecture on poetry and poetics has received less attention, except when used in a loosely descriptive but nontechnical way. The reason for this restraint is no doubt fear of the many pitfalls in a field that is notoriously open to impressionist criticism. These are real pitfalls, unless we can find—as Wittkower put it—"practical prescriptions of ratios supplied by the arts themselves."[35] When discussing the topic in *Mnemosyne: The Parallel Between Literature and the Visual Arts*, Mario Praz considered such a project to be impossible and concluded that it "would be useless to try to find in poets such strict rules as those practised by architects."[36] He was content to confine the similarities to aural euphony and rhythm alone, comparing music to the modulations of poetry. This opinion would have been wholly unacceptable to Renaissance poets who wrote on "proportion poeticall," since they considered poetry to be a divine art. It would have been unacceptable, because it stresses the practical, aural, and local aspects of a poem rather than its theoretical and visual aspects. Like the division of music into speculative and practical branches, poetry in cinquecento poetics had a conceptual side and a practical side, and the practical or elocutionary aspect depended in various ways upon the underlying structural subtext. When these points are considered we must conclude that Praz was so unnecessarily negative about the possibility of finding strict architectonic rules in poetry that his conclusion becomes too summary. Such rules did indeed exist, and, as we have seen, they can be tested against actual poetic practice. There is nothing arcane about this practice, as the poet and dramatist Ben Jonson reveals when he aligns architecture and poetry:

> As, for example, if a man would build a house, he would first appoint a place to build it in, which he would define within certain bounds; so, in the constitution of a poem, the action is aimed at by the poet, which answers place in a building, and that action hath his largeness, compass, and proportion. So the epic asks a magnitude, from other poems: since, what is place in the one is action in the other, the difference is in space.[37]

To Jonson, then, action in drama or poetry corresponds to place in a building, so that the collective actions of a play as written or printed form a configuration of textual "places," or actions recorded in, and confined to, particular textual segments. Such a series of actions—the plot—can be abstracted and represented as a drawing or figure projected unto a flat surface. The plot of a play or poem might simply have started out as something not unrelated to the plan for a building, which inevitably is the impression we get from studying the distribution of rhetorically adorned places ("topoi") in Renaissance literature.[38]

One starting point for such practices is the art of rhetoric, particularly in the descriptions of the periodic style. To remain with Jonson, let us consult his description of a period executed according to the ideal of *symmetria*. Here we find the notion that: "[t]he congruent and harmonious fitting of parts in a sentence hath almost the fastening and force of knitting and connection, as in stones well squared, which will rise strong a great way without mortar."[39] We readily recognize ideals of rhetorical composition that stem from classical rhetoric: syntactic or ornamental figurations linking together the beginning, middle, and end of a period. Indeed, the basic implied metaphor of text as architecture appears already in Demetrius's *De elocutione*, a treatise inspired by the third book of Aristotle's *Rhetoric*. Here we are told that "the members in a periodic style may, in fact, be compared to the stones which support and hold together a vaulted dome" (I.13).[40] Although this metaphor may be read in a loose and noncommittal sense, it draws attention to the way in which a concept of an orblike design is connected with the rules for creating a perfect period, as already mentioned. Thus the alignment between architectural and literary structure is no figment of the twentieth-century critic's imagination. Discussions of Italian Renaissance and Elizabethan poetics often neglect these aspects of rhetorical composition, because many scholars are still reluctant to think about works of literature as spatial artifacts.[41]

The discussion by Italian artist and theorist Zuccari of inner design in *L'Idea de' pittori, scultori e architetti* (1607) provides clues that allow us to see why Shakespeare and Jonson could take such an interest in architectural terminology. Zuccari summarizes a debate on aesthetics that had been going on for more than half a century and had given birth to numerous academies throughout Italian cities; among these learned bodies was the illustrious Academia del disegno founded by Vasari in 1563. One writer whose treatise had contributed to giving the concept of design such an increasingly prominent role was Benedetto Varchi, who gives several alternative terms for design that emerge in Elizabethan writers: "idea, . . .essemplare . . . esempio, e più volgarmente modello."[42] Of Platonic origin, the term "idea" became a central concept in cinquecento discourses on art in the widest sense of the word: in rhetoric it came to play an important role through the widely disseminated arguments of the Byzantine rhetorician Hermogenes,[43] whereas Scaliger treated it in the "Liber Tertius Qui et Idea" of his monumental *Poet-*

*ices libri septem.*[44] In an Elizabethan context the term is associated with poetry and poetics rather than with painting, sculpture, and architecture. We recall Sidney's famous phrase concerning the poet's "Idea, or fore-conceit," his insistent use of "example," and the alignment between a literary text and a work of architecture, where he applies the term "model."[45] Then too this terminology is shared by the various arts, and in the moral sense of the word literary art and the art of building are equally *architectonike*,[46] hence Sidney's use of the term in the *Apology.*[47]

These various terms, and the implied alignment between architecture and the construction of texts, must have entered England quite early to appear so frequently in Elizabethan and Jacobean poetical treatises, probably before the works of Varchi and Zuccari came to be known. To discover the first expression of these ideals in England, it will be best to work backward in history from the first known references to Albertian aesthetics in Henry Wotton, Richard Wills, and John Dee to what I take to be the foundation of such influence in John Shute. The diplomat Henry Wotton, the contemporary of Jonson as well as Shakespeare, may appropriately be chosen as our guide into the field. A former ambassador to Venice, Wotton published upon his return to England a remarkable treatise on architecture, *The Elements of Architecture* (1624), which presents an important survey of Late Renaissance aesthetics. His reliance on a number of treatises, ranging from Vitruvius through Alberti to the most recent theoretical work on architecture, makes him a particularly valuable source for early seventeenth-century late sixteenth-century aesthetic thinking in England. He had the decided advantage of having lived and traveled extensively in Italy, so his opinions are based on study and experience. The distinction he draws in the preface between two kinds of treatises reveals a decided preference for the kind of treatise Alberti had written. Wotton writes:

> There were two wayes to be deliuered, the one *Historicall,* by description of the principall workes, performed already in good part, by *Giorgio Vasari* in the liues of *Architects:* The other *Logicall,* by casting the rules and cautions of the *Art,* into some comportable *Method.* (Sig. A.i.r)

Wotton's "historical" here also carries the implication of "rhetorical," and he personally prefers the *genus dialectice,* or "the Logicall," which is also the choice Alberti made when he wrote his *De re aedificatoria.* It comes as no surprise that he considers "Alberti the Florentine, . . . the first learned Archi-

tecte, beyond the Alpes" (Sig. A.i.r). Moreover, he refers repeatedly to
Alberti's work, and what seems to have appealed to him is precisely his predecessor's rationalist and utilitarian approach. Wotton's opening sentence
proclaims his preference: "As in all other Operatiue Arts, the end must direct
the Operation. The end of Architecture is to build well" (Sig. q.3.r). He is
certainly familiar with Alberti's work in Italy, and he mentions the kind of
harmonious church construction Alberti perfected when he distinguishes
between the artisan and

> the Architect, whose glory doth more consist, in the Designement
> and Idea of the whole Worke, and his truest ambition should be to
> make the Forme, which is the nobler Part (as it were) triumph ouer the
> Matter: whereof I cannot but mention by the way, a forreigne Paterne,
> namely the Church of Santa Giustina in Padoua: In truth a sound piece
> of good Art, where the Materials being but ordinarie stone, . . .doe yet
> rauish the Beholder, . . .by a secret Harmony in the Proportions. (Sig.
> B.2.r-v)

Here we notice the familiar Albertian preference for abstract form and the
somewhat awkward term "designement," which may be Wotton's compro-
mise rendering of Varchi's and Vasari's "disegno" and Alberti's "lineamentum."[48] Wotton was aware of the problem of finding apt English renderings
of Latin and Italian terms, "bewayling . . . some defect of Artificiall tearmes
in [Gualterus Riuius], as I must likewise" in his own "Saxon" tongue (Sig.
A.i.r). His phrasing also recalls Sidney's famous line in *An Apology for Poetry*
that "the skill of each artificer standeth in the Idea or fore-conceit of the
work."[49] This might be an intended reference to Sir Philip's seminal treatise,
which suggests that Wotton consciously adjusts his phrasing to views on
poetry current in the circles where Sidney was still an influential source of
inspiration.

Although Wotton acknowledges his indebtedness to Alberti only occasionally, the latter's influence is pervasive. Thus unacknowledged borrow-
ing occurs as in the phrase concerning "the casting and the comparting of
the whole Worke (being indeede the very Definitue Summe of this Art, to
distribute usefully and gracefully a well chosen Plot)" (Sig. G.3.r), which
leans on *De re aedificatoria* I.ix.65: "Tota vis ingenii: omnisque rerum aedificandarum ars et peritia una in partitione consumitur." Other examples occur
throughout and often in conjunction with direct quotations. Although Wot-

ton is the first Englishman to discuss these principles at length and the underlying Vitruvian definition of beauty, Jonson had already referred to them in 1603 in his description of triumphal architecture,[50] and John Dee had praised Alberti in a book published as early as 1570.

The multifaceted Elizabethan John Dee can also be considered a pioneer in English architectural theory. In that capacity he too was greatly hampered by the lack of adequate English terms, but the "Mathematicall Praeface" to *The Elements of Geometrie of Euclid of Megara* (1570) bears witness to the Italian influence. Dee had the largest library in England, he received visits from royalty who wanted to admire his collection, and "he frequently had students in residence."[51] In the words of Frances A. Yates, "the whole Renaissance was in his library."[52] Among his books were copies of both Vitruvius and Alberti. In the preface to *The Elements of Geometrie* Alberti is praised before being cited at length: "We thanke you Master Baptist, that you haue so aptly brought your Arte, and phrase thereof, to haue some Mathematicall perfection: by certaine order, number, forme, figure, and Symmetrie mentall: all naturall & sensible stuffe set a part."[53] In this sentence we recognize the phrase quoted above about the need for "certum numerum dignumque modum et gratum ordinem" in the fashioning of an "aedificii forma et figura" (I.i.19). In fact, Dee also translates in full the crucial passage on design, meticulously rendering its balanced figural form: "And it is the property of Lineamentes, to prescribe vnto buildinges, and every part of them, an apt place, & certaine nûber: a worthy maner, and a semely order: that so, ye whole forme and figure of the buildyng, may rest in the very Lineamentes. &." Following Alberti, Dee defines architecture as a mathematical discipline, listing it "in the honest Company of the Artes Mathematicall Deriuatiue" (Sig. d.iij). In Dee's view on architecture, art is "immaterial" and is based on imagination; for Dee the essence of art is found in abstract principles of mathematical proportion and cosmic harmony.[54] When rendering Alberti's definition of design (*lineamenta*), Dee therefore adheres to Alberti's Latinate terminology: "Lineamente, shalbe the certaine and constant prescribyng, conceiued in the mynde: made in lines and angels: and finished with a learned minde and wyt" (Sig. d.iiij). The results were not slow to come: Only three years later Richard Wills published his treatise *De re poetica*, in which he applies the term *lineamenta* to literary structure.[55] Dee's choice of wording is understandable because he had no experience as an architect himself, yet he could have found a basis for a native terminology in a work published in 1563: *The First and Chief Groundes of Architecture*, by John Shute.[56]

Although recognized as a pioneer, Shute does not figure prominently in the written histories of English architecture. He is, for instance, given only a few lines by Peter Murray in *A History of English Architecture* (1962), and in Anthony Blunt's article "Des origines de la critique et de l'histoire de l'art en Angleterre" his importance is proclaimed, but the following is all that is said on the topic: "Plus intéressant est le petit traité publié par John Shute en 1563, Shute a passé plusieurs années à Rome, mais son livre, qui vaut plus par ses planches que par le texte, est un mélange d'éléments tirés de Serlio et du Vitruve de Philander."[57] Shute was sent to the Continent by the Duke of Northumberland in 1550, and he visited Italy, where he studied both Renaissance buildings and such Italian treatises of architecture as Sebastiano Serlio's *Regole generali di architettura* (1537–47).[58] He was "one of those Tudor travellers such as Wyatt and Hoby who physically imported the Renaissance to England."[59] In addition to Serlio's and Philander's editions of Vitruvius, Dee seems to have known Giacomo da Vignola's *Regole delli Cinque Ordini di Architettura* (1562) well.[60]

Today Shute is remembered primarily because he wrote the first treatise on architecture, scarcely more than a primer, and because his illustrations of the five classical orders greatly influenced Elizabethan architectural ornamentation—for example, at Longleat House.[61] About architecture he writes: "And among all other studies there is none in my simple iudgement of this sorte that diserueth greater prayse, then that whiche is of the grekes named *Architectonica*, and of the latines *Architectura* (I thinke not altogither vnfite nor vnaptlie by me termed in Englishe, the arte and trade to rayse vp and make excellent edifices and buildinges) the whiche like in all other ages before hath bene in meruelous accoumpte and estimation." Although Shute's mode of presentation probably would qualify for inclusion in the category "historical" rather than "logicall," to use Wotton's distinction, his brisk treatise also reveals a strong thrust toward abstract design. In his view architecture "hath a natural societie and as it were by sertaine kindred & affinitie is knit vnto all the Mathematicalls." On several occasions Shute presents the idea of design or of conceiving a plan in the mind before transferring it onto paper and realizing it materially: the architect should "haue expert knowladge in drawing and protracting the thinge, which he hath conceyued" (Sig. B.iii) and "through drawing vtter his fantasie and shewe the trike and fascion of the thing that he goeth about to make" (Sig. B.iii). In these passages terms like "protracting," meaning to "draw a plan of ground to scale," "fantasie," which means a mental image, and "fascion," which denotes "form," all suggest Alberti's idea of working from an abstract plan in a general manner. On the third occasion, when Shute describes the process of working from an abstract plan, he turns to an established English term: *plot*.[62] In consonance with the Vitruvian ideal, he argues that the architect must be trained in all the arts, so as to

> shewe what ground plottes stande in the most holsom ayer to builde vpon. And which also be the swet and holsome waters; the moste fertill and frutefull places, as namely for those plottes stand contrary to thys order are not mete or necessarie to build vpon. This holsome ground so found whereon Ye shall build, ye must furst haue knowlaige how to cast your ground plotte, wherein you must deuide all your seuerall places of offices appertayning to the furniture of your house. (Sig. B.iii-iiij)

"Plot" is here used in two senses, corresponding to Alberti's "area" and "partitio," both of which reappear in Shakespeare. Here the traditional term has caused Shute to ignore the need for terminological precision recommended in Dee's treatise, where "plot" does not occur. Although Shute's usage may be inconsistent, we should not be deceived by his prose, or by the fact that Alberti is not named, into discarding the Italian as a source. Before examining the above-cited passage more closely, let us consider what Shute actually states about his sources: "I thought it therefore good to sette out and commit to writing in our natiue language, parte of those thinges whiche (both by great labour and trauaile, at first for my priuate commoditie I searched out and for my owne pleasure out of diuers as well Latin and Italian, as french and dowche writers) I haue diligently gathered" (Sig. A.iijr). What is surprising here is that he does not mention Vignola, because he must have used him for his illustrations.[63] Similarly, Alberti, although unnamed, informs his text. In fact, on closer inspection we find that the cited passage combines three different stages in the argument of Book One of *De re aedificatoria*: How to find a suitable region for a building, how to find an appropriate site, and how to go about distributing the plan or plot for the building. When Alberti advises on the proper region in which to build, he writes:

> Atqui erunt quidem inditia optimi aeris integrarumque aquarum, si ea regio feret bonorum fructum copiam. (I.viii)

> [And indications that the place has excellent air and pure water, will be that the area yields well and in abundance.] (I.vii.53)

This specification crops up in Shute's argument about the necessity of know-ing "what ground plottes stande in the most holsom ayer to builde vpon. And which also be the swet and holsome waters; the most fertill and frute-full places." Interference from Philander's French is reflected in the preced-ing phrase about "vnderstanding of the *plages* or *Coastes* of the World," but when he becomes more specific his phrasing reproduces Alberti.

The next step in his prescription—that is, having "the knowledge how to cast your ground plotte"—seems similarly to derive from Alberti's Latin: what to do when an appropriate site has been chosen ("This holsome ground so found"). More particularly, the point derives from Alberti's sum-mary that "ita et area totius regionis praescriptum et definitum quodam spatium, quod quidem ad aedificium habendum occupatur" ("similarly the site is a definite space chosen within a larger area and destined for the plac-ing of the building"). Like Alberti, Shute stresses the point that the same procedure applies to the selection of both area and site *("so found"* versus *ita).* With regard to tracing the plot in "lines" (Alberti's "lineis et angulis"), Shute returns to the already familiar emphasis on abstract design in the dis-tribution of the parts of the building: "ye must furst haue the knowlaige of how to cast your ground plotte, wherein you must deuide all your seuerall places of offices appartayning to the furniture of your house" (Sig. B.iii.v). Behind this phrase looms Alberti's phrases about the "lineamenti munus et officium praescribere aedificiis et partibus aedificiorum aptum locum" and the "[t]ota vis ingenii: omnisque rerum aedificandarum ars et peritia una in partitione consumitur" (p. 65). While retaining the order of his arguments, Shute appears to have compressed Alberti's line of reasoning.

On the basis of these parallels I would therefore argue that Shute's de-scription of how to go about building a house suggests that he not only had a working knowledge of the principles of Albertian architecture, but also comes close to quoting him verbatim. The "strangeness" experienced when confronted with his rendering of Alberti's Latin—Shute simply could not cope satisfactorily with his predecessor's terminology—obscures his indebt-edness. In general, however, there are few direct borrowings,[64] and he is careful not to enter too much in detail into the "hard sentences or questions of Symetrie" (Sig. B.iii.r). Instead he repeatedly underlines the practical and the profitable aspects of architecture. Similarly, his style is characterized by a matter-of-fact attitude and does not display any great attention to periodic sophistication and the use of rhetorical ornaments.[65]

Then too, Shute's little book agrees perfectly with the Protestant hu-manist doctrine of "profitable discourse," which was ubiquitous in the 1560s

and the following decades.[66] The emphasis on utility and practical application of theoretically elaborated grammars of action dominates all sectors of
social life in the period and channeled intellectual life largely in one direction, that all activities should make the commonwealth pros-per, and in this
enterprise rhetoric was a key element.[67] It is in this context that Shute emphasizes the profitable character of his project and that he is anxious that
the "forsayd foundatio[n], stocke, or science shall bring forthe the frutes of
it to their great profites, and Commoditie of the Realme."[68] These are ideas
that accorded well with the civic spirit and practical nature of Alberti's theories of architecture, and that made Alberti more palatable to the Elizabethans than the Italian's later and more sophisticated compatriots. When
the poet George Gascoigne talks about the need to stick to one's projected
"platforme of inuention," or when Sidney describes "the narration . . . as an
imaginative ground-plot of a profitable invention" (p. 124), each in fact remains well within the context both of Alberti's architectural theory and of
Elizabethan ideals of social, economic, and ethical edification.

Sidney could have known the work, for example, of Lomazzo,[69] but in
the cases of Gascoigne, Wills, and Shute, Alberti himself may have played a
major role, in view of their remarks on abstract design and related topics.[70]
We may therefore reasonably assume that "Albertian" compositional ideals
in general exerted a shaping influence on Elizabethan intellectuals from the
1560s onward. Shakespeare's impressive command of this aesthetic appears
clearly in the elegant exposition offered in Lord Bardolph's speech. But,
more important, the currency of architectural terminology in Renaissance
poetics makes it necessary to speak about an architecture of the text, a kind
of "fortifying with words" directly inspired by current Italian aesthetic theory and practice. And before concluding this chapter and going on to explore some of the roots of that practice, I want to show how a poet could
dramatize the use of architectural symbolism and design in various contexts.
Two brief examples will illustrate the point.

My first example is drawn from Shakespeare's comic erotic poem *Venus
and Adonis* (1592), a delightfully suggestive topos of female courtship contained in two stanzas in which he sets out to metamorphose the body of
Venus into a park within the confines of a firmly controlled textual shape.
Upon entering the poem we hear Venus addressing Adonis:

230     "Fondling," she saith, "since I have hemmed thee here
        Within the circuit of this ivory pale,
        I'll be a park, and thou shalt be my deer;

Feed where thou wilt, on mountain or in dale;
Graze on my lips, and if those hills be dry,
235    Stray lower, where the pleasant fountains lie.
Within this limit is relief enough,
Sweet bottom-grass and high delightful plain,
Round rising hillocks, brakes obscure and rough,
To shelter thee from tempest and from rain;
240    Then be my deer, since I am such a park;
No dog shall rouse thee, though a thousand bark."

(230–41)

We cannot but notice how the goddess is transformed into a park, a park anthropomorphosed into body, as the park's lineaments merge with the embracing limbs of the goddess: "I have hemmed thee here / Within the circuit of this ivory pale, / I'll be a park." What the reader and Adonis find "[w]ithin this limit" (235) is a sensuous landscape where intimate details of female anatomy are translated into the artfully cultivated elements of a park. Lips, breasts, and private parts become pastures on which to "graze" (233) and "pleasant fountains" (234) from which to drink, "round rising hillocks" (238) to climb, and finally "brakes obscure and rough" (238) that offer "shelter" (239). These metamorphoses are executed in the spirit of Naso himself in their use of the female body, giving us a sexually coded version of the lay of the land.

    Yet there is more to these stanzas than Ovid's transgressive art: in keeping with cinquecento bravura gardening, the witnessed *bizarrie* are integrated into an elegantly controlled design. Thus the two stanzas form the two halves of an enclosing figuration whose constituent elements are the following repetitions:

*park   deer   Graze   hills   //   grass   hillocks   deer   park*

These repetitions create a combination of chiasmus and sequential repetition as expressed in the formula *a-b-c-d-c-d-b-a*. Moreover, in addition to including these markers that serve as thematic key-words, Shakespeare joins the initial statement of the topos to its middle via the parallel phrases "[w]ithin this circuit" and "[w]ithin this limit," thus completing a design that imitates the patterned plot or plan of a park. And because the focus of the topos is the situation of Adonis within the circuit of Cytherea's "ivory pale," we cannot but enjoy the poet's witty reformulation in the key image of Renaissance architectural anthropomorphism: Vitruvian man. Unfortunate and overpowered, Adonis is effectively inscribed within a circle, but it is a circle that adds to the parodic tone of the scene rather than presenting him as the master and measure of creation. The several references to enclosure and to circles should therefore be taken to refer not only to the topomorphic structure of the two stanzas but also to this important embedded emblem.

In my second example, Sonnet 55, we move from the threefold alignment between the female body and park as topomorphic structure, to a contrast between the wonders of architectural structures and the kind of "room" created in poetry:

| | |
|---|---|
| 1 | Not marble, nor the gilded monuments |
| | Of princes shall outlive this powerful rhyme, |
| | But you shall shine more bright in these contents |
| | Than unswept stone, besmeared with sluttish time. |
| 5 | When wasteful war shall statues overturn, |
| | And broils root out the work of masonry, |
| | Nor Mars his sword, nor war's quick fire shall burn: |
| | The living record of your memory. |
| | 'Gainst death, and all-oblivious enmity |
| 10 | Shall you pace forth, your praise shall still find room, |
| | Even in the eyes of all posterity |
| | That wear this world to the ending doom. |
| | So till the judgment that your self rise, |
| 14 | You live in this, and dwell in lovers' eyes. |

What is striking in this context is not only the poet's emphasis on the verse to outlast the material monuments to human greatness on earth, but also his prominent combination of architectural terms and a stunning tectonic structure of repetitions. The metaphoric references to building and to buildings are plentiful: "marble" (1), "monuments" (1), "stone" (4), "the work of masonry" (7) and "room" (9), and "dwell" (14). These references stress that poetry differs from built architecture in that it is an immaterial but lasting structure in which the poet's praise of the beloved "shall . . . find room" and "dwell" forever. At the heart of this idea, of course, lies the notion that the most important stage in architectural and poetic creation is the initial mental phase, what Alberti refers to as "innata ratio" and "prescriptio concepta animo"—the idea conceived in the mind of the divine architect. In poetry, however, we cannot expect such a pattern to be represented by "lines and angles" as in architectural plans.

As we have seen above, such textual platforms are frequently established by means of verbal repetitions, and the repetition causes such words to stand out and shine in the readers' eyes. Not unexpectedly, Shakespeare alludes to this technique early in the sonnet, "But you shall *shine* more bright in these contents" (3; italics added), thus drawing attention to the inner design of his creation, which is as symmetrical as any Renaissance architectural plan. In fact, he creates a balanced pattern that strives against the conventional divisions of the sonnet into eight plus six verses or twelve plus two verses. He does so by superimposing a configuration that divides it into seven plus seven lines and that emphasizes the beginning, middle, and end of the poem. Typically, these resumptions are found in the two initial lines, the two central ones, and the concluding couplet, and are combined so as to link lines one and seven ("Not marble, nor . . ." versus "Not Mars. . . , nor . . .") and lines two, eight, and fourteen by means of references to life and to the poem itself: *"outlive this* powerful rhyme," "the *living* record," and "You *live* in *this."* Thus he creates an embedded structure based on equal distribution and on the Aristotelian formula of wholeness—a structure whose praise is sounded through the pages of Renaissance treatises on poetics— "totum veró est, quod principium, medium, atque finem habet."[71] The promise to erect a lasting memory to his beloved makes the choice of repeated key words *(outlive, living, live)* most appropriate.

These examples may appear anything but edifying in an ethical sense, but it is important to realize that although there are obvious links between textual architecture and ethics, the use of architectural principles and metaphors in Renaissance literature should primarily be seen as a method to achieve effective communication and persuasion. These examples also embody discursive strategies for teaching young male readers how to obtain a desired love. My second chapter will study these formal techniques as they appear in the Latin love elegies termed *paraclausithyra,* a type of poem that is intrinsically connected with architecture by being focused on the door leading into the beloved's house.

*Pulcherrimum Carmen*

Latin *Paraclausithyra* and the Period as a Poetic Ideal

The art of making poetry was always, so it seems, associated in the human mind with the act of divine creation, the second world or nature of the poet being fashioned in imitation of, and in response to, the primary *poësis* of the deity.[1] Thus when discussing the problem of evil in relation to the creation of the universe, Saint Augustine, the father of Christian rhetoric, typically compares the universe to a beautiful poem:

> Neque enim Deus ullum, non dico angelorum, sed vel hominem crearet, quem malum futurum esse praescisset, nisi pariter nosset quibus eos bonorum usibus commodaret atque ita ordinem saeculorum tanquam *pulcherrimum carmen* etiam ex quibusdam quasi antithesis honestaret.

> [Now God would never create any man, much less any angel, if he already knew that he was destined to be evil, were he not equally aware how he was to turn them to account in the interest of the good and thereby add lustre to the succession of the ages as if it were *an exquisite poem* enhanced by what might be called antitheses.] (*De civitate Dei* XI.xviii.494–95; italics added)

This often-quoted alignment between God's creation and the world of words is revealing for various reasons. Leaving questions of doctrine aside, let us consider the aesthetic implications of the rhetorical and poetic terms employed. More particularly, I would argue that Augustine's chosen terms shed light on aspects of classical poetry as presented in his aesthetics of *aequalitas*, aspects that I consider essential for our understanding of how and why Augustine's work came to play such a decisive role in the cultivation of classical ideals of order and harmony in the Renaissance. Augustine's "rhetorical patterning of philosophical ideas lent itself," it has been said, "to the renaissance composition and the reading of literature in 'literary architectonics.' "[2] It is a much-repeated fact that in the Renaissance the key discipline was rhetoric, which provided the vocabulary for the arts as well as for literature. Indeed, in this period it regained the position it had enjoyed at the time Augustine wrote his famous treatise.

The Renaissance emphasis on rhetoric often caused the well-formed and balanced sentence to be used as a metaphor in the description of all kinds of artistic creation, speech being the prime expression of, and medium for, man's humanity. In his comment on the "necessary balance of opposites" in Renaissance art, James Mirollo notes its almost universal application: "In literature it ranges from the antithesis within a single line of poetry to the alignment of phrases and clauses in a Ciceronian period and from the employment of contrasting plots and ideas in individual plays and poems to the pairing of separate works espousing different concepts."[3] The ideal of *concinnitas* is associated with a well-formed sentence; the narrative structure of Catullus LXVI is analogous to the structure of a full-bodied period. The poem's order, concentric and parenthetic, is like that of a Latin periodic sentence."[4] This device of arranging "subject matter to achieve a structural symmetry not only with echoes of language but also themes" has been found in a wide variety of Greek and Roman prose and verse.[5]

A similar line of reasoning is found at the heart of the Augustinian passage already quoted, where the notion of a planned, ordered progression in time, "ordinem saeculorum," alludes to the way in which poems like Catullus's *Carmina* are often organized as patterned sequences, ordered "fine usque ad finem," to use the biblical idiom. Various arrangements existed, but, as a vast body of classical scholarship has shown,[6] two basic dispositional schemes dominated: poems could be organized either according to the principle of "ring composition" or according to the principle of "parallel composition."[7] ring composition the parts of a poem are arranged on a principle of mirror or recessed symmetry (ABCDED$^1$C$^1$B$^1$A$^1$), whereas in "parallel construction" or "linear construction"[8] the repeated elements follow in a series in which the same order is observed in the constituent members (ABCDEA$^1$B$^1$C$^1$D$^1$E$^1$). There is good cause to assume that Augustine's use of "ordo" in the passage above implies one of these structural arrangements (or a related one), especially when we take into account his discussion of the concept in *De ordine*.[9] However, he does not content himself only with references to the *dispositio* of the divine poem in time; he also specifically mentions how words combine and contrast at the level of *elocutio*. Although he uses terms drawn from Cicero and Quintilian, Augustine turns to Scripture when he offers examples of "the most elegant ornaments of style."[10] These ornaments—*antitheses* and *contraposita*—belong to the repertoire of schemes recommended for a perfect *periodos*, a concept that, ever since Aristotle, had been associated with antithesis or other correlational syntactical systems used to produce a long and tightly organized sentence.[11] One of Augustine's periods may serve to illustrate this rhetoric of *contraposita*:

> Sicut ergo ista contraria contrariis opposita sermonis pulchritudinem reddunt, ita quadam non verborum, sed rerum eloquentia contrarium oppositione saeculi pulchritudo componitur.

> [Just as a contrast of opposites produces the beauty of language; not words, but things combine by the same contrast of opposites to form a kind of beauteous eloquence of the ages.] (*De civitate Dei* XI.xviii.496–97; my translation)

We note how the writer carefully balances and shapes his sentence into a well-composed whole, filling in by means of figures of repetition some of the "structural slots" favored in periodic rhetoric—that is, the frontal, medial, and final positions of the clause. In this respect, the expression "the beauty of language" ("sermonis pulchritudinem") parallels "the beauty of time" ("saeculi pulchritudo"), and that parallel is underlined by the position of the two expressions toward the end of the two cola. Although the repetitions in question do not conform to the rule of similar endings as outlined by Aristotle in *The Art of Rhetoric*, Book Three, Augustine's period nevertheless exhibits a number of conspicuous repetitions. Thus we can see that the ordered repetition of entire words in a sequence (*contraria contrariis opposita pulchritudinem . . . contrarium oppositione . . . pulchritudo*) constitutes the most striking way of creating balance within the period, forming as it does an example of what is commonly referred to as "parallel composition."[12] This technique entails repeating entire words, not just inflexions and suffixes. As shown elsewhere in his writings,[13] such iterated words may be part of a strategy to indicate structurally significant positions.[14] Moreover, we observe the same kind of rhetorical structure in the prose of Philo Judaeus in his description in the *De genesi* of the way in which the divine architect establishes harmony.[15] Augustine, then, like Philo before him, draws on the syntactic and figurative conventions of the grammatical period to describe the cosmos.[16]

These verbal schemes nevertheless represent some of the formal dispositions possible in, and associated with, the ideal of *aequalitas* or *convenientia*, where equal division and the graded arrangement of unequal parts are essential strategies.[17] These are aesthetic formulas that Augustine holds to be operative in all the arts: "in omnibus artibus convenientia placeat."[18]

Regrettably, Augustine's prose examples do not tell us what type of poem he had in mind, but obviously it was a type in which rhetorical schemes like *opposita* and *contraposita* serve to create harmony. When *opposita* are used in single lines or members of periods, local effects of harmony and balance are achieved, but when they are employed to keep together a multi-member period or a poem, the effect is akin to the structure of Catullus LXVI. Such arrangements are often found in Alexandrian and Roman epics, but I do not believe that the kind of *carmen* Augustine had in mind alluded primarily to epic poems like *The Aeneid* or the *Argonautica*, although he repeatedly quotes Vergil's epic and modeled his spiritual epic on it.[19] I suggest instead that the kind of harmonious poem he has in mind belongs to a category of shorter, formally sophisticated poems, the daring elegies referred to as *paraclausithyra*, whose appeal was both sensuous and sensational.

Because *paraclausithyra* often had a splendid rhetorical finish they were closely studied and imitated with respect to style and technique, at the same time that their ticklish topics and salacious comedy appealed to many. The dubious morality and careless humor of these poems turn them into classical equivalents of Renaissance love sonnets where aesthetic pleasure and sexual innuendo vie with the ultimate defeat and moral reformation of the poet-lover. On the whole, they emerge as rhetorical bravura pieces on the topic of *amor furtivus*, which most educated and literary-minded persons knew and were able to quote. Also, it is distinctly possible that this mini-genre may incorporate witty elaborations of now-lost hymns to the god Janus,[20] whose cult was important in pre-Christian Rome.

The cult was one of Augustine's main targets in the *De civitate Dei*, where he writes at length about Janus, presumably because the deity was closely connected with the cult of Jupiter and was associated with a symbolism that in some respects competed with that of Christians. Janus was one of the *di indigetes*, and in the *Carmen saliare* he was termed creator and father of all things.[21] One symbolic nexus associated with Janus is the notion of the doorway and its trinity of deities—Limentinus, Forculus, and Cardinea—which Augustine derides.[22] I would therefore suggest that a mythological substratum relating to Janus is present in the *paraclausithyra* of Propertius, Tibullus, and Ovid and that their literary treatment of shared cultic material may have prompted Augustine's attack on the pagan deities.

But how do we pass from Augustine to the poetry that exhibits the poetic style he obviously cherished? Rhetorically sophisticated and witty these elegies may be, but their themes certainly were contrary to the edifying strategies favored by the church. These poems nevertheless had some themes and metaphors in common with biblical poetry so that they could be exploited for didactic purposes. Thus the psalmist often expresses his frustrations in words that bring to mind the feelings described in Latin love elegies. This parallel makes the *paraclausithyron* a particularly interesting mini-genre. The Christian's fervent desire to break through the barrier of the flesh to reach the heavenly bridegroom could easily merge with the frustrated lover's complaint outside the closed door of his beloved.

Bearing this in mind, let us briefly consider the lover in Propertius I.xvi ("Quae fueram magnis olim patefacta triumphis"). The lover is not admitted by his former mistress and therefore cannot decide who is the more cruel, the mistress or the door, because neither responds to his advances:

> ianua vel domina penitus crudelior ipsa,
> quid mihi tam duris clausa taces foribus?
> cur numquam reserata meos admittis amores.
> nescia furtivas reddere mota preces?

(17–20)

> [Door, crueller to the core, yea than thy mistress herself,
> why art thou shut against me with those grim silent leaves.
> Why art thou ne'er unbarred to let my love in?
> Can nothing teach thee to relent and be the herald of my stealthy prayers?]

The contrast between the drunken lover who beats his fists against domina Tarpeia's barred door and a pious Christian is admittedly marked. But if we consider Augustine's phrasing in the *Enarratio in psalmum* CIII, where the Christian is said to knock with invisible hands on the invisible door of the Lord ("manibus invisibilius ad invisibilem ianuam pulsatis"), the contrast cannot invalidate the thematic and verbal resemblance, particularly when we remember the door's complaint in Propertius:

> nunc ego, nocturnis potorum saucia rixis,
> pulsata indignis saepe queror manibus.

> (5–6)

> [(I) am now wounded in the nightly brawls of revellers
> and have oft to complain of blows from unworthy hands.]

Then too, Augustine contrasts two different categories of lovers. Thus, in the *De libero arbitrio* those who believe it is possible to enter heaven are contrasted with those who fear predestination to inevitable defeat: "You have knocked vigorously at the door of God's mercy. May it be opened to those who knock. Yet I do believe that a great number of men are tormented by this question [of inevitable necessity], . . .abandoning themselves, their spirits, and their bodies to the accidents of chance, they give themselves to be battered and torn by lusts."[23] The lover of Propertius I.xvi is obviously "torn by lusts," for his intention is clearly dictated by a desire for sexual gratification rather than for God. Nothing in Augustine quite matches the outspoken sensuality of Propertius, but at times Augustine is surprisingly profane. Thus he describes Wisdom as a woman who, though pursued and embraced by all, remains chaste to all men.[24]

In fact, the sensuous representation and experience of beauty is an essential element in Augustine's perception of the divine.[25] We encounter the emphasis on the sensuous everywhere in Augustine. Rather than positing a contradiction to the more familiar definition of *ordo* and *aequalitas* in strict geometrico-mathematical terms, the sensuous merely constitutes a complementary aspect of the *ars divina*, since Augustine's notion of visual-artistic beauty embraces both the sensible and the intelligible. Typical in this respect is the fusion of visionary and concrete images found in the introductory Sermo I(a) to the *Enarratio in psalmum* CIII.

As so often, Augustine's point of departure is his architectural concept of the world, whose magnitude and beauty appeal to the eye and teach us to love: "Videmus enim fabricam mundi amplam quamdam ex coelo et terra."[26] And God is the *fabricator* of the construction whose beauty impels us to want to enter:

> [Q]uibus quasi manibus invisibilius ad invisibilem ianuam pulsatis, ut invisilibiter vobis aperiatur, et invisibiliter intretis, et invisibilibiter sanemini. (col. 1338)

> [(A)lmost as if you beat with your hands invisibly on the invisible door, in that it be invisibly opened onto you, you shall invisibly enter, and you will invisibly be cured.]

These images suggest a possible allusion to the poetic genre, which displays especially striking examples of the antitheses and contraposita that Augustine considered so essential in the composition of an exquisite poem.

The *paraclausithyron* containing phrases that come the closest to Augustine's door metaphor is Propertius I.xvi, one of four extant Latin paraclausithyra, the others being Catullus LXVII, Tibullus, I.iii, and Ovid's *Amores* I.vi. The genre seems to have originated in Hellenistic poetry with such elegant and skilled poets as Callimachos and the Alexandrians. The earliest of the poems, Catullus LXVII, is no fully developed *paraclausithyron*[27] but nevertheless establishes some of the typical elements. The first is the device of casting the poem as a dialogue between the door of the domina's house and a lover, while a second characteristic is a witty and harsh tone.[28] Here, however, the poem commands interest mainly as the starting-point for Propertius I.xvi.

Inventiveness and design are key elements in Propertius's poem on the door lamenting the wrongdoings of the house's residents, yet the source is evident.[29] But rather than taking over the cryptic topical allusions and the spontaneous style of its source, Propertius's poem is characterized by greater weight and a clearer narrative focus. The situation has been developed to a considerable extent and a firm story line has been added. The poet also introduces a greater number of ironic allusions to religious practice, thus adding comic depth and ironic distance.

The poem is conceived as a narrative addressed by the door to the reader, and the narrative consists of four segments of varying length, each well defined and distinct from the others. In the initial segment (verses 1–4) the door tells the story of its glorious past, before its reputation was blackened by Tarpeia's dissolute life. Next comes the door's detailed description of the frequent nightly brawls and the many indignities committed by the mistress:

> nec possum infamis dominae defendere noctes
> nobilis obscenis tradita caminibus. (9–10)

> [Nor can I protect the nights of my mistress from dishonor,
> but, though once so honored, am the prey of ribald songs.]

Then, in the longest section (verses 17–44), we listen to one suitor's poetic complaint, a paraclausithyron presented as an inset song. The introit to the song, "arguta referens carmina blanditia," states that the flattering songs had been composed and rehearsed at home. The song itself is interesting for its use of alliteration and other rhetorical repetitions (see 23–24 and 29–30), but equally prominent is the systematic introduction of allusions to religious practices in the suitor's inset *carmen*. The first is the reference to prayer in verse 20, "nescia furtivas reddere mota preces?" ("can nothing teach thee to relent and be the herald of stealthy prayers?"), but further on the allusions become more detailed and sustained:

> at tibi saepe novo deduxi carmina versu,
> osculaque inpressis nixa dedi gradibus
> ante tuos quotiens verti me, perfida, postes.
> debitaque occultis vota tuli manibus!

> (41–44)

> [Nay, I have often spun the thread of song for thee in novel verse,
> and bent me down to print the gift of kisses on thy steps.
> How many a time, traitress, have I turned round before thy posts
> and paid the votive offering with hidden hands!]

The *osculum* was "a mark of respect usually paid to sacred buildings," and Vulpius saw the turning-round mentioned in verse 43 as an ancient religious custom.[30] The mock-religious subtext is evident throughout verses 40–44, and the cult of Janus might have inspired the account. By way of conclusion, Propertius lets the suitor's elaborate complaint be followed by four verses given to the door (45–48). Thus the poem ends with two distichs that return to the point of view with which it began: the door's complaint that it has been "defamed with everlasting obloquy" ("aeterna differor inividia").

Considering the poem as a whole, we note that the four parts are patterned in interesting ways. The references to time are nicely grouped both as a sequence and spatially: the action outlines a movement from night "nocturnis . . . rixis," verse 5), through midnight, "mediae noctes," verse 24, to the break of day ("matutinis . . . alitibus," verse 46). A particular finesse is seen in the placement of the reference to midnight in the central distich. Moreover, this temporal scheme coincides with another scheme: the opening section focuses on the past, signaled by the temporal adverb *olim*, while the two central sections focus on the present as heralded by the initial adverb *nunc*, and the final section is spoken in the present but with a view to the future (*semper . . . aeterna*). The three sections are grouped into the balanced constellation of 4 + 40 + 4 verses.

These patterns are clearly significant, but we find more obvious patterns in a number of verbal repetitions of interest with regard to the symbolism of Janus[31] as well as to Augustine's carmen of antitheses. It so happens that at the transition between the door's complaint and the suitor's inset song, Propertius refers to the shrill sound of the songs: *arguta . . . carmina* (16). The reference comes strategically in the sixteenth of the forty-eight verses, which divides the poem into 16 : 32 verses, or an inverted version of the diapason (2 : 1). This emphasis on the contrast between what has passed and what is to come at this point of division suggests an allusion to Janus bifrons, the two-faced god who "alone of all the heavenly ones . . . see[s] both back and front" (verse 92). Thus Ovid explains in the *Fasti* that Janus is a god of creation:

me penes est unum vasti custodia mundi,
et ius vertendi cardinis omne meum est.

(119–20)

[The guardianship of this vast universe is in my hands alone,
and none but me may rule the wheeling pole.]

On a more prosaic level, Janus was the guardian of the threshold, because

> Every door has two fronts,
> this way and that, whereof one faces the people
> and the other the house-god.

(134–36)

Apart from this prosaic fact of domestic architecture, the principle of two into one is also reflected in the fact that the deity shared his temple in Rome with Jupiter, which led Augustine to claim that Jupiter and Janus were one and the same god.[32] Ovid explains:

> Iuppiter in parte est; cepit locus unus utrumque
> iunctaque sunt magno templa nepotis avo.

(293–94)

> [One place found room for both, and the temples
> of the mighty grandsire and the grandson are joined together.]

We see, then, that there are several good reasons for dividing a poem centered on a door according to the most basic of proportions, the diapason. The musical symbolism (*arguta . . . carmina*) strengthens this impression, while at the same time producing an analogue in textual form that harmonizes with the act of creation as reflected by Ovid's Janus in *The Fasti*.[33]

As a "builder" with words, Propertius weaves the various parts of the poem together with a subtle network of carefully placed verbal repetitions. These are often placed at opposite ends of the poem so that they in some sense become structural *contraposita*, albeit not *antitheses* proper. These repetitions may single out other structurally significant points within the poem's structure, such as the textual center and the points at which the text divides into the proportion 1 : 2—that is, after verses 16 and 32. Of these points, the transition from the door's account to the suitor's paraclausithyron is unquestionably due to the change in narrative focus and the embedded allusion. The point of division is furthermore marked and supported by iterated words, and thus the word *ianua* in the opening distich is repeated as the initial word of the inset poem, and the thematically significant word "postes" in the distich preceding is repeated in the final distich (verse 43). In this way Propertius weaves a careful web of correspondences between the poem's different parts. Not only are words from the beginning of the second part ("nunc ego noctis . . . rixis"; verse 5) inverted and antithetically balanced in the fourth part ("matutinis . . . alitibus. / sic ego nunc"; verses 46–47), they are also rehearsed after the second structural division in verse 32: "*nunc* iacet alterius felici nixa lacerto: / ut mea *nocturno* verba cadunt *Zephyro*" ("Now she is leaning in repose on another's happy arm, while my words are scattered by the zephyrs of the night"; 33–34). We note that verse 32 incorporates a musical allusion to ascent comparable to the one found in verse 16: "surget et invitis spiritus in lacrimis" ("and the sigh will arise amongst unbidden tears"). The "musical" points of the poem thus relate as in Fig. 2.

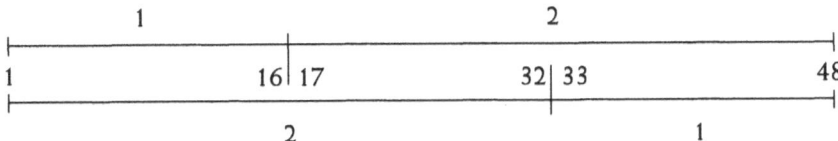

**FIG. 2**

Diapasic points of division in Propertius I.xvi

This double musical and architectural division into the graded arrangement of 1 : 2 (2 : 1) finds confirmation in Tibullus's Elegy I.iii.[34]

Returning to Propertius, we find that the distich following upon the division (33–34) dramatizes the fact that the suitor's song will fail by establishing an antithetical relationship to the preceding passionate outburst. Thus the lover's soaring sigh is said to fall prey to the wind (verse 33). The effect is that of a peripety in the poem's dramatic trajectory indicated in a way that was to become conventional in Renaissance poetry.[35] Can this be a striking example of the *contraposita* that Augustine associated with a *carmen pulcherrimum?* I believe so, and propose that a further examination of the verbal texture will uncover a series of examples of distributed verbal signs where the thematic or verbal similarity is accompanied by a significant contrast, or what we may refer to as antithesis. The following repetitions encircle the central distich (verses 23–24) containing the reference to midnight:

## The Contraposita of Propertius I.xvi

captorum lacrimis (4)
   indignis . . . manibus (6)
      querelas, / supplicibus a longis (14–15)
         duris clausa taces foribus (18)
           nostro . . . dolori (21)
*Textual center:* me mediae noctes . . . (24)
            humanos . . . dolores (25)
         respondes tacitis mutua cardinibus (26)
      longa . . . querela (39)
    occultis . . . manibus (44)
amantis / fletibus (47–48)

This already exhaustive list shows how at that time such *contraposita* could be said to enhance the harmony of an excellent poem, although several of the pairings are mere *contraposita*, not antitheses proper. Propertius here appears as a verbal "builder," and his verbal art became the starting-point for the creative endeavors of Ovid.

In fact, Ovid's *Amores* I.vi, affords the most highly rhetorically developed example of the genre. His poem is a kind of dramatic monologue addressed to the doorkeeper:

Ianitor—indignum!—dura religate catena,
Difficilem moto cardine pande forem!

[Janitor—unworthy fate!—bound with the hard chain,
move on its hinge the surly portal, and open it!]

Throughout we hear only the outbursts and frustrations of the increasingly embittered lover. The lack of response from the janitor, and the poet's insistent pleas, are emphasized by an unusually high frequency of repetitions, the most striking feature undoubtedly being the exact repetition of the line "tempora noctis eunt; excute poste seram!" as many as five times (24, 32, 40, 48, and 56). Each repetition occurs at an interval of eight verses, a number traditionally associated with harmony, but the musical aspects here are probably of secondary importance, unless they point to an ironic contrast. The chief purpose, no doubt, is to suggest that the door is as fixed as the verse itself.

The concept of harmony enters the poem in a more conspicuous sense when Ovid develops the metaphor of no response used by both Propertius and Tibullus to establish structural divisions matching those found in the creations of his fellow poets. In Ovid's elegy the "critical" point comes after verse 48, and at the very moment when the lover first imagines he is hearing the hinges turn to allow him to enter:

Fallimur, an verso sonuerunt cardine postes,
Raucaque concussae signa dedere fores?

[Am I deceived, or did the post sound with the hinge,
and was that the hoarse signal given by the shaken door?]

This distich of doubt keeps the suitor and the reader for a moment in suspense before we realize the suitor's mistake, and we soon get the prosaic explanation: "Fallimur; inpulsa est animoso ianua vento" ("I am deceived—it was only the beating of a gusty wind upon the portal").

The punning reference in verses 49–50 to the absence of the desired sound falls at what can be termed a pivotal point in the poem's structure, because it separates the introductory forty-eight verses from the concluding twenty-four verses of the elegy. Thematically and in mood, this is also the point at which the *historia* of the poem changes direction and a distinctly downbeat, pessimistic mood is introduced. The repetition of the word *fallimur* (in verses 49 and 51) dramatizes the fact that the poem (and the poet's hope) remains undecided and in the balance for a brief moment. With the second, correcting "fallimur," the wheel of fortune has, as it were, turned.

In terms of elocution, we notice that Ovid links the beginning and the end to the point of division. Most notably, a nexus of key words found at the beginning—*dura, catenae, cardine,* and *forem*—appears in the distichs before and after the point of division, and again in the elegy's final distich:

Ianitor—indignum!—*dura* religate catena,
Difficilem moto *cardine* pande *forem*.

(1–2)

Dummodo sic, in me *durae* transite catenae!
Tempora noctis eunt; excute *poste* seram!

Fallimur, an verso sonuerunt *cardine postes*,
Raucaque concussae signa dedere *fores?*

(47–50)

Vos quoque, crudeles rigido cum limine *postes*
*Duraque* conservae ligna, valete, *fores!*

(73–74)

It is certainly possible to describe these verbal recurrences in various suggestive ways. One might say that the poem hinges on them or that the structure is indicated or cemented by the repetition of words like *dura* and *postes*, but whatever the metaphor chosen, the fact remains that Ovid took considerable care to connect these parts verbally, so that he treats the poem as if it constitutes one long period.

Ovid's use of artful rhetorical resumptions does not end here. He adds other types of ornament as well, adornment revealing that he wanted the reader to take in and contemplate the whole structure of the poem at once, as if it had been a patterned mosaic. The focal point for this secondary extrasyntactic pattern coincides with the textual center by line count in verses 36–38, which contain self-referring passages alluding to its centrality: first, of course, we note the mock reference to coronation ("lapsa corona," 38; "the fallen coronet"), but also the allusion to division ("a membris dividar ipse meis," 36) and circular structure ("circa mea tempora vinum," 37). As Alastair Fowler has shown, this technique of indicating the center became conventional in Renaissance literature.[36] The constitutive elements in the secondary structure appear more clearly when we make the passage at the center our starting-point so that we read the text spatially. A spatial reading allows us to perceive how Ovid has encircled the textual center with a chiastic verbal arrangement. Thus the phrase "in media pace" (30) and the words "amantem" (31) and "seram" (32) are balanced in inverse order by the words "seram" (40) and "amantis" (41) and the phrase "in mediae sidera" (44). This mosaic-like pattern[37] is detected only when the reader has processed the entire textual field and considers all of it at once, an operation facilitated by the scrolls on which the text was written in antiquity. A poem like *Amores* I.vi (74 lines) would probably have filled three or more columns or blocks of text capable of being surveyed visually at one glance. Thus the reader would have perceived how key words in the opening distich ("Ianitor indignum, *dura* religate catena, / Difficilem moto cardine pande *forem*") reemerge in the final line: *"Duraque conservae ligna, valete, fores!"*

It so happens that the circular return of words in the poems of Propertius and Ovid accords well with what is the probable substratum provided by the hymns of the ancient Janus cult, although the textual evidence is slender, with the exception of the fragmentary *Carmina Saliorum.*[38] Macrobius comments in the *Saturnalia* that Janus was indeed associated with the sun, the annual cycle, and the orbit of the earth:

> ad demonstrandum anni dimensionem, quae praecipua est solis potestas, alii mundum, id est, coelum esse voluerint; Ianumque ab eundo dictum, quod mundus semper eat dum in orbem volvitur, et ex se initium faciens in se refertur.

> [(some say) Janus symbolizes the shape of the year, which is close to the power of the sun, others take him to be the world, that is, the heavens; and Janus is termed so from going (*eundo*), because the world always turns in a circle, and from the point of beginning returns to itself.][39]

Supporting evidence is in the third of the *Carmen saliare* fragments, which contains the chiastic verse "es iáneús, ianés es" (thou art Janus, Janus art):

> Ozeúl, o dómine, es omnium
> patér! Patúlci, Cloési,
> es iáneús, ianés es!
> duonús cerus es oénus,
> promélius déuom récum.

(p. 30)[40]

This archaic invocation aligning Janus with the sun and giving him the title of father and creator attests to the important role of the god as one of the *di indigetes* and shows how intrinsically he was associated with a principle of circular return. The poem suggests how the cult of the *Janus bifrons* came to furnish poets like Propertius and Ovid with a symbolic and formal subtext for their *paraclausithyra.*

The composition of poetry where important divisions are indicated by means of rhetorical repetitions encouraged a visual approach unfamiliar to us today. Unfamiliar though it may be, we must acknowledge that this dimension may have been an important factor in the transmission and enjoyment of many poems on a par with the more familiar figure poem, where the graphic shape expressed its subject.[41] We find the visual approach in medieval religious poetry—for example, in the poems of Hrabanus Maurus (780–856), who composed a cycle of twenty-eight poems on the cross, "De laudibus sanctae crucis," where the message of the cross and its very shape are found in figures created by the poetic text.[42] We witness a less figural and more abstract and hidden method of celebrating divine order in the Anglo-Saxon poem entitled "Cleanness" included in the manuscript Cotton Nero A.x,[43] where the poet uses "simple geometrical constructions" as his basis.[44] Such constructions embody the medieval concept of the divinity as either architect or geometer who imposes form on the cosmos by using a compass.[45] It is therefore fascinating to see that the author of the *Poetria nova* (ca. 1208–13) recommends a similar method:

> Circinus interior mentis praecircinet omne
> Materiae spatium. Certus praelimitet ordo
> Unde praearripiat cursum stylus, at ubi Gades / Figat.

(55–57)

[Let the inner compasses of the mind lay out the entire range of the material. Let a certain order predetermine from what point the pen should start on its course, and where the utmost limits shall be fixed.]

(p. 16)

Here we clearly recognize the idea of working from an abstract plan such as that of a geometrical construction on a planar surface.

The examples of structural poësis uncovered in classical *paraclausithyra* do not quite reach the level of difficulty or abstraction encountered in *Cleanness*, or the poetry of Hrabanus Maurus for that matter, but they nevertheless mark the inception of the kind of artful proportioning that we find in medieval and Renaissance religious poetry. Notable in this context is the persistent use in *Cleanness* of the ratio of 1 : 2 combined with a preoccupation with the concept of threshold. This concept seems to have played an important role in this medieval poem too, thus forging a link between *Cleanness* and Latin elegiac poetry.[46] The genre of the *paraclausithyron* and its poetic techniques may also be traced in the "modern" examples provided by de Vinsauf himself, and then notably in the *Sanctae Crucis querela* ("The lament of the holy cross").

De Vinsauf's *prosopopeia* is a vigorous religious poem where the holy cross accuses Christians of having abandoned it. The cross, then, has been granted "the power of speech" (p. 39) in a way that recalls the indignant door's address in the poem by Propertius. Let us listen to the opening verses:

Crux ego rapta queror, vi raptaque manuque canina
Et tactu polluta canum. Sum rapta pudenter
A veteri, nec adhuc extorta, nec ense redempta.

(469–71)

[I, the ravished cross, lament, being snatched away by the force of rabid hands and polluted by the touch of dogs. I was shamefully taken away long ago; to this time I have not been wrested back by force nor redeemed by the sword] (p. 39)

The lament echoes the indignant complaint spoken by the Propertian door: "I am now wounded in nightly brawls of revellers / And have oft to complain of blows from unworthy hands." We perceive how the classical poetic mode has been transferred and reinterpreted to fit a Christian framework.[47] Technique and tone are not the only elements that point to an ongoing dialogue with the pagan past, because de Vinsauf also displays a use of verbal ornament similar to that of his predecessor. Particularly striking is the use of repetitions to mark the equal division into equal parts, which is a basic ingredient in the *paraclausithyra*.

The *Sanctae Crucis querela* consists of thirty-nine lines, which is the number of the cross.[48] The poem is divided into two main parts, separated by a centrally placed insistent appeal to the Christian to turn back, followed by a promise to return: "Ego, si verteris, ad te / Vertar et instanter ad corda reversa revertar" (19–20). The first half (1–20) contains primarily rebuke and lament, whereas the second half (21–39) is more inviting and persuasive, ending on a distinct note of hope. The central line (20), with its strong emphasis on conversion, constitutes, so to speak, the poem's peripety, and line 21 emerges as a new beginning with the image of the soaring turtle from the Song of Songs: "Surge cito, propera, te citat et excitat hora." The image also crops up in the last verse as winged will, "voluntas alata" (39), thus connecting the middle to the end.[49]

The first three lines and the lines that follow immediately after the central line are linked also by a series of tangible verbal repetitions, which underline the new beginning. The words repeated (*Crux-ego-ense-redempta* // *Ego-crux-redemit-ense-crucem-redimas*) follow a partly linear and partly chiastic pattern, both patterns being frequently used in classical elegies. Chiasmus is the obvious figure for a poem about the cross, because the Greek letter Chi (X) is the first letter in the name of Christ. Its very shape was explained as referring to the cross. Consequently, the "Hermogenis figura" was often used to allude to the cross in medieval religious poetry.[50] We observe that the system of repetitions serves to link the beginning, middle, and end, so that the technique obeys the rule recommended in antiquity for rounded sentences. We find this rule among de Vinsauf's own recommendations in the *Poetria nova*.

The structural aesthetics developed from the theory of the period caused Tasso to claim, like Augustine, that "the art of composing a poem resembles the plan of the universe, which is composed of contraries, as that of music is."[51] This claim had a great impact on Renaissance aesthetics. Leading critics of Renaissance structural poetics such as Alastair Fowler, S. K. Heninger Jr., Thomas P. Roche Jr., Maren-Sofie Røstvig, and others, have shown the degree to which many Italian and English Renaissance poets applied the principles associated with this aesthetic in their work. Nevertheless, surprisingly little attention has been devoted to the study of the decisive role of periodic rhetoric for such patterns and their presence in classical poetry. The preceding analyses show that Latin *paraclausithyra* provide practical examples of how the period functioned as an aesthetic ideal. As instances of the formally perfect *carmen pulcherrimum* praised by Saint Augustine, these elegies served as a basis for imitation in a Christian context by a medieval theorist and poet like de Vinsauf.

Because of the great cultural changes that occurred between antiquity and the Renaissance, the *paraclausithyron* could not remain a vital genre except as an object of study or translation. Its role was taken over by shorter forms, such as the sonnet, a new type of poem focused on the frustrations of the poet as lover placed in a strong ethical framework. With the renewed interest in rhetoric in the Renaissance, it is nevertheless clear that the periodic rhetoric embodied in the *paraclausithyra* analyzed here furnished poets with important formal models.[52] This seminal influence is most apparent in cinquecento commentaries on Aristotle's *Poetics,* one of the centers of Renaissance literary theory. Thus such theorists as Robortello and Castelvetro relate what Aristotle says about plot in tragedy to his account of the rhetorical period in *The Rhetoric,* Book Three.[53] In the definition of unity of action—"totum verò est, quod principium, medium, atque finem habet"—Robortello explicitly draws attention to the similarity between the unity of plot and the definition of the unity of the period:

> Aristitotelis libro Rhetoricorum tertio, vbi loquitur de periodo in oratione, habet quiddam, quod simillimum est his verbis, quibus vtitur nunc in declarando.[54]

> [The Third Book of Aristotle's Rhetoric, where the period in speech is treated, states much the same, being very similar in phrasing to what is being said now.]

The basis for making the comparison, as Robortello points out, is both the similar phrasing and that Aristotle compares the structure of a long period to the structure of speeches and dithyrambs. He thus suggests the extension of the formal matrix to larger compositions,[55] and also practices ring composition himself.[56] The degree to which a Renaissance poem or play was thought of in terms of a macro-period is demonstrated by Christopher Marlowe. In *1 Tamburlaine the Great,* the pioneering dramatist and translator of the *Amores* applies the aesthetic ideal to love poetry in general when the protagonist discusses the inadequacy of poetry to capture beauty:

> What is beauty, saith my sufferings then?
> If all the pens that ever poets held,
> Had fed the feeling of their masters' thoughts,
> And every sweetness that inspired their hearts,
> Their minds, and muses on admired themes:
> If all the heavenly quintessence they still
> From their immortal flowers of poesy,
> wherein as in a mirror we perceive
> The highest reaches of a human wit,

If all had made *one poem's period,*
And all combin'd in beauty's worthiness,
Yet should there hover in their restless heads
One thought, one grace, one wonder at the least,
Which into words no virtue can digest.

(V.i.165–78; italics added)

It has been documented that Marlowe practiced the ideal of "one poem's period" when structuring speeches by means of rhetorical repetitions and that he structured a play as a whole in the same way.[57] In this context it is also useful to consult his poetic practice in the translation of the *Amores* I.vi to see how he responds to Ovid's verbal artistry.

When we take into account the obvious differences between a poem composed in hexameters and one in rhymed pentameters couplets, it is interesting to note that Marlowe seems to have appreciated the musical division of the elegy into a graded arrangement of 2 : 1. In keeping with the structural use of rhyme in Renaissance poetry, Marlowe repeats rhyme sounds to create an effect similar to that which he studied in Ovid. Thus the rhyme sound of the opening couplet crops up in the crucial verses 47–48:

Unworthy porter, bound in chains full *sore,*
On moved hooks *set ope the* churlish *door.*

(1–2)

Though it be so, shut me not out there*fore,*
Night goes away, I pray thee *ope the door.*

(47–48; italics added)

When Marlowe thus substitutes one set of structural markers for another, more appropriate for his age, he confirms his awareness of the presence of a graded division around a central unit—48-2-24 verses—in the original poem.[58] It must be added that this is the only time this particular rhyme sound is used in the seventy-four-line poem. Note too that Marlowe repeats not only rhyme words but also the same verb in the same form, "ope the door." He also stresses the point of division by adding a chiasmus not found in Ovid when he lets the question "Err we" be balanced by the answer "We err," whereas the Roman poet uses "fallimur" twice. On the whole, however, Marlowe reduces the number of repetitions in his version, focusing his attention instead on the principal thematic and structural division.

Marlowe is not the only poet to refer to how "the flowers of poesy" may be combined into "one poem's period." This ideal is alluded to in several sixteenth-century treatises on poetics, but it is nevertheless rarely explained and illustrated in detail. There are, however, some notable exceptions. Thus Samuel Daniel describes in detail the act of writing poetry as being both architectural in its verbal structure and edifying in the sense of an architectonic structure,[59] at the same that he offers valuable, explicit information about the role of rhyme when shaping a poem into "an Orbe of order and form."[60]

In the *Defence of ryme* (1603) he first defines rhyme as: "number and harmonie of words, consisting of an agreeing sound in the last silables of seuerall verses, giuing both to the Eare an Eccho of a delightfull report & to the Memorie a deeper impression of what is deliuered therein" (pp. 7–8). The phrase "a deeper impression" indicates that, like Landino and Sidney before him, Daniel considers rhyme not simply in terms of pleasing sound effects. He actually attributes more important functions to rhyme than most modern readers would allow, for to him rhyme is "comparable to the best inventions of the world" and begets "conceit beyond expectation" (p. 16). Then too, a proper use of rhyme actually appeals to the mind and invests a poem with *enargia*, a quality Renaissance poets and theorists attributed to well-ordered poetry. George Puttenham explains *enargia* as the "glorious lustre and light" uniting the "outward shew" and the "inward working" of figurative language (III.iii.142–43),[61] whereas Torquato Tasso emphasizes the visibility implied by *enargia*.[62] This twofold function of verbal ornament is identical to the double effect Daniel attributes to rhyme: the "delightful report . . . to the Eare" and the "deeper impression . . . to the Memorie."[63] The key concepts are Daniel's "report," in the double sense of "message" and "repetition," and Puttenham's "glorious lustre and light," and we must remember that *lumen* and *lux* were commonly used to denote rhetorical figures. *Enargia (illustratio)* therefore refers to the impact made by the configuration of visible and audible rhetorical figures *(lumina)* in a given text. Although Daniel introduces his argument by referring to the effect on the ear, other terms employed by Daniel and Puttenham ("shew," "lustre," and "light"), and indeed the etymology of *enargia*, presuppose "that verbal vision is possible."[64] Puttenham and Daniel both offer examples of how "figure breedeth . . . light" and "vertuous operation" in poetry, but for convenience I here limit myself to the latter's Platonizing description of how "the unformed Chaos" of the imagination may be "wrought into an Orbe of order and forme . . . by the divine power of the spirit."[65] The terminology used is once again that of creation, but we are wrong if we think that this way of composing is restricted to religious poetry.

The terms Daniel employs to describe poetry characterized by a proper use of rhymes—"Orbe," "girum," "circuit," and "periode"—are all terms drawn from rhetoricians' definitions,[66] which suggests that he favored cyclical textual arrangements in his poetry. He tells us that this method is practiced in "some" of his sonnets and that its use may entail breaking up expected rhyme schemes, as when he argues that a "manumission from bondage" is achieved when rhyme is reduced "in girum, and a iust forme" (p. 16). The sonnets alluded to must be *Delia* IX and XXXVIII, which display circular rhyme schemes and a variety of verbal figures of the kind analyzed earlier in this chapter. In *Delia* IX, rhymes and other key words are arranged so as to encircle the mythological image of Sisyphus at the poem's center (italics added):

| | |
|---|---|
| *If this be loue, to drawe a weary breath,* | a |
| Paine on flowdes, till the shore, crye to th'ayre: | b |
| With downward lookes, still reading on the earth; | c |
| The sad memorials of my loues despaire. | b |
| *If this be loue,* to warre against my soule, | d |
| Lye downe *to waile,* rise vp to sigh and *grieue me* | e |
| The neuer-resting stone of care to roule, | d |
| Still to complaine *my greifes,* and none releiue me. | e |
| *If this be loue,* to cloth me with darke thoughts, | f |
| Haunting vntrodden pathes *to waile* apart; | g |
| My pleasures horror, Musiques tragicke notes, | f |
| Teares in my eyes, and sorrowe at my heart. | g |
| *If this be loue,* to liue a liuing death; | a |
| O then loue I, and *drawe this weary breath.* | a |

The sonnet's rhyme scheme is surprisingly "imperfect" and exhibits several half-rhymes before the initial rhyme word *breath* is repeated in the concluding couplet, thus creating an enclosing verbal *circuitus*. The iterated rhyme-

words in verses 1, 6, 8, and 14 (*breath-me-me-breath*) encircle and give prominence to the lover's hardships as a circular image: "The neuer-resting stone
of care to roule"; 7). As in "The Roundell or Spheare" quoted by Puttenham
(II.xi.98–99), Daniel's rhymes produce *enargia* visually observed on the page.
When the phrase "If this be loue" occurs four times (lines 2, 5, 9, and 13),
this recalls *Amores* I.vi. This anaphoric repetition and the twice-iterated verb
"to waile" (lines 5 and 9) further strengthen the impression of futile movement within a restricted space. The poem, so to speak, folds back upon itself
as in the chiasmus included in the couplet "If this be *loue,* to *liue* a *liuing* death;
O then *loue* I" (13–14; italics added). As in Shakespeare's Sonnet 129 the
many rhetorical repetitions provide a striking example of mannered
artifice.[67]

We have seen such Renaissance poets as Marlowe and Daniel openly
refer to the period as a formal matrix for artists to imitate. We have seen too
that they compare poetic structure to the structure of the universe and that
the effect of poetry resembles heavenly music in its measured harmonies.
They therefore adopt the very techniques favored by Propertius and Ovid.
Daniel also introduces architectural metaphors into his writing, as when he
likens his rhymed "orbs" to well-ordered rooms (p. 17).[68] Thus, he fully acknowledges that the rhetorically formulated principles that poetry shares
with architecture and the other arts are universal, a notion suggested by
Scamozzi's title, *L'Idea dell'architettura universale.*[69]

Stressing the interdependence of the arts while celebrating the role of
poetry, Daniel differs from his rival Campion, who claims that poetry is less
directly linked with that higher music than practical music. Practical music
"held its place in an interdependence with celestial harmony,"[70] although
"simmetry and proportion" in poetry was believed to stem ultimately from
the same source. In Chapter 3 we shall see how one of the most influential
theorists and architects of the early Renaissance, Leon Battista Alberti, illustrates the importance of rhetorical rules of composition when describing
Filippo Brunelleschi's cupola of Santa Maria del Fiore.

FIG. 3
Filippo Brunelleschi, rear view of S. Maria del Fiore, Florence

*Edificare*

Representing Brunelleschi's Dome of Santa Maria del Fiore

> The final end of the orator is to persuade,
> that is, to move somebody to act, or to compel
> him to pursue goodness, and to flee evil.

—Vossius, *Rhetorica* I.1.4

Early Renaissance authors were invariably more concerned with the ethical and religious aspects of their written creations than many twentieth-century scholars seem to believe. To explain the insistence of the former on order and proportion solely in terms of a cultivation of form for its own sake is therefore unhelpful. It would be equally misleading, though, to try to ignore the element of playfulness and the studied use of ambiguity in works of art and poetry, however elevated. The mixture of high seriousness and playful attentiveness to form, and thus also an inclusive and inviting attitude toward reader and spectator participation, are almost omnipresent in Renaissance poetry and art. What, then, is the relationship between such playful compositional practices and the ethical and aesthetic suppositions prompting the production of an edifying text? In Chapter 1 we saw that when a character in a play by Shakespeare talks about fortifying in paper, the allusion does not primarily concern spiritual *aedificatio*,[1] but bears on a process of planning for action; it is this planning that is expressed in terms of a preplanned architectural design. Such allusions are evident also when Vasari, in the *Life of Michelangelo*, relates that Buonarroti in a dispute with San Gallo over the plans for fortifications at San Miniato in Monte declared that he had gained experience by fortifying his thoughts.[2] Such examples of sixteenth-century planning practices have fifteenth-century roots in humanist theories of education and in the humanists' classical training.[3]

This connection between ethics, rhetoric, and aesthetics is presented in a highly illustrative and suggestive manner by Leon Battista Alberti in his *Profugiorum ab aerumna* ("On the Tranquillity of the Soul").[4] This dialogue in three books was written in 1441–42, a few years before Alberti began working on his massive treatise on architecture, composed between 1443 and 1452. Although the topic of the dialogue is how one should proceed to shield the mind from distress, it begins, surprisingly enough, with a long ekphrastic passage on Brunelleschi's recently completed dome of Santa Maria del Fiore at Firenze. The passage is unique in Alberti's oeuvre, because as a rule Alberti does not describe or refer to contemporary buildings in his writings on art. This description is included not primarily as a contribution to architectural theory or as a record of building practices, but as an architectural example of a different kind.[5] To investigate exactly how that ethical purpose is expressed rhetorically, I propose to read the passage in relation to similar descriptions elsewhere in the *Profugiorum*, as a guide to understanding the close interrelationship between rhetorical composition and ethics in Alberti's writings.

With this relationship in view, let us turn our attention to a passage on architecture at the end of the dialogue, when Alberti has fully developed his theme. Here one of the interlocutors, Agnolo di Filippo Pandolfini, tells us about various intellectual exercises he has devised in order to soothe his agitated mind ("mie agitazioni d'animo") and fortify it against external influences that may beset a man's mind at night. One of these nocturnal exercises involves the imagined construction of a classically inspired edifice:

E talora . . . , composi a mente e coedificai qualche compositissimo edificio, e disposivi più ordini e numeri di colonne con vari capitelli e base inusitate, e collega'vi conveniente e nuova grazia di cornici e tavolati. (III.182)

[And at one time . . . I composed in mind and put together some well-assembled edifice, and there arranged various storeys (*ordini*) and numbers of columns with diverse capitals and unusual bases, and I added to it a convenient and novel grace by means of cornices and marble plaques.]

Alberti's use of the term *ordini* suggests that in this passage the term may have begun to acquire the expanded meaning of "the Orders," for the *genera* of columns.[6] Probably, "ordini" here primarily refers to storeys of columns, but the ethical context extends its semantic reach to include aspects of Augustine's *ordo* as described in *De ordine*. Order is a crucial concept that is used repeatedly in the third and final book of the *Profugiorum*, as applied to various subjects and with different yet related meanings.[7] The emphasis on columns here and elsewhere in the *Profugiorum* may reflect the "ethical interpretation of a column as a symbol of balance, purity and incorruptibility."[8] We are told how the mind may be trained to create a bulwark against adversity by creating an architectural fantasy. Judging by the details of that fiction, the fantasy is characterized both by *concinnitas* and by *varietas*. Symmetry is suggested by such terms as "coedificai qualche compositissimo edificio" and "conveniente . . . grazia," which bring to mind the Latin term *convenientia* in both a Ciceronian and an Augustinian sense (that is, harmony). Variety is equally prominent in terms such as "vari capitelli e basi inusitate" and "nuova grazia."[9]

Abstract, mental speculations are not merely aids to sound sleep; they also occupy a place in his more vast project of *utilitas*. In fact, the investigation comprises and culminates in "mathematical demonstrations," seen as most valuable when developed for practical use ("qualche utile pratica in vita"). And here Agnolo specifically mentions the experimental and practical work of the author himself:

> massime quando io studio ridurle a qualche utile pratica in vita; come fece qui Battista, qual cavò e' suoi rudimenti di pittura anch'i suoi elementi da' matematice, e cavonne quelle incredibili preposizioni *de motibus ponderis*. (III.182).

> [especially when I tried to reduce these to some practical purpose in life; the way our Battista did when he developed his elements of painting from his mathematical ones, and developed those incredible propositions in *De motibus ponderis*.]

The mental preparations outlined by Alberti are the creation of "another nature within ourselves." "[S]piritual tranquillity . . . is a human creation," it
has been written, "built up as a moral edifice through human intention,
knowledge, and skill."[10] Although Alberti appears not to have used the term
*altra natura* explicitly, we discern behind this kind of reasoning that became
current in the century to follow[11] the ancient description of how man mod-
ified the natural environment for his own benefit by using nature as a
model.[12] Cicero, who is everywhere present in Alberti's thinking, had outlined that process in *De natura deorum*, where he explains how: "We sow corn
and plant trees. We fertilize the soil by irrigation. We dam the rivers, to
guide them where we will. One may say that we seek with our human hands
to create a second nature [*alteram naturam*] in the natural world."[13] To Cicero
"[n]ature is our teacher and guide,"[14] and he numbers architecture among
the useful arts—"[artes] illa necessitatis, cultus dico agrorum extruc-
tionesque tectorum"[15]—in which man exerts his capacity to create another
nature. This combination of ethics and building, so essential to Cicero's influential treatise, was taken over and developed in *De re aedificatoria*.[16] No
wonder, then, that a house may reflect the owner's character: "a man's dignity may be enhanced by the house he lives in, but not wholly secured by
it," Cicero explains, as he warns against excess and luxury (I.xxxix.139). Alberti utilizes this argument in Book Nine of his treatise when he transferred
it from the private to the public sphere: "because we decorate our house as
much to adorn our fatherland and family [*patriae familiaeque condecorandae*] as
for the sake of elegance, who will deny that such activity is the duty of a
good man [*boni viri officium*]?" Alberti here comes close "to admitting his debt
[to Cicero] . . . by his use of the word *officium*."[17] Then too, Alberti's choice
of a model contributed to the structure of his treatise on architecture, by
prompting its division into five initial books on *usus* and four books on *pulchritudo* and *ornamentum*, a choice that conditioned "the future history of architecture and architectural theory."[18] However, the division does not entail
an absolute opposition between the two aspects of the art, for Alberti works
from "the premise that composition (*opus*) and refinement (*ornamentum*) are
inseparable components of the art of building."[19] Nevertheless, he takes a
radical step away from the Vitruvian view of ornament when he defines it as
"a Kind of auxiliary Brightness and Improvement to Beauty. So that then
Beauty is somewhat lovely which is proper and innate, and diffused over the
whole Body, and Ornament somewhat added and fastened on, rather than
proper and innate."[20] Although this entails no absolute opposition between

*Body* and *Ornament*, Alberti here "anticipates the trend towards an ever-widening divergence between form and decoration."[21] On the whole, however, adornment is acceptable to Alberti when controlled by utility and informed by the same principles of classical beauty as the structure of the work itself.[22]

In other words, an apt correspondence must prevail between the interior and exterior parts of a work, for—as de Vinsauf put it—"unless the inner ornament corresponds to the outer requirement, the relationship between the two is worthless."[23] Alberti's aesthetic ideas are consistent with this Ciceronian tradition in rhetoric, here cited in a high medieval version.[24]

Cicero had stated that a house should exhibit both utility and beauty ("ornanda enim est dignitas domo") because the dignity of the house depends on the moderation ("modestia") or moral rectitude ("honestas") exhibited in its execution.[25] Following the doctrines of the Stoics, Cicero had defined moderation as "the science of disposing aright everything that is done and said,"[26] thus invoking a notion of rhetorical composition that celebrates "the essence of orderliness and of right-placing."[27] Comparing ethics to oratory, he had also explicitly applied this principle to textual composition: "Such orderliness of conduct, therefore, is to be observed, that everything in the conduct of our life shall balance and harmonize, as in a finished speech" (I.xl.144).[28] The well-made or balanced structure of a speech, its *concinnitas*, serves as a formal ideal for the design of a building and at the same time for the virtue of prudence.[29] In a number of passages Cicero describes the distribution of words in a speech or its miniature exemplar, the period, always stressing the importance of verbal ornament along with structure: "Words when connected together embellish a style if they produce a certain symmetry (*concinnitas*) that disappears when the words are changed, though the thought remains the same; for the figures of thought that remain even if the words are changed are to be sure numerous, but relatively few are noticeable."[30] Style, then, is related to morals through a shared intrinsic mental dynamics; both are in turn related to the principles that define Alberti's theory of civic architecture, and indeed his theory of painting.[31] It is clear, therefore, that within the context of Alberti's ethical and rhetorical sources the concept of the architect includes strong elements of the moral philosopher and orator, a person who in addition to using "his mind and his intellect to shape a building" also functions as an erudite adviser.[32] Vincenzo Scamozzi sums up this fundamental similarity between the work of the orator and the architect:

Hà l'Oratore à provare la verità della sua causa, con testimonij, e scrit-ture autentiche, e trattare tutte le cose ornatamente, e con parole chiare, & appropriate alla materia: altresi l'Architetto dee fare i suoi disegni con Moduli regolari, e ben intesi, e . . . con approvare anco in particolare gli ornamenti, le parti, e le membra.[33]

[The orator proves the truthfulness of his case by testimonies and au-thentic writs, and by treating all things ornately and with words that are clear and suited to the matter: for his part the architect must make his designs with regular and easily perceived modules, and . . . ap-prove in detail the ornaments, the parts and the members.]

While bearing this interdependence in mind, let us now see in closer detail how these various aspects of the architect's function are described in Alberti's *Profugiorum*. Like his model Cicero, Alberti extends his ethical de-liberation to include a number of disciplines; thus in Book One he couches his argument in architectural terms:

E parmi accomodata similitudine questa. Come alle tempeste del verno ne addestriamo e apparecchiamo, coperti e difesi dalle veste, dalle mura, da' nostri refugi e redutti, e se pure el tedio delle nevi, la molestia de' venti, le durezze de' freddi ne assedia e costringe, noi op-pogniamo e' vetri alle finestri, e' tappeti agli usci, e precludiamo ogni adito onde a noi possa espirare alcuna ingiuria del verno; . . . così alla volubilità e impeti e tempeste della fortuna bisogna addestrarsi e ap-parecchiarsi con l'animo precludersi dalle perturbazione ogni adito, ed eccitare e susservare in noi quello ignicolo innato e insito ne' nostri animi quale v'aggiune e infuse la natura ad immortale eternità. (III.121)

[This appears to me to be a most appropriate simile. Just as we prepare and equip ourselves against the storms of winter, covered and pro-tected by clothing, by walls, by our shelters and also against the in-convenience of the snow, the ravages of winds, the severity of the cold which beleaguer and hamper us, we put up panes of glass in the win-dows, and append carpets at the entries, and close every exit through which any kind of wintry discomfort may penetrate; . . . likewise it is necessary to train and prepare oneself against the volubility and impe-tus and storms of fortune and mentally block all perturbations from entering, and to excite and further in us that small innate and internal fire of our minds which nature added and infused for immortal eternity.]

Here the terminology found in *De officiis* and *De natura deorum*[34] is directly applied to the process of moral edification and formation by describing how the nature of man may be refined and strengthened. Nor can we avoid noticing the similarity of expression between the above passage ("quello ignicolo inato e insito ne' nostri animi") and the expression "animis innata quaedam ratio" (the reason innate in our minds) in *De re aedificatoria,* where Alberti describes the laws of beauty inherent in man.[35]

Still another way of reinforcing one's mind against adversity consisted in memorizing an already existing poem or excellent piece of prose, thus establishing a link with poetic theory. But it is not sufficient to learn it by heart; it is better still to develop a text through amplification and ornament. Alberti writes:

Soglio darmi a imparare a mente qualche poema o qualche ottima prosa; soglio darmi a commentare qualche essornazione, ad amplificare qualche argumentazione. (III.181)

[I often engage in learning some poem or some piece of excellent prose at heart; I usually busy myself with commenting on some adornment, with the amplification of some argument.]

The phrase "imparare a mente" inevitably makes one think of the *ars memoriae,* and such mnemotechnic exercises are also included among the practices recommended in manuals. But the passage is interesting also because the difference between amplifying an existing text and creating a new one would appear to be minimal. It is fairly easy to imagine how a text may be built by accretion and elaboration, while the basic structure remains the same or is strengthened. The original text would then function as the sketch or *congetto* for the fully finished artifact.[36] And again we see that architectural terminology is employed when a poetic creation—be it that of others or Alberti's own—is compared to the construction of an edifice:

Così avvien presso de' litterati. Gl'ingegni d'Asia e massime e' Greci, in più anni, tutti insieme furono inventori di tutte l'arte e discipline; construssero uno quasi tempio e domicilio in suoi scritti a Pallade e a quella Pronea, da de' filosofi stoici, ed estesero le pareti colla investigazione del vero e del falso: statuirono le colonne col discernere e annotare gli effetti le forze della natura, apposervi el tetto qual difendesse tanta opera dalle tempeste avverse. (III. 161)

[This also authors do. The minds of Asia and especially of the Greeks for many years together invented all the arts and disciplines; they almost built a temple and abode in their works on Pallas and to the goddess Pronea, (and based on) the Stoic philosophers they erected walls in their investigation of the true and the false: they established the diverse kinds of columns after discerning and observing the effects and forces of nature, and there placed a roof which was to defend such a work from adverse tempests.]

We note the parallel drawn between the writings of the Greeks and a temple—that is, between written compositions and architecture—which recalls the similar alignment in Lorenzo Valla between *Verbum Dei / Templum Dei*.[37] The study of Valla's *Encomion sancti Thomae* and the *Elegantiae* (pre-1440) and the *Collatio N. Testamentii* (1453) reveals that rhetoric is a perfect science ("perfecta sapientia") and an instrument to restore Holy Writ, on an analogy with the restoration of the Temple of God.[38] Inevitably, we recall here Alberti's own restoration of San Teodoro and Santo Stefano Rotondo at Rome as architectural analogies.

If we read on in Alberti's text at this point, we note another interesting architectural metaphor for a written composition: the metaphor connects the laying of *tesserae* in a mosaic with the distribution of materials in written work.[39] The metaphor is interesting because it reveals the presence of a written outline for the work, a process dwelt on in detail in *De pictura*.[40] Still Alberti is careful to distinguish between the more or less random piecing together of surplus *tesserae* at Ephesos and his own premeditated and thoughtful mode of composing. Rather than working from previous inventions, however rich and splendid, Alberti says that he has exclusively selected what is suited to his initial design, that these elements have been distributed accordingly:

Noi vero, dove io come colui e come quell'altro volli ornare un mio picciolo e privato diverserio tolsi da quel pubblico e nobilissimo edifi-

cio quel che mi parse accomodato a' miei disegni, e divisolo in più par-
ticelle distribuendole ove a me parse. (III.161)

[But for my part, when like him (Cipreste) or another (architect) I
wished to adorn one of my small and private trifles, I took from a public and most noble edifice what seemed suited to my drawings, and divided it in smaller parts and distributed it where I thought fit.]

Alberti employed this technique also when designing the Tempio Malat-
esta, where structural elements are taken from an imperial Roman building
and reduplicated in the new design.[41] In writing, the same procedure of
adornment would result in the repetition of syntactical and verbal elements
within a global design. Cardini, who is primarily interested in quotations
from ancient authors, not in words repeated within a *lineamentum*, observes
that Alberti's strategy is "rigorous and complex," consisting of "a lucid and I
would say a geometrical strategy of the page within which every "scrap"
finds a new meaning and function."[42] As I show below, this approach is evident in the style chosen for the panegyric narrative about the Florentine
Temple. The narrative is similarly characterized by a desire to create a piece
of ekphrastic writing that matches the *concinnitas* of the building.

   Alberti's chosen style of composition is mixed; he combines elements
of a rational and scientific character and elements typical of architecture and
art.[43] In the opening books of *De re aedificatoria* and *De pictura* he stresses the
links between mathematics and artistic composition, thus laying down a
firm and rational basis for his theories of beauty and utility. To him the laws
of beauty have been given to man as a language "innate in our minds" ("animis innata quaedam ratio").[44] In an Italian Renaissance rendering the rhetorical and logocentric bias of his theory appears clearly, where "ratio" is
rendered "uno discorso, & . . . una ragione" (IX.v.337) in keeping with the
common alignment between *ratio* and *oratio*.[45] The earliest translation into
English ("a secret Argument and Discourse") demonstrates the same connection.[46] When Alberti advocates *concinnitas*, what he presents is an expanded and Christianized version of the Ciceronian rhetorical concept, as
Paolo Portoghesi points out: "Alberti tends however to force its meaning
making it into a conventional category connected to the *unitas* and symmetry as understood in Augustine's *De vera religione* (VI.32)."[47] *Concinnitas*, however, may have other connotations. In the *De re aedificatoria* it appears to mean
harmony, because it refers to the formal principle by which elements are

grouped together so as to produce perfection. As such it is linked to the concept of *mediocritas* and to composition by antitheses. Then too, in the *Profugiorum, concinnitas* is primarily a quality of the finished building. To this end Christine Smith offers an excellent analysis of the antithetical structure of Alberti's description of the cupola of Santa Maria del Fiore. To do justice to her rich argument, I quote part of her analysis:

> The first portion . . . proceeds by pairs of opposites. The first of these, "grazia" and "maiestà," is borrowed from definitions of the stylistic differences between rhetorical styles. . . . In his next pair of opposites, Alberti transforms these general stylistic principles into terms of architectural description: "grace" becomes "charming slenderness," and "majesty" becomes "robust and full solidity." In this way, categories of linguistic styles evolve into terms of architectural description. . . . His last pair of opposites, "designed for pleasure" and "built for perpetuity," at first seem to bring the descriptive criteria within Vitruvius's principles of firmness and delight (*firmitas* and *venustas*), but may depend directly on Vitruvius's source in Cicero's *De Oratore* (III.xlvi). This fundamental antithesis—beauty and necessity—underlies, for Alberti, all architectural design.[48]

On the basis of this analysis, Smith urges: "the harmony evoked in *Profugiorum* must be understood within the context of rhetoric rather than philosophy: it concerns the senses before the intellect and seeks to persuade rather than to move."[49] She relates the described harmony to the instrumental music of Dufay, whose motet *Nuper rosarum flores* had been composed for the consecration ceremony.[50] It is surprising, however, that she does not extend her rhetorical analysis to comprise the entire opening section of Alberti's work. As we shall see, a topomorphical analysis of its internal arrangement and finish lends strong support to the general argument concerning Alberti's strategy of persuasion, as it reveals that Alberti has created a textual web whose overall form reflects the *lineamenta* of the dome itself. In other words, the witty verbal design emulates the splendor of the dome so that the verbal patterning becomes a significant part of the description—a verbal sign pointing to the architectural design (Fig. 7).

My point of departure is Alberti's general argument about the importance of *lineamenta*. As S. Lang has pointed out, *lineamenta*, or "a measured ground-plan" is a key element in Alberti's theory of composition: "To sum up: the ground-plan incorporated the design; those features that could be read from the plan were the essential ones; the measurement of the ground-plan would form the foundations for the dimensions of the height; all measurements are linked by the rules of proportions."[51] If Smith is correct in arguing that to Alberti *mediocritas* represents ethical, aesthetic, and stylistic categories, then a style that combines elements taken from the well-rounded periodic as well as the plain style would seem to be inherently anti-thetical in character. And antitheses are precisely what Alberti used in his description of Brunelleschi's dome.[52] Still, this does not mean that antitheses were applied everywhere, because variety was a highly valued aesthetic quality.[53] For Alberti, *concinnitas* does not necessarily entail symmetrically balanced members or ornaments, but he clearly enjoyed shaping his otherwise sober prescriptions rhetorically so as to render them visible in the verbal texture. In fact, his definition of *lineamenta* itself displays such a well-rounded period in its distribution of verbal lights:

> Atqui est quidem lineamenti munus et officium praescribere aedificiis et partibus aedificiorum aptum locum et certum numerum dignumque modum et gratum ordinem, ut iam tota aedificii forma et figura ipsis in lineamentis conquiescat. (I.i.19)

> [Thus the purpose and function of the design is to bestow on buildings and their parts, an appropriate placing, an exact proportion, a suitable disposition, and a harmonious order, so as to make the whole form and figure of the composition reside entirely in the design itself.]

Alberti's cultivation of a precise Latin style often resulted in his impatience with Vitruvius (VI.5);[54] his own clear period-structure reveals a thorough familiarity with classical authors and their style, and he was as concerned about restoring *Latinitas* as Valla was. Considering Alberti's definition, we recall how Aristotle discusses the rhetorical repetitions to be deployed to adorn the beginnings and ends of sentences.[55] The period contains a crucial part of his argument and accordingly receives special attention in terms of rhetorical finish. Its elaborate positioning of verbal and conceptual repetitions is striking, including an obvious tendency to cluster elements in groups of two, a stylistic trait that has been traced in Alberti's vernacular style as well.

   If we survey the sound-patterns in Alberti's tripartite period, we note that the initial "Atqui est" is balanced and inverted in the concluding word "conquiescat." Thus the sound of these words establishes a firm link between beginning and end, while the second part located in the middle ("aptum locum et certum numerum dignumque modum et gratum ordinem") exhibits a sequence of similar endings. This makes it very different indeed from the remaining parts of the period. We find no repetitions between beginning and middle, or middle and end, so that the sentence cannot be said to be perfectly balanced, but it has a "firm" center indicated, perhaps, by the phrase "certum numerum." On the other hand, the words *lineamenti* and *aedificiis* in the opening segment balance *aedificii* and *lineamentis* in its third segment.[56] This structure squares with Aristotle's account of *paromoiosis*, "the similarity of the final syllables of each clause," where he stresses the point that "[a]t the beginning the similarity is always shown in entire words; at the end, in the last syllables, or the inflexions of one and the same word, or the repetition of one and the same word" (*Rhetoric* III.ix.9). However, Cicero and Quintilian are more likely to have furnished more accessible sources.[57]

The analysis of Alberti's definition of *lineamenta* affords instances of well-placed verbal ornaments, a practice Alberti describes in detail when he stresses the necessity of placing architectural ornaments correctly. This is what Alberti says, as rendered in the translation by James Leoni:

> First of all your Ornaments must be exactly regular, and be perfectly distinct, and without Confusion. . . . There is no Part whatsoever but what the Artist ought to adorn; but there is no Occasion that all should be adorned equally, or that every Thing should be enriched with equall Expense; for indeed I would not haue the Work consist so much in Plenty as in Variety. Let the Builder fix his richest Ornaments in the principal Places; those of a middling Sort, in Places of less Note, and the meanest in the meanest. (IX.ix.204)

In his own writing too, Alberti fixes "his richest Ornaments in the principal Places"—that is, at the beginning and the end, which are the most important "places" in a periodic construction. In fact, embellishment by means of ornaments contributes to producing the brilliance of sentences and buildings alike.[58] This basic fact is much in evidence because the terms used ("tota aedificii forma et figura" [the whole form and figure of the composition]), are rhetorical terms used by Cicero in the *De finibus* and the *De oratione*.[59] As already remarked, the reverse argument about the introduction of architectural terminology into poetry and poetics has received less attention. Such terminology has been seen mainly as a descriptive, not as a functional or analytical, metaphor.

The textual web found in Alberti's definition of *lineamenta* represents a more integrating kind of *concinnitas*, and the purpose of artfully repeated words clearly is to appeal to the senses or, if you wish, to persuade by framing the described object. A similar intention to persuade is apparent in the opening passage of the *Profugiorum ab aerumna*, where the temple is offered to the citizens of Florence as an edifying and inspiring example. Upon closer inspection, therefore, we shall find that the famous description of the "tempio" is but a part, albeit a very important part, of a long and well-disposed prose passage in Ms. Palatino 112(L1), totaling forty-six printed lines in the *Opere volgari*.[60]

As a rhetorically shaped piece of writing, this long passage possesses a structure of argument and a verbal finish that accord well with its crucial function as the opening section, because such a section "should be full of grandeur, magnificence and splendor, like the facade of palaces."[61] The main topics in the opening paragraph of the *Profugiorum ab aerumna*, or—in Cicero's phrasing—its *loci actionis*, are:

| **Topics:** | **Lines (in ed. Grayson):** |
|---|---|
| (a)  The interlocutors, the setting, and the action are identified. | 1–8 |
| (b)  Agnolo praises Alberti for coming often to the *tempio*, whose antithetical qualities he then describes, | 9–25 |
| including its compatibility with sacred music. | 26–28 |
| (c)  He contrasts secular and sacred music, describing the antithetical qualities of sacred music, and its power to temper the soul. | 28–45 |
| (d)  Agnolo excuses his long apostrophe and returns to the introductory topic. | 45–46 |

The organization of this extended prose paragraph has a striking shapeliness. First, we see that lines 1–8 function as a general introduction by identifying the three interlocutors: Niccola de messer Veri de' Medici, Agnolo di

Filippo Pandolfini, and the speaker ("io," that is, Leon Battista Alberti) who is identified by name in line 9 ("Te, Battista"). The setting is the "tempio massimo" of Brunelleschi, and the action is a discussion concerning "dottrina e investigazione de cose degne e rare" (doctrine and investigation of worthy and rare things). At this point Agnolo commends the piety of Battista (the author), who frequently visits the church, before he launches into a detailed description of the sensuous quality of the building itself. As Smith already has shown in her analysis of the first part of the speech, Agnolo's description is conspicuously rhetorical; it progresses by a series of opposite qualities: *grazia* and *maiestà, gracilità* and *sodezza, amenità* and *perpetuità*.[62] The praise of the building as a *locus amoenus* reaches a climax when Agnolo states that what he enjoys the most is the marvelous sweetness produced when the Mass is sung:

> *Qui*, dovunque tu miri, vedi ogni parte esposta a giocondità, e letizia; *qui* sempre odoratissimo; e, quali ch'io sopra tutto stimo, *qui* senti in queste voci al sacrificio, e in questi quali gli antichi chiamano misteri, una soavità maravigliosa. (lines 25–28; p. 107; italics added)

> [Here, wherever you look, you see the expression of happiness and gaiety; here it is always fragrant; and, that which I prize above all, here you listen to the voices during Mass, during that which the ancients called the mysteries, with their marvellous beauty.][63]

Here we are also close to the center of Brunelleschi's dome, whose circular outline and concave shape is alluded to as the nest of delights ("il nido delle delizie"), another reference to the primacy of the senses in our response to the edifice. When Agnolo addresses Battista for the second time—"Here, wherever you look, you will see each part arranged to produce happiness and pleasure"—the interlocutors are probably standing at a vantage point in the middle of the floor directly beneath the cupola. Thus the men are close to the center of its *lineamenta* as projected onto the floor, and in the near vicinity of the present-day altar. And as if by geometrical precision, the sentence just quoted occupies the privileged middle section of the prose paragraph. In Ms. Palatino 112(L1) the sentence begins at the numerical center of the passage, which in Grayson's edition occurs in lines 25–28 within the total of forty-six lines. Alberti here seems to combine the notion of the first page as the facade of the work with that of an architectural plan for the cupola in a way recalling how Fortunatus Venantius (c. 540-c. 605) com-

AVGVSTIDVNENSISOPVSTIBISOLVOSTAGRI

✠

```
DIVSAPEXADAMVTFECITDATSOMNIADONEC
AVVLSACOSTAPLASMATAESTEVANECINPAR
FELICESPARITERDIPLOIDELVCISOPERTI
ORECORVSCANTESINTERPIARVRAIVGALES
RIPAEIVCVNDAENARIGRATAAVRAREDIBAT
TVRISDELICIAESATVEABANTVDEREFLATV
VNAFOVESSAMBOSFLOROSASEDEVOLVPTAS
NOTABONISREGIOPASCEBATTEMPEBEATOS
ATCVMTAMMAGNOPOLLERENTMAIVSHONORE
TOTADOMINVMMIREPAREBATTERRADVORVM
OCCVLTVSMENDAXMOXEXEBITARMAVENENI
SERPENSELATVSZELATORLARVEVSHOSTIS
ATROXINNOCVGSEVINCENSPELLENOCENTI
CONLISITSVASVQVOSGRATIADIVABEARAT
ETHOMODETERRATVMDENVODECIDITILLVC
REPTANTISQ:DOLOEOOISEXCLVDITVRORTV
HACNATIMORIMVEDAMNATILEGEPARENTVM
ATDEVSEXCELLENSAIEETDELVMINELVMEN
ECAELISOLIODVMMVNERAPROVIDETVLTRO
CASTAECAENERVDIVIVANINTROIITAGNVS
PRODIITINDESALVSMATVTINIVELVCERNA
INTACTAEPARTVLVNERVITEXCITAMVNDVM
APATREIVREDSHOMODEHINCCARNEVSALVO
VTNOSERIPERETVILISEDETRAHITAVCTOR
OREGISVENALECAPVTQVODDECRVCEFIXIT
TELOVOCEMANVMALFACTVSVERBEREFELLE
ACTVHACSOLVISCAPTIVOSSORTECREATOR
SEROVERADATAESTVITALISEMPTIOMORTE
YNNOSVNDEDEOLOQVORABSOLVENTEBEATV
ATVOSAETERNAESVFFVLTILAVDECORONAE
GALLORVMRADIIVOBISQVOFVLGEATETNOX
RVMPITELORAIVGISETSVMITISARMADIEI
IPSAVELIBERTASVOSLIBERATATQ:BEABIT
```

**FIG. 4**

Venantius Fortunatus, acrostic poem

bines the image of a temple front with his Christocentric acrostic "Ad Sya-grium Augustdunensem," which consists of 33 x 33 letters (Fig. 4).[64] Charac-teristically, Alberti furnishes the sentence with a number of rhetorical markers of the kind conventionally used in classical and Renaissance litera-ture to indicate centrality. Among such markers are the insistent anaphoric repetition of "qui" three times in frontal position, the use of similar endings ("odoratissimo . . . stimo"), and a pervasive tendency to favor alliteration (quel . . . questi . . . questi quali; senti . . . sacrificio . . . soavita . . . misteri . . . mar-avigliosa). But more important, the phrase "quel ch'io sopra tutto stimo" con-tains a multiple punning allusion to the cupola above the head of the speaker, a cupola that is the fulcrum and central point of his description, just as it is of the central mysteries of the Christian religion. As a piece of ver-nacular oratory, the sentence justifies Cristoforo Landino's praise of Alberti's style.[65]

Once the climactic description of the dome has been completed, Ag-nolo goes on to praise the wonderful power of sacred music, which, unlike the varieties of secular singing, never tires the ear of the listener. Here too Alberti develops his argument in a rhetoric of opposita, corresponding to the technique employed in the first part in the depiction of architectural quali-ties. All profane song is said to cause displeasure in its repeated modes and varieties ("tutti gli altri modi e varietà de' canti reiterati fastidiano"), thus contrasting unfavorably with the undiminished pleasure offered by sacred song ("solo questo cantar religioso mai meno diletta"). A distempered mind and a hardened heart are softened by the beautiful ascending and descend-ing patterns of hymns ("bello ascendere e poi descendere"). In fact, music has the marvelous capacity to render us peaceful at heart ("mi maraviglio . . . quanta forza portino seco quelle a intenerirci"). At this point we should re-member that the interlocutors would have seen the two beautiful organ lofts once located inside the cupola, now on view in the Museo dell'Opera del Duomo. The lively and playful cantoria by Donatello portrays singing and dancing (Fig. 5), while the more graceful cantoria by Luca della Robbia por-trays scenes of playing and singing (Fig. 6). The della Robbia cantoria is dec-orated with three bands containing quotations from the Psalms on the topic of singing and playing in praise of the Lord ("Laudate eum in sono tubae"). Within the context of the solemn and austere dome the two cantorie strike a note of playfulness and joyous praise.

Agnolo's final exemplum concerns the influence of music on Alexander the Great, one of the Seven Worthies of Antiquity. Alberti seems to draw a parallel between the profane ruler swayed by music to abandon arms and turn to peaceful communion at the table, and the Christian called to the *mensa* of God in Brunelleschi's church.

The long opening prose paragraph concludes with Agnolo excusing himself—"Ma fec'io bene?" Enraptured, he has held forth at length about subjects not agreed upon in advance, thus testifying to the power of the dome to move the faithful to spontaneous praise. As the rhetorician Demetrius had put it, "amplified beginnings have a stately effect."[66] It is only after this remark has been made that the dialogue proper can begin, and it is not surprising that it continues with a detailed recapitulation of the theme as initially stated. The introductory phrase *"ragionavamo,* come era nostro costume, *di cose* gioconde e ch'appartenevano a *dottrina* e investigazione *di cose degne* e rare"(107.4–6; italics added) is briefly recapitulated as *"ragionare* e disputare *di cose dotte* e *degne"* (108.24–25; italics added). And with the new beginning the topos of the citizen as ornament (107.1 and 108) of the *civitas* reemerges again.[67] Then too, verbal repetitions are important building-blocks in Alberti's shaping of his argument, so that they can reasonably be referred to as stones or bricks in a wall, as in Demetrius's metaphorical description of the contrast between the periodic and the disconnected style: "The members in a periodic style may, in fact, be compared to the stones that support and hold together a vaulted dome. The members of the disconnected style resemble stones that are simply thrown about near one another and not built into a structure" (I.12.307). Examining the description of the dome to ascertain the extent to which it contains verbal repetitions that may function like these metaphorical stones, we discover the following configuration of repeated verbal "lights" or "verbal tesserae":

### Alberti's Verbal Tesserae

a   Nicola (1)
b   ragionavamo (3)
c   gioconde (4)
d   quel detto di que' buoni antiqui (11)
e   delizie (22)
e   delizie (24)
c   giocondità (25)
d   que' versiculi greci (39–40)
b   ragionamenti (46)
a   Nicola (46)

(Numbers refer to the lines in Grayson's edition.)

FIG. 5
Donatello, *Cantoria* (organ loft), Museo dell'Opera del Duomo, Florence

FIG. 6

Luca della Robbia, *Cantoria* (organ loft), detail: angels singing from a scroll, Museo dell'Opera del Duomo

Although they are scarcely impressive, these words—with one exception, the name "Nicola"—are important thematic words bearing on the project of moral edification. Thus *ragionavamo* and *ragionamenti* define the interlocutors' reasoned discourse on worthy topics, while *gioconde* and *giocondità* underline the unity of purpose that informs their discourse as well as Brunelleschi's edifice. Similarly, the repeated references to antiquity ("quel detto di que' buoni antiqui" and "que' versiculi greci") help to moor the achievement of the present in a venerable past; as such, this technique recalls the use of ancient architectural backgrounds in *quattrocento* paintings.[68]

We notice that the repetitions are situated at definite points within the compass of the prose paragraph, more particularly its beginning, middle, and end sections, thus indicating that Alberti treats it as one long prose period. Thus one of the repetitions, *gioconde-giocondità* (4, 24), linking the beginning of the segment to the middle, is precisely the word used later n to describe the beautifully ornamented floor of the Temple at Ephesos in the phrase "opera . . . grata e *iocunda*" (III.161). He distributes iterated words like *tesserae* in a mosaic floor so as to form *una designata forma*. The paragraph contains further repetitions of potential importance in this context.[69] Of these, the combinations including the word *cose*, seem to stress structure as well as theme on three occasions. Thus the phrase *"cose* gioconde . . . ch'appartenevano a dottrina"(4) used initially is played off against Agnolo's concluding excuse for having strayed from the agreed topic of their discussion: "distesimi in *cose* non accomodate" (45–46), thus establishing antithesis and creating *frisson*. Of course, Agnolo's praise of the dome does not constitute a deviation from the argument, but it does serve as a most appropriate exemplary introduction to their theme, for in it he has drawn attention to things that agree with nature, when at the center of the paragraph he defines delight and sees the church itself as a very "nest of delight":

> le delizie sono quando a' nostri sensi s'aggiungono *le cose quanto e quali le richiede la natura*, chi dubiterà appellare questo tempio il nido delle delizie?

> [delights result when to our senses are added things that are required by nature; who will then hesitate to call this temple the nest of delights?]

These carefully ordered repetitions involving the word "cose" at the beginning, middle, and end are significant in that they show Alberti's exercise of prudence, the virtue he specifically refers to initially (I.107), for as already stated prudence entails "orderliness and right-placing," as Cicero explains in *De officiis* (I.xl.143). Order, both tectonic and ethical, is what the argument of the opening paragraph is all about. In fact, the paragraph presents a rare example where ekphrasis and textual tectonics coincide, as when the textual circular *lineamenta* approach the architectural design or the frame for a picture. The embedded verbal pattern constitutes, as it were, a "frozen" music characterized by "the same minute divisions" that mark the architect's and the musician's mode of composition.[70] Naturally, this analysis implies a predominantly spatial, rather than linear, concept of the text that reveals how Alberti's approach to the various disciplines is perfectly unified in thought and methodology. This spatial concept of the text is his "hidden" theory of visual art.[71]

It is logical to relate Alberti's rhetorical fashioning to his theory of perspective in painting, although prose would not appear to invite the same kind of stringent spatial organization as pictorial representations or the rhythmically ordered texture of poetry. But like a painting or like epic poetry Alberti's prose actually presents a narrative with a *historia* for the reader to consider, and moreover, this narrative possesses a unified perspective orchestrated by *one* narrative voice aimed at an implied reader. In order to ensure that his narrative has an impact, Alberti adds to the text some of the characteristics of visual art. Thus he channels the attention of the reader in the right direction by "framing" or fixing the outer perimeters of his narrative segment by means of verbal repetitions.

His use of the frame entails distributing signs on the planar surface of the page in the same way that he would have plotted the outline of an architectural drawing or a painting. This process is in perfect agreement with Alberti's modification of Cicero's phrasing in the *Orator* in his own treatise *De pictura*. Alberti let "the ornamented or 'luminous' words that define and embellish thoughts in oratory become the lines *(fimbriae)* *lumina* which shape and adorn surfaces in painting."[72] We see a similar transformation in the *Profugiorum*, where Alberti observes the rules for adornment outlined later in *De re aedificatoria*.[73]

Alberti is the first theorist to use a physical frame to organize the *historia* of a painting executed according to the rules of single-point perspective, and he employs a similar technique when he frames the "visual" field recreated in the reader's imagination during the act of reading. Once the outer perimeters have been fixed, the reader experiences the gravitational force of what has been termed "the power of the center."[74] This force enables the reader to survey the enclosed visual field, the mental field as well as the space on the page, as a separate entity. The repetitions compel the mind to reconsider the area of prose it has just perused, and the attentive reader will note that the center of the segment coincides with that of the described object, the cupola (Fig. 7). Although most modern readers will notice the embedded symmetrical structure only on a subliminal level, it is plain that Alberti's *historia* of Santa Maria del Fiore has also achieved coherence because it has been architecturally conceived. The architectural beauty of the resulting composition is representable as a geometrical figure, possibly as concentric circles inscribed within a square (Fig. 8). And at the center of this circular frame Alberti situated his speaking subject and Vitruvian man.

The description of the temple communicates the idea that it is not the precise geometrical or mathematical operation called for in the design of the cupola that occupies the place of honor, but the immediately appreciable sensuous quality of the building that constitutes its most valuable and persuasive characteristic. Through his interlocutor Agnolo Pandolfini, Alberti sets out to describe the total impact and impression of the *machina* as perceived by the pious spectator. This visual and sensuous aspect of the description can be associated with the thinking of Augustine, who preferred a vision of delight to the certainty offered by geometry.[75] But does a contradiction really exist between Alberti's preference for a sensuous enjoyment of architecture and his repeated emphasis on the musical proportions and mathematical ratios with which a work of architecture should be calculated? Of course not. The contradiction is only apparent. Alberti's *ars divina* has two complementary aspects; his "notion of visual-artistic beauty embraces both the sensible and the intelligible."[76]

For an influential early writer who stresses the same points, we must turn to Philo Judaeus, who focuses on topics bearing on the theological and ethical approach to architecture. Smith has shown that Alberti's praise of Brunelleschi's church has a Greek background, because it was influenced by Manuel Chrysoloras's praise of Hagia Sophia in his *Comparison of Old and New Rome*.[77] Chrysoloras in his turn was undoubtedly influenced by Philo. The relevant work is his *On the Creation*, where the sensuous quality of divine architecture is strongly stressed. In fact, Philo presents God's creation as a banquet offered to man:

> He desired that on coming into the world man might at once find both
> a banquet and a most sacred display, the one full of all things that earth

and rivers and sea and air bring forth for use and for enjoyment, the other of all sorts of spectacles, most impressive in their substance, most impressive in their qualities, and circling with most wondrous movements, in an order fitly determined always with the proportion of numbers and harmony of revolutions. In all these one might rightly say that there was the real music, the original and model of all others, from which the men of subsequent ages, when they had painted the images in their own souls, handed down an art most vital and beneficial to human life. (XXV.78 [63])

In Philo's account we recognize a strong emphasis on harmony, proportion, and utility, all of which qualities Alberti attributes to Brunelleschi's dome and the sacred music performed in it. We also note that the term "period," used about the revolutions of the stars, traditionally denotes the syntactic unit as well as the planetary motion, so that the universe literally becomes a well-ordered speech.[78] Although the world emerged from chaos, matter was capable of receiving form by the divine architect who modeled it harmoniously according to his preconceived plan in the manner of a rhetorician who arranges his words. Philo's own antithetical style presents a good example of the resulting order when he explains the shaping power of the divine plan: "For of itself it was without order, without quality, without soul, (without likeness); it was full of inconsistency, ill-adjustment, disharmony; but it was capable of turning and undergoing a complete change to the best, the very contrary of all of these, to order, quality, life, [. . .] identity, likeness, perfect adjustment, to harmony, to all that is characteristic of the more excellent model" (VI.22 [19]). We cannot fail to notice how Philo playfully creates a well-formed, circular period in imitation of God's work: a series of negative terms are related antithetically to a second series of positive qualities, qualities that are grouped around the chiastic presentation of change at the center of the phrase: "but it was capable of *turning* and undergoing a complete *change* to the best, the very *contrary* of all these" (italics added). The positive qualities are repeated in the same order as the negative ones, thus establishing a perfect example of "parallel construction."[79] Thus the phrase is self-referential, because syntax and verbal configurations provide a structural projection of the argument.

The divine art that orders everything "in mensura et numero et pondere" (Sapientia 11:21) is aesthetically stimulating, which is why Philo may have wanted to describe it as a banquet and a spectacle pleasing to the

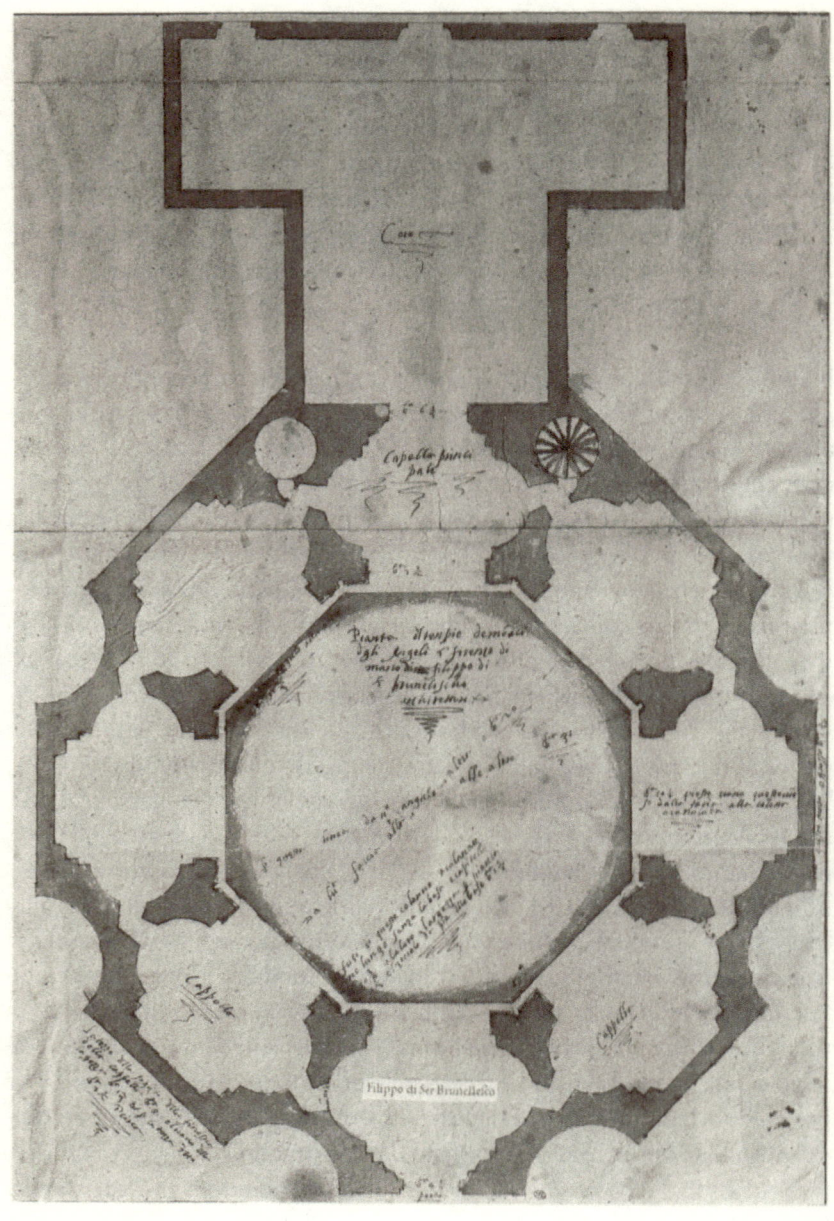

**FIG. 7**

Filippo Brunelleschi, plan of the cupola of S. Maria del Fiore, Florence

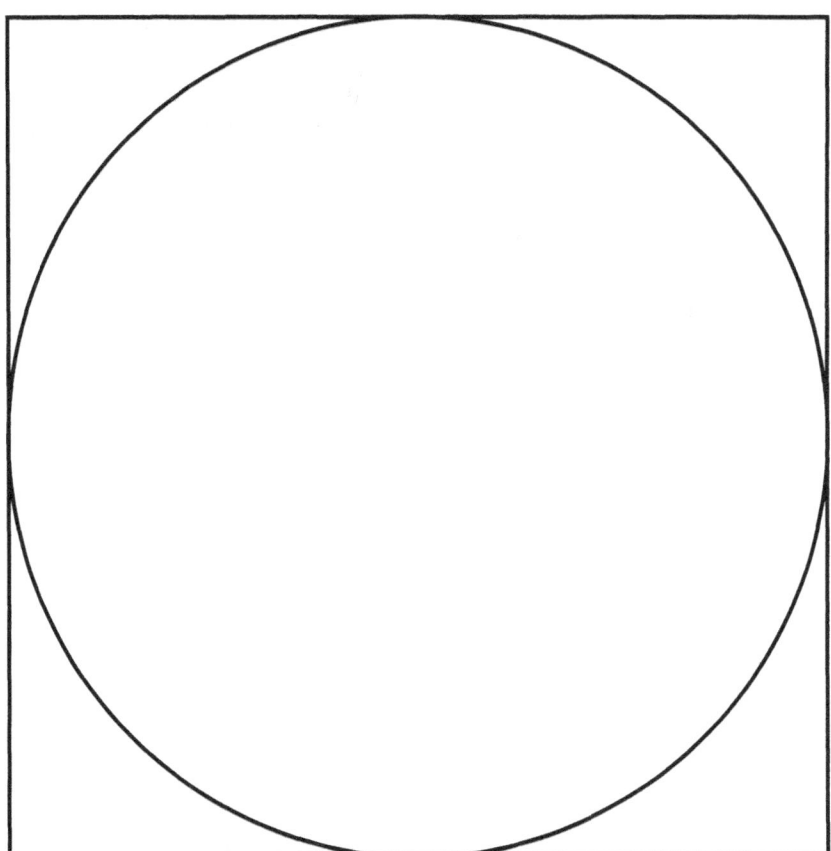

**FIG. 8**
Circle inscribed within a square

human eye. What we find here, then, is a complex of metaphors and aesthetic notions that ultimately reappear in Alberti's narrative as he emphasizes the sensuous aspect of Brunelleschi's architecture, for the basic metaphor in Philo is precisely that of God as an architect-designer who produces a pleasing work on the basis of an abstract model. Philo is much more explicit on that point than Plato in the *Timaeus:*

> We must suppose that, when He was minded to found the one great city, He conceived beforehand the models of its parts, and that out of

these He constituted and brought to completion a world discernible only by the mind, and then, with that for a pattern, the world which our senses can perceive. As, then, the city which was fashioned beforehand within the mind of the architect held no place in the outer world; . . . even so the universe that consisted of ideas which would have no other location than the Divine Reason. (*On the Creation* V.19–V.20)

These are ideas with which Chrysoloras is likely to have been familiar when he praised the actual architects who projected and executed the Hagia Sophia: "those men who mentally conceived of such a great work without the help of any similar model and who, having formed a mental image, believed themselves to be capable of actually realising it and bringing it to completion. What I said about the work as a whole is particularly true of the dome, which the architect must have envisioned as we see it now from the moment the foundations were laid, or even before that" (Smith, 212–13). Chrysoloras introduces his account with the inevitable comparison of the Hagia Sophia to the heavenly vault: "just as it amazes us that the heavenly sphere revolves by itself, so we are at a loss to understand how this inimitable and heavenly vault and ceiling was built and continues to stand," a statement that calls to mind Demetrius's striking alignment between a *periodos* and a well-constructed vault in *On Style*. Of course, I do not want to argue that Philo is a source for Alberti's presentation of Brunelleschi's *capolavoro*; my purpose is to suggest a general theological context for the thinking that went into the creation of such visionary works of art.[80] Although Alberti's antithetical style matches that of Philo, the same stylistic traits appear in Chrysoloras, who in turn was inspired by the Byzantine rhetorician Hermogenes, as explained by Smith. Nevertheless, Philo's treatise affords a striking context for the thinking at the heart of Alberti's "connection between the persuasive effect of oratory and of architecture"[81] and the emotional response to beauty that it advocates. These connections add perspective to the marked interaction between ethics and *elocutio* in Alberti's writings on art, for Alberti is indeed an orator or a designer in words; he creates what he elsewhere refers to as "una forma designata" with a clear intention to persuade his readers to engage in virtuous action and to turn "to doctrine and investigation of worthy and excellent things" (1.108).[82] As Philo put it, the perfect work is "beneficial to human life."

The highly ordered description of the dome of Santa Maria del Fiore serves as the exordium to this important statement of purpose. And just as Alberti's prose *historia* is patterned according to "the rhetoric of perspective" so as to communicate the qualities of the dome, so are the topoi of the *Profugiorum* as a whole. Thus Smith points out that Book One is arranged antithetically in relation to Book Three, and that "the treatise closes, as it opened, with an image of pleasurable absorption and tranquillity of the soul."[83] In other words, the difference between the two images reflects the well-known principle of repetition with a significant change: the change from a situation of passionate response to a situation of active search for mastery via the investigation Alberti presented in the treatise *De motibus ponderis.*

In this chapter I have tacitly rejected the view expressed by Mario Praz that it is useless to try to find in writers "such strict rules as those practiced by architects."[84] Instead I have advocated a study of the relationship between architecture and the art of writing, and I have done so on the basis of Alberti's concept of edification, for when a writer is both an architect and a moral philosopher, we have a basis for examining the interface of his various roles. In this context Alberti is of exceptional value because he fuses the embodiment of the various aspects of *architettura* just as he contributed to shaping the Renaissance conception of the term architect.[85] Then too, Alberti openly explains his aesthetic choices and his preferred techniques of edification. No doubt some of the repetitional patterns visible in the textual web of Renaissance texts like the *Profugiorum ab aerumna* will appear to many as trivial and pedantic, but we must remember that *elocutio* includes all the rhetorical features of a text and that these features have been created with a view to persuading and edifying. Alberti's narrator addresses this issue when he asks, "[a]nd who will be so stupid as not to approve and praise the man, who has spent his industry and diligence in such a well-composed work?"[86] This insistence on a well-composed work owes a great deal to the symbolic import of such a composition as a type of moral edification. This view is entirely compatible with the attitude of Renaissance artists toward perspective as a "symbolic form."[87]

The emphasis on form and preplanned design in Alberti's oeuvre influenced coming generations to a considerable extent, and one writer and artist who remembered his example is Giorgio Vasari, in *The Lives of the Artists.* The encyclopedic and epic biography was his chosen genre in which his ability to shape both his periods and the individual lives into an overall architectural design is shown to great advantage. Nowhere is his will to form more evident in *The Life of Michelangelo.*

## Appendix to Chapter 3: Profugiorum ab Aerumna (1441), Opening Paragraph

Niccola di messer Veri de' Medici, uomo ornatissimo d'ogni costume e d'ogni virtù, e io insieme passeggiando nel nostro tempio massimo ragionavamo, come era nostro costume, di cose gioconde e ch'appartenevano a dottrina e investigzione di cose degne e rare. Sopragiunse Agnolo di Filippo Pandolfini, uomo grave, maturo, integro, quale e per età e per prudenza sempre fu richiesto e reputato fra' primi nostri cittadini. Salutocci e disse:—Te, Battista, lodo io; e piacemi che, come in altre cose, così e in questo tuo ridurti qui assiduo in questo tempio ti veggo religiossisimo. E' non fu sanza cagione quel detto di que' buoni antiqui che massime allora sì dà opera al culto divino quando si frequentano e' luoghi sacrati a Dio. E certo questo tempio ha in sé grazia e maiestà: e, quello ch'io spesso considerai, mi diletta ch'io veggo in questo tempio iunta insieme una gracilità vezzosa con una sodezza robusta e piena, tale che da una parte compreendo che ogni cosa qui è fatta e offirmata a perpetuità. Aggiugni che qui abita continuo la temperie, si può dire, della primavera: fuori vento, gelo, brina; qui entro socchiuso da' venti, qui tiepido aere e quieto: fuori vampe estive e autunnali; qui entro temperatissimo refrigerio. E s'egl'è, come e' dicono, che le delizie sono quando a' nostri sensi s'aggiungono le cose quanto e quali le richiede la natura, chi dubiterà appellare questo tempio nido delle delizie? Qui, dovunque tu miri, vedi ogni parte esposta a giocondità e letizia; qui sempre odoratissimo; e, quali ch'io sopra tutto stimo, qui senti in queste voci al sacrificio, e in questi quali gli antichi chiamano misteri, una soavità maravigliosa. Che è a dire che tutti gli altri modi e varietà de' canti reiterati fastidiano: solo questo cantare religioso mai meno ti diletta. Quando fu ingegno in quel Timoteo musico, inventore di tanta cosa! Non so quello s'inter-venga agli altri; questo affermo io di me, che e' possono in me questi canti e inni della chiesa quello a che fine e' dicono che furono trovati: troppo m'acquetano da ogni altra perturbazione d'animo, e commuovonmi a certa non so quale io la chiami lentezza d'animo pieno di riverenza verso Dio. E qual cuore sì bravo si truova che non mansueti sé stessi quando e' sente su bello ascendere e poi descendere quelle intere e vere voci con tanta tenterezza e flessitudine? Affermovi questo, che mai sento in que' misteri e cerimonie funerali invocare da Dio con que' versiculi greci aiuto alle nostre miserie umane ch'io non lacrimi. E fra me talora mi maraviglio, e penso quanta forza portino seco quelle a intenerirci. E quinci avviene ch'io credo quello che si dice ch'e' musici potessero esortare Alessandro Macedone ad arme cantando, e rivocarlo in cena. Ma fec'io bene? Io ruppi forse e' vostri ragionamenti, Niccola, e distesimi in cose non accomodate.

(ed. Grayson, 107)

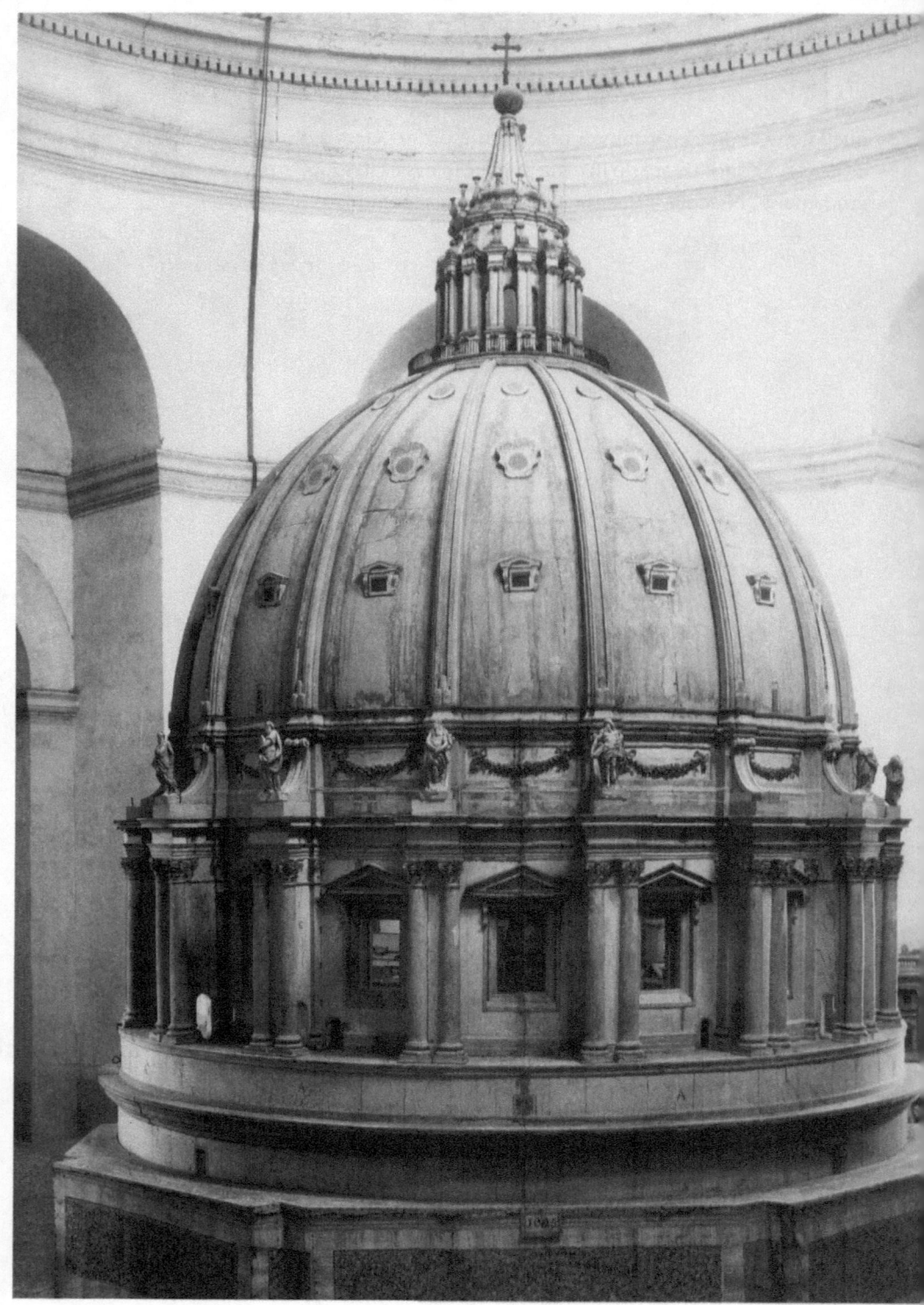

**FIG. 9**
Michelangelo, Maderno, and Vanvitelli, model of the cupola of
Saint Peter's, Rome

"Ordine con più ornamento"

Vasari's *Lives of Michelangelo* (1550 and 1568)

While the most noble and industrious spirits were striving, by the light of the famous Giotto and of his followers, to give to the world a proof of the ability that the benign influence of the stars and the proportionate admixture of humours had given to their intellects, and while, desirous to imitate with the excellence of their art the grandeur of Nature in order to approach as near as possible to that supreme knowledge that many call understanding, they were universally toiling, although in vain, the most benign Ruler of Heaven in His clemency turned His eyes to the earth. And, having perceived the infinite vanity of all those labours, the ardent studies without any fruit, and the presumptuous self-sufficiency of man, desiring to deliver us from such great errors, became minded to send down to earth a spirit with the universal ability in every art and every profession, who might be able, working by himself alone, to show what manner of thing is the perfection of the art of design in executing the lines, contours, shadows, and high lights, so as to give relief to works of painting, and what it is to work with correct judgment in sculpture, and how in architecture it is well-proportioned, and rich with varied ornaments.

—De Vere, III: 1832

"Giorgio Vasari was not a profound or original thinker."[1] Those are T. S. R. Boase's apologetic words from 1979, which remind us just how fashionable it was to portray Vasari as a prolific but mediocre artist who won fame either by imitating the maniera of other and better artists or by immortalizing their lives and works in the volume in which he invented the discipline of art history. Where he has been granted originality and fame is in architecture and biography. However difficult it seems to disentangle Vasari from the fate and fame of his hero Michelangelo, we should recognize that the impression we have today of many artists, and not least of Michelangelo, was originally created by Vasari's powerful and eternalizing pen.[2] Vasari is an accomplished fashioner of words, arguably one of the greatest fiction writers of the Italian Renaissance, and certainly one of the most influential.[3] Leaving the afterlife of the *Lives* aside, I here want to consider Vasari's remarkable literary art in relation to the concept of design. Vasari here provides an indispensable focus of attention: he unites in one person several disciplines crucial to the concept and its material expression, being painter, sculptor, architect, theorist, and writer. He may even be said to surpass Alberti in the sheer breadth and variety of his oeuvre. His actual accomplishment offers unusual opportunities for cross-disciplinary research into the particular aspect of Renaissance artistic creation that is my topic. True enough, Vasari does not openly include history among the arts subject to the operations of design, but the interpenetration of terms drawn from rhetoric and the arts, and the compositional practice of Renaissance poets, strongly suggests that prose composition too may be informed by the same aesthetic thinking. Recent scholarship on Vasari has shown the extent to which Vasari was conscious of his relationship to the historiographical tradition and that his mastery of the genre was recognized by contemporary historians.[4]

The interest in the *Vite* as fiction also entails an interest in Vasari's emplotment of a particular interpretation of history, of which he was a "very creative interpreter" indeed.[5] In view of this creative aspect, it was only to be expected that scholars from the very beginning discovered a considerable degree of inexactness in the work and many have delighted in mapping all the points on which the author was misinformed: he nodded, or he misconstrued the facts.[6] The situation has been not unlike that of the venerable *OED*, where myriad plodders have cataloged omissions, deviations, and mistaken dates. This has not, however, diminished the value of the original work, and it has rightly been pointed out that neither Vasari nor his chosen genre needs an apology.[7] Rather than focusing on its factual shortcomings, I want to explore it as a piece of literary architecture.

More particularly, I want to concentrate on the 1550 and the 1568 versions of the *Life of Michelangelo*, and the changes Vasari introduced in the long initial period of the *Life* and in the section to which it belongs, with the further purpose of analyzing both in relation to the shape of the *Life* as a whole. I believe that this limited focus is justified, although my purpose is to make a general point about Vasari's aesthetic, because the *Life of Michelangelo*, in which he exhibits his best art, constitutes Vasari's peak achievement. My purpose is to assess the rhetorical nature and effect of the novel constellations as a guide to the possible changes in the author's aesthetic preferences. Thus I argue that Vasari's stylistic shift is consistent with major developments in Late Renaissance style.

As argued in the preceding chapters, the elocutionary patterns found at the micro-level of Renaissance texts are important because they carry the visible imprint of the author's formal intention, the *dispositio* given to his original invention. In the case of such self-conscious writers as Vasari, analysis may provide vital clues to his overall design in the two versions of the *Life of Michelangelo*. A close analysis enables us to map and so to understand the rationale behind the stylistic differences between the two versions.

The shorter and less read 1550 *Life of Michelangelo* is just as polished as the 1568 version, which concludes with the death and funeral of Michelangelo. The impact of the end clearly bears on the differences between the Torrentiniana edition of *Le Vite* published in 1550 before Michelangelo died, and the Giuntina edition published in 1568, four years after the artist's death. In fact, the Torrentiniana was reprinted only once in a limited diplomatic edition, whereas the longer 1568 edition was reprinted eighteen times and appeared in eight translations.[8] Nevertheless, in one respect the shorter version, strangely enough, may be said to provide a more complete picture of Vasari's achievement, as it concludes with the climactic life of Michelangelo, who then was still alive and active. It thus presents the ascent of art at a moment when it could still be said to be ascending. It spells out the basic typological design of the entire work in a direct manner: Michelangelo's life is an *imitatio Christi*, and his advent matches that of Christ in sacred and world history.[9] In addition, because the *Life of Michelangelo* does not end the way all the other lives do, it is possible to see in its special rhetorical form a playful allusion to the artist's "immortality." This aspect is seen *in nuce* in the sweeping opening period of the 1550 *Life*:

Mentre gl'industriosi et egregii spiriti col lume del famosissimo Giotto e de gli altri sequaci suoi si sforzavano dar saggio al mondo de 'l valore che la benignità delle stelle e la proporzionata mistione degli umori aveva dato agli ingegni loro, e, desiderosi di imitare con la eccellenzia della arte la grandezza della natura, per venire il piú che e' potevano a quella somma cognizione che molti chiamano intelligenzia, universalmente, ancora che indarno, si affaticavano, il benignissimo Rettore del cielo volse clementemente gli occhi alla terra, e veduta la vana infinità di tante fatiche, gli ardentissimi studii senza alcun frutto e la opinione prosuntosa degli uomini, assai piú lontana da 'l vero che le tenebre dalla luce, per cavarci di tanti errori si dispose mandare in terra uno spirito che universalmente in ciascheduna arte et in ogni professione fusse abile, operando per sé solo, a mostrare che cosa siano le difficultà nella scienza delle linee, nella pittura, nel giudizio della scultura e nella invenzione della veramente garbata architettura.

This period is one of the grandest in Italian literature, which establishes Michelangelo as a God-sent bringer of light. Barolsky suggests that Vasari here turns to liturgy, specifically the Introit of the Mass at Christmastide, for this passage, which presents a similar image.[10] I find the topos of divine intervention in human affairs in Psalm 101:19–20 more to the point:

For he hathe loked downe fro[m] the height of his Sanctuarie:
out of the heauen did the Lord beholde the earth,
That he might heare the mourning of the prisoner,
and deliuer the children of death.

(*The Geneva Bible* [1560], 256v)

Whatever the source, Vasari's period not only serves as an introduction to, and summary of, the *Life of Michelangelo*; it serves other important functions as well. As the beginning of the pivotal life, it harks back to the opening sentence of the Preface—"Solevano gli spiriti egregii in tutte le azzioni loro, per uno acceso desiderio di gloria, non perdonar alcuna fatica, quantunque gravissima, per condurre le opere loro a quella perfezzione che rendesse stupende a maravigliose a tutto il mondo"[11]—at the same time that it echoes the creation of Adam and the discovery of painting and sculpture, that Vasari placed at the very beginning of the Preface.[12]

In this way Vasari indicates that we have reached an important new beginning. Accordingly, the first period in the *Life* summarizes within its confines the entire structure of Vasari's work, so that it serves as its formal matrix; or, as Scamozzi would have put it, "by way of design it reduces the entire world . . . to a tiny form."[13] It also bears on the basic theme and design of the work as a whole—the ascent of Florentine art from Giotto to Michelangelo—for in Vasari's own typology of art Michelangelo is the greatest artist of all time and all previous artists have only prefigured and prepared the way for his arrival, just as important Old Testament figures and events are types of Christ and of events in his life. Thus in the opening period Giotto emerges as the Old Adam, whereas Michelangelo is presented as the Second Adam, the Son of Man who appears as *sol iustitiae* to dispel darkness and doubt. From one point of view, therefore, the *Lives* is a series of saints' lives culminating in the revelation of Michelangelo. Giotto in this respect is to Michelangelo what Virgil was to Dante; he is Michelangelo "avanti la lettera," a guide along the way to Paradise.[14] Both Laura Riccò and Roland Le Mollé have sought to redress the strange lack of scholarly interest in Vasari's literary accomplishment, a situation that Le Mollé considered "assez singulier": "quatre siècles d'exégèse vasarienne ont relativement peu apporté à la connaissance profonde de la langue des *Vite*."[15] This situation, however, has changed significantly in recent criticism, which pays greater attention to Vasari's literary techniques.

Of course, Vasari the rhetorician does not actually say that Giotto *is* Adam and that Michelangelo is Christ or the Archangel Michael. Adroitly he uses the indirect method, already favored in the program for the frescoes in the Sala dei Cento Giorni in Rome some years earlier (1546). There too the rhetorical figure of *synchresis*—"la comparazione del soggetto con i famosi eroi del passato"—had suited his purpose to praise Paulo III, turning the frescoes into a laudatory speech of visible images.[16] This point is made more than evident by the important position he attributes to the personification of Eloquentia in the program.

The period, then, imitates the pattern traditionally attributed to God's scheme of creation and redemption. Vasari had already used this technique in his account of the birth of the arts in the Proemio to the *Lives;* art conforms to God's plan when "the Divine Architect of time and nature" becomes the model for the artist, as in the well-known metaphors employed by Plato, Philo, Augustine, and Bonaventura.[17] When the divine architect created the world and adorned it with lights ("quando l'altissimo Dio, fatto il gran corpo del mondo et ornato il cielo de' suoi chiarissimi lumi"), he also established a pattern for poets or rhetoricians to imitate in their distribution of verbal "lights." This mimetic process and its inherent "disegno interno"[18] may in fact be studied at various points in Vasari's narrative of commemoration, as well as in the configuration of major episodes in the *Life* itself. The carefully balanced structure of repetitions in Vasari's description of how God creates by adding and subtracting according to a preconceived design thus shows how crucial rhetorical shaping is in his method of persuasion:

> il divino architetto del tempo e della natura, come perfettisssimo, volse mostrare nella *imperfezzione* della materia la via del *levare* e dell'*aggiugnere* nel medesimo che sogliono fare i buoni scultori e pittori, i quali ne' lor modelli *aggiugnendo* e *levando*, riducono le *imperfette* bozze a quel fine e *perfezzione* ch' e' vogliono. (II: 4; italics added)

> [the Divine Architect of time and of nature, being Himself most perfect, wished to show in the imperfection of the material the way to add and to take away; in the same manner wherein good sculptors and painters are wont to work, who, adding and taking away in their models, bring their imperfect sketches to that final perfection which they desire.] (Trans. de Vere I: 27)[19]

The verbal recurrences in this passage are conspicuous, and when we isolate them we note that they form a structural grid or modello of ten related words repeated in two subseries of five words each. All but two of the key words (*volse* and *vogliono*) occur in inverse order (see diagram):

> (ab) perfettissimo . . . volse
>   (c) imperfezzione
>     (d) levare,
>       (e) aggiugnere
>       (e) aggiugnendo
>     (d) levando
>   (c) imperfette
> (ab) perfezzione . . . vogliono

Monotony is avoided because the words repeated, although derived from the same root, are not exactly identical. The technique ensures variety in sameness, and variety was a much cherished quality. On the whole the distribution of repetitions confirms the division of the period into the two parts of a comparison; "Il divino architetto . . . volse" in the first part matches "e' [that is, *i buoni scultori e pittori*] vogliono" in the second. In this way the parallel between divine and artistic creation is clear enough, albeit with the significant difference between divine will and human desire. The pattern is sufficiently obvious for us to conclude that Vasari manipulates the sentence structure and distributes its verbal "lights" in order to emphasize his argument. The pattern has been cleverly put there for skilled readers to perceive and enjoy, which they no doubt did.

While bearing in mind this technique and the resulting structure, let us now return to the opening sentence of the 1550 *Life*, where related images of divine intervention and inspiration recur in similar fashion. Here the analogy is not between the artist and God, but between imperfect though ambitious artists of the past and the God-sent perfect artist, Michelangelo. The period would therefore seem to invite a rhetorical structuring of the same kind that we have just observed. It contains three parts. The first describes the many futile attempts by Giotto and his followers, while the divine intervention into human history appropriately occupies the central position: "il benignissimo Rettore del cielo volse clementemente gli occhi alla terra." The third and climactic part presents the divine act of artistic redemption when God sends Michelangelo, a man skilled in the laws of perspective and design ("le difficultá nella scienza delle linee") and an expert in painting, sculpture, and architecture.

This important argument has been shaped rhetorically in such a way that it harbors a conspicuous number of repeated words and concepts. A semantic scanning yields the following pattern (identified by letters from *a* to *f*):

### 1550 Life of Michelangelo, Repetitions in the Initial Period

| | | | | | |
|---|---|---|---|---|---|
| (f) | si affaticavano | tante fatiche | (f) |
| (e) | indarno | senza alcun frutto | (e) |
| (d) | universalmente | luce | (b) |
| (c) | arte | spirito | (a) |
| (b) | lume | universalmente | (d) |
| (a) | spiriti | arte | (c) |

Although less symmetrical than that of the period on divine creation analyzed above, the pattern is clear enough, and it does underline the combined
syntactic and semantic structure. In fact, the basic pattern is one of mirror
symmetry, where the words are iterated around the centrally situated image
of God. In all, eight words and synonyms are repeated chiastically (a-b-e-f-f-
e-b-a) around the phrase "il Rettore del ciel," whereas the remaining four
words of the pattern (*arte* and *universalmente*) are arranged as sequential repetition (a-b-a-b). This is a form of recurrence that suits the kind of progressive
and open-ended structure readily associated with literary maniera. In fact,
the critical terms stressed in the concluding part of the period emphasize the
role that theory and practice gave to invention, elegance, and difficulty:

> le *difficultà* nella scienza delle linee, nella pittura, nel giudizio della
> scultura e nella invenzione della *veramente garbata architettura*. (Italics
> added)

> [the difficulty of the art of drawing, in painting, in the judging of
> sculpture and in the invention of truly elegant architecture.]

The contrived rhetoric of the passages analyzed here refutes the view advanced in scholarship that Vasari's style is uniform and additive. Vasari's *Vite*,
it has been said, is "a construction characterized by successive additions that
obey the desire to relate incidents in a narrow space, producing a paratactic
style that is also devoid of lexical variety."[20] While rightly stressing the
dominance of "un registro espressivo tanto uniforme" in long stretches of
narrative, this view nevertheless underestimates the function of *ornatus* and
Vasari's conscious use of verbal artifice to shape the work as a whole and individual *vite*.

   This reassessment receives further support when we consider the entire opening paragraph of the *Life*.[21] This paragraph serves as an introduction
to the life story proper, and hence it has been written so as to prefigure the
end. Thus its last period underlines the unique character of Michelangelo's
infinite wit by concluding with a paradox: He was "un ingegno che mos-
trasse perfettissimamente (mercé della sua bontà) l'infinito del fine" ("an in-
genium that [given his goodness] showed most perfectly the infinity of the
end"; p. 948) This emphasis on "the open-endedness of the end" thus prefig-
ures the open end of the *Life* as a whole. To grasp the full implication of how
the structure of the opening sentence and paragraph relates to the shape of

Vasari's commemorative narrative, we need to consider how the *Lives* relates to the dominant narrative genre of the period, the epic, and to examine how the celebration of the artists' *res gestae* relates to current theories of the epic.

In his introduction to the 1550 edition of the *Vite*, Giovanni Previtali compares the relationship between the two *Vite* to that between Tasso's *La Gerusalemme liberata* and *La Gerusalemme Conquistata*.[22] The comparison is interesting as far as the question of the two editions is concerned, though essentially misguided if we want to relate Tasso's theory of the epic to his epic practice. But in this context it is not necessary to rehearse the basic elements in Tasso's concept of *unità mista* and his distinctly personal brand of neoclassical poetics.[23] I want instead to consider here the interdisciplinary aspects of cinquecento aesthetics, focusing first on a famous cinquecento commentary on Tasso's epic and its relationship to Ariosto's. The commentary marks the beginning of a long and virulent debate about the relative poetic merits of *Orlando furioso* (1532) and *La Gerusalemme liberata* (1581). Written in the form of a dialogue entitled *Il Carrafà, ovvero della epica poesia*, it was published by Giulio Camillo Delminio in 1584. In so doing, I focus on design, which Vasari contributed to making so prominent in late cinquecento and seicento art theory, and my use of the term will reflect the practice of Benedetto Varchi and Vincenzo Danti.[24]

We recall Vasari's well-known statement that

il disegno, padre delle tre arti nostre architettura, scultura e pittura, procedendo dall'intelletto cava di molte cose un giudizio universale simile a una forma overo idea di tutte le cose della natura. (Vasari 1966: 111)

[issuing from the intellect, design, the father of our three arts of architecture, sculpture, and painting, draws from many things a universal judgement, which resembles a form or idea of all things in nature.]

We note the close connection between the notions of *disegno, forma,* and *giudizio*—that is, plan, structure, and judgment—a combination that is crucial to an understanding of Vasari's textual architecture and that reflects the desire to communicate and persuade that it proclaims. We are mistaken if we assume that this scheme is to be understood entirely in terms of Neoplatonist idealism or abstraction, because Vasari's project aims at teaching. It reveals a will to shape his message rhetorically so that it will be in accord with his pro-

Florentine and Medici point of view. The *Lives* reflects the same concern with dynastic issues as the epic and the frescoes executed by Vasari (and Paolo Giovio) in the Sala dei cento giorni in the Cancelleria at Rome.[25] This shared concern appears not least in Vasari's calculated use of the terms *luce* and *lume* (literally "light") throughout the *Lives*. As I argue below, light acquires a spiritual and ethical dimension in addition to its role as a structural marker.

Notwithstanding the spiritual dimension, I believe it would be wrong to underestimate the joco-serious element in Vasari's depictions of his great hero, a stance frequently adopted by an artist who is so renowned for his ironic wit. If we read carefully we perceive a built-in safeguard in many of Vasari's most adulatory passages, even in the initial sentence on Michelangelo, where "la opinione prosuntosa degli uomini" may be included not only for the sake of contrast but also as a warning against making claims that are too lofty. Consider, for instance, Ariosto's account of the fictional history of the d'Este family in *Orlando furioso* in relation to the apotheosis of Michelangelo to sainthood and divinity as described by Vasari. Both are conspicuously rhetorical exercises set within a firm dynastic framework to further the interests of the patron.

Some may object that Vasari did not write epic poetry or moral philosophy, but then neither did he write "pure" history, if such a genre can be said to exist. Rather, Vasari comes far closer to being a "poet historical" like Augustine or Tasso,[26] or a "spiritual historian" who draws on various types of written and narrated documentation, and—in Vasari's case—on extant physical objects to compose a continuous work of epic scope and intention. It is in this sense, I suggest, that Henry Wotton in 1624 was to use the term "historical" when discussing different modes of writing on art: "There were two wayes to be deliuered, the one Historicall, by description of the principall workes, performed already in good part, by Giorgio Vasari in the liues of Architects: The other Logicall, by casting the rules and cautions of the Art, into some comportable Method."[27] "Historical" here carries the implication of "rhetorical" and should be related to Quintilian's distinction between "the two kinds of speech": "duo . . . genera orationis, altera perpetua, quae rhetorice dicitur, altera concisa, quae dialectice" ("the continuous which is called rhetorical, and the concise which is called dialectic"; II.xx.7). In one sense, therefore, Vasari's *Vite* presents an instance of *oratio perpetua* that is not unrelated to how, for example, Ovid's *Metamorphoses* is a *perpetuum . . . carmen* (I.4). Vasari presents a sequence of stories bound together by a shared design and embellished in accordance with the rules of rhetoric.[28] In fact,

Vasari establishes this mode of continuous representation in the Proemio to Part Three when he refers to "l'ordine, il quale aveva di bisogno di una invenzione copiosa di tutte le cose e d'una certa bellezza continuata ["a certain sustained beauty"]."[29] The rhetorical and essentially fictional character of this mode of writing has been described as a "fictional pageant," "an important rootstock of the modern historical novel, especially the novel about the life and times of the artist."[30] In the writing of such a work, an author would invariably fall back on his own powers of *inventio* and *prudentia* to teach and promote his personal vision of truth.

Turning to Delminio's dialogue on the comparison between Ariosto and Tasso and its basic metaphors, we notice that the author throughout aligns poets and architects in a conspicuous manner:

> Come, per essempio, se un architetto avrà mal intesa la fabrica di un palagio, avendo preso errore nel disegno della pianta, onde l'erto poi ne sia falso riuscito, non già per questo fallo diremo costui non esser architteto, ma non buon architteto. (III: 312)

> [If, for example, an architect has conceived the body of a building badly, in that he has erred when drawing the plan, so as to make the erected building a failure, we do not on account of this mistake say that he is no architect, but that he is no good architect.]

According to Delminio, Tasso the elder [Bernardo], is a less accomplished poet, and the son is an excellent poet, but both are poets. He praises Torquato Tasso for having followed the rules of Aristotle ("il Tasso figlio ha . . . ordito il suo Epico poema con le vere regole insegnatoci da Aristotile") and for taking care to imitate "una sola attione" (one single action).[31] This statement seems baffling in view of the plethora of dramatic actions encountered in the *Liberata*, but we should not let it lead us astray. Delminio immediately qualifies his statement by explaining that what is required is a poem that can be surveyed in one mental effort ("in una sola speculazione")—that is, an object can be grasped even if extensive, provided it is ordered. He likens the poem's plan to that of a palace:

> immaginatevi che la Gerusalemme liberata sia una fabrica di non tanta grandezza, ma bene intesa, con le misure, & proportioni di architettura; et adorna secondo il convenevole di veri fregi, & colori. (III: 318)

[try to imagine that the Gerusalemme liberata is a building, whose size is not too large, but well conceived in its measurements and architectural proportions; and that it is aptly adorned with true friezes and colors.]

Ornaments and colors in the sense mentioned here would of course refer to the various kinds of rhetorical embellishment, including verbal repetitions and figures of thought. These types of ornatus are naturally present in Ariosto's poem too, and Delminio does not deny that it is worthy of praise, but in his view it does not deserve praise for the same reasons as Tasso's poem. *Orlando furioso* should be compared to "un palagio . . . falso di modello" (III.318)—that is, a palace with a faulty design. Delminio could not expect such criticism to go unanswered, and Ariosto's supporters retaliated by using the same metaphors. To the author of the *Difesa dell'Orlando furioso*, Tasso's poem is

vna casetta picciola, povera, e sproporzionata, per lo esser bassa, e lunga, oltre ogni corrispondenza di convenevol misura, oltr'à cio murata in sul vecchio.[32]

[a small, poor, and disproportionate hut, that in addition to lacking all correspondence of a suitable measure, is base and long, and also erected on old foundations.]

This passage recalls Vasari's *paragone* between Michelangelo and Tiziano. The latter—despite many excellent qualities—similarly meets with censure on account of his imperfect mastery of design, a defect Vasari attributes to Venetian artists in general.

But how exactly can a poem or a written life be compared to, or be seen to function as, an edifice? The obvious answer is that this occurs when they conform to the rules for creating "one poem's period," or a plot that is whole in the sense that it has a beginning, a middle, and an end. As such it should be adorned with the appropriate rhetorical "lights."

This aesthetic ideal will then be realized in specific ways at the levels of structure, segmentation, and verbal finish—that is, it will be manifested and be traceable at the level of *elocutio* or —to put it in Vasari's own words— "in ogni minima cosa." In fact, the elocutionary patterns constitute the end product of the various operations codified in rhetorical theory. Similarly, to

Vossius "elocutio alia philosophica est, alia oratoria, alia historica, alia poetica" ("elocution is both philosophical, or rhetorical, or historical, or poetical"),[33] and we may also add "architectural" to the list. In other words, elocution is flexible and all-embracing.

How do we identify, then, an integrated design, and its constituent parts? Sperone Speroni, Torquato Tasso's teacher of rhetoric, provides us with an important clue to a spatial reading when he argues that "solo il sito delle parole è tutta l'arte oratoria" ("the whole art of rhetoric resides entirely in the placing of the words").[34] Now the term *sito* ("place"), used by Tasso for placing an episode within the fabric of a plot, or by Speroni for he positioning words in a sentence, is also the Italian word for the architectural term "area." As shown in Chapter 1, poetry shares with architecture a reliance on a preconceived plan or design. Ben Jonson states, we recall, that in "the constitution of a poem, the action is aimed at by the poet, which answers place in a building"[35] or, in Daniel Heinsius's own words, "hic actio, ibi locus" ("this the action, here the place").

In this usage, theorists like Speroni and Tasso most likely recalled that Demetrius and Quintilian compared the placing of words to the placing of ones in a wall: "and [words] are therefore transferred from place to place to form the most suitable combinations, just as in the case of unhewn stones in a wall."[36] If we were to define the difference between a poem or narrative and a building, it could be said to reside in the building's realization in space: the building becomes a physical object, whereas the poem becomes a thing that is more intellectual than material,[37] possibly to be compared to a hologram or a product of virtual reality. Still in the first stage of planning—that is, in the plotting and projection onto a one-dimensional surface—the two are alike in the reliance on inner design. What about Vasari's epic narrative concerning the ascent of art in general, and more specifically the ascendancy of Florentine art? Can the wealth of materials, the multitude of luminaries and their works of art described in its three books, be considered in *una sola specolatione?* The answer is in the affirmative, because Vasari too bases himself on design—that is, a preexistent "true pattern" to which he frequently returns:

> ma io dirò bene che l'essere dell'una e dell'altra arte et il disegno—che è il fondamento di quelle, anzi l'istessa anima che concèpe e nutrisce in se medesima tutti i parti degli intelletti, fusse perfettissimo in su l'origine di tutte l'altre cose. (Vasari 1568: 3)

[But surely I will say that of both one and the other of these arts [paint-ing and sculpture] the design, which is their foundation, nay rather, the very soul that conceives and nourishes within itself all the parts of man's intellect, was already perfect before the creation of other things.]

Here preexistent, "inner" design plays the same role with respect to art and "all the parts of man's intellect," as does plot in epic and tragic structure in Aristotle's *Poetics*, and we must of course notice the architectural metaphor: *il fondamento*. On this point, therefore, Vasari anticipates Tasso and Delminio in his conception of the text as an ordered artifact existing in space.

Surveying the narrative line of the 1550 *Life* with these ideas in mind, we discover that Vasari's *Life* displays the same proportions as his encomium on the *res gestae* of Paul III. We see too that the main episodes have been or-dered virtually like the places ("loci") in a house or theater of memory as de-scribed by Francesco Sansovino or Thomas Wilson. In this respect these "loci" resemble Vasari's cycle of frescoes in the Cancelleria. In his descrip-tion of the *Sala dei cento giorni*, Kliemann argues that we can "interpret the frescoes within a rhetorical framework not only because they relate familiar topoi, but also because their very distribution can be connected with a rhetorical procedure known as *ars memoriae*."[38] When seen as a whole, the episodes and personifications depicted constitute a series of topoi for an en-comium of the pope, their function being similar to that of the episodes in the *Life of Michelangelo*.

The fact that Michelangelo was alive and active in 1550 may have pre-sented Vasari with a problem. In 1550 Michelangelo had already for three years been Chief Architect, responsible for the rebuilding of San Pietro, but the work progressed slowly and no end was in sight when Vasari first pub-lished his work. Vasari obviously did not want to conclude the *Life* (and the *Lives*) by emphasizing an unfinished and hotly disputed work like San Pietro. He was at pains, therefore, to create a finale that would not lessen the great-ness of Michelangelo, but in 1550 no recent completed work had sufficient unequaled merit to serve as the crowning achievement of the artist's career. Hence Vasari had to find a different solution, because the burial monument for Julius II, if completed, would become that final masterpiece:

la quale opera può pensarsi, che se da lui finita al mondo restasse, ogni altra opra sua da quella superata sarebbe per la difficoltà del cavar di quel sasso tante cose perfette. (III: 989)

[one can imagine if this work, had it been left to the world in finished state, would have surpassed any of his work due to the difficulty of carving so perfect things from that stone.]

But Vasari does not seem convinced that this work would merit such a role, or that it would ever be finished, in view of Michelangelo's advanced age—which he wrongly gives as seventy-three (for seventy-five). Why should he stress the difficulty of carving the stone rather than inventing the design? This uncertainty may explain why he plays down the important commissions Michelangelo received upon the death of San Gallo.[39] In Vasari's account of the life proper of Michelangelo, the year 1550 is reached already on page 989 of the Torrentiniana, just as the description of the artist at this point suggests that his best work has been done "Dopo tante sue fatiche, già alla età di LXXIII anni s'è condotto" ("After so many efforts, he had already reached the age of seventy-three"),[40] and instead he somewhat clumsily gives an assessment of the artist's character:

> e di continuo sino al presente con bellissime e savie risposte s'ha fatto conoscere com' uom prudente, e stato nel suo dire molto coperto et ambiguo, avendo le cose sue quasi due sensi.

> [always and to the present he has been known as a prudent man in his beautiful and wise answers, and he has been very guarded and ambiguous in that his statements almost always had two senses.]

The concluding three pages of the *Life* are anecdotal and exemplary; they provide us with a number of *exampla* of that prudent wisdom that most modern readers probably would interpret as devious, and with a final *peroratio* of Michelangelo's genius. Thus the text ends quite in keeping with Renaissance conventions of closure. The final paragraph not only reverts to the imagery of the first period but specifically refers to it: "come nel principio dissi, il Cielo per esempio nella vita, ne' costumi e nelle opere l'ha giù mandato" ("as I stated in the beginning, Heaven has sent him down to us to serve as an example in life, customs, and works").[41]

This somewhat surprising ending has the virtue of allowing the *Last Judgment* of the Capella Sistina to remain the last major work to remember Michelangelo by, which is most appropriate because in it "he even surpassed himself" (III: 982). In fact, the two cycles of frescoes executed in the Sistina occupy significant positions in the narrative of the life and works of the artist, coming as they do at the center and again at the very end of the narrative. I find it aesthetically pleasing that Vasari situates the frescoes in the Sistina ceiling at the textual center, because in Renaissance poetics the center was conceived as the high point or peak of the narrative, whereas the frescoes behind the altar are the last great work. This structural analogy must be the result of studied and conscious art, for the description, which occupies eight pages in the Torrentiniana (III: 965–72), being the longest one of all, is preceded and followed by a roughly equal number of pages of text (19–8–19). It is not that Vasari counted lines to achieve this effect, but he seems to have had a good idea of the text's proportions. Furthermore, the glorified position of the ceiling is enhanced by the character of the description. The frescoes are introduced as "having truly been a beacon," so that they hark back to the symbolism of light and darkness used in the opening sentence of the *Life*:

> La quale opera è veramente stata la lucerna che ha fatto tanto giovamento e lume all'arte della pittura, che ha bastato a illuminare il mondo per tanti anni in tenebre stato. (III: 965; italics added)

> [The ceiling has proved a veritable beacon to our art, of inestimable benefit to all painters, restoring light to a world that for centuries had been plunged into darkness.] (Bull, I: 354)

Once Vasari has completed his long and detailed account of the many scenes that are part of the plan for the ceiling, he addresses his own age in an apostrophe that once again presents Michelangelo as the bringer of light:

> O veramente felice età nostra, o beati artefici, che ben cosí vi dovere chiamare, da che nel tempo vostro avete potuto al fonte di tanta chiarezza rischiare le tenebrose luci degli occhi e vedere fattovi piano tutto quel ch'era difficile da sí maraviglioso e singulare artefice. (III: 972; italics added)

> [What a happy age we live in! And how fortunate are our craftsmen, who have been given light and vision by Michelangelo and whose difficulties have been smoothed away by this marvellous and incomparable artist!] (Bull, I: 360)

Again we notice how the key concepts of light and darkness keep reappearing at important structural points, for the two passages cited enclose and serve as a narrative frame around the ekphrasis itself. In this manner Vasari compels us to rethink the narrative as a spatial structure. No doubt this is also why he specifically makes perception both spatial and architectural, stating that Michelangelo illuminated the mind's eye and removed the falseness that darkened the rooms of the intellect ("le bellissime stanze dell' intelletto"; III: 972). It was conventional to place the peripety, or "mutamento di fortuna," at the textual center of a plot in dramatic and epic poetry, and when he reaches the end, Vasari refers to how "invidious Fortune" opposes Michelangelo, thus linking the middle and the end. For the Pope dies when Michelangelo is at the height of his career and when he has resumed his work on the burial monument for Julius II. The new Medici Pope Leo X makes it impossible to complete the monument by instead sending him to Firenze for the completion of San Lorenzo. This is how we learn that the peak has been passed ("volse *la fortuna invidiosa* che di tal memoria non si lasciasse quel fine"; III: 972; italics added).

The second great work in the Sistina, the frescoes of the *Last Judgment*, occupies less space within the *Life* than that given to the frescoes on the ceiling (III: 982–85), but they are signaled to the reader in much the same way when the painting is said to have been "mandata da Dio a gli uomini" (III: 985). Thematic decorum is shown by replacing the references to light with a strong emphasis on terror and the aspect of *terribilità*. Instead of dwelling on the victory of light over darkness, Vasari in this case creates a narrative frame presenting Michelangelo himself as victorious. Michelangelo not only conquered all other artists who had worked in the chapel before him, he surpassed even himself:

> mostrò non solo essere vincitore de' primi artefici, ma ancora nella volta ch'egli tanto celebrata avea fatta, volse vincere se stesso, et in quella, di gran lunga passatosi, superò se medesimo. (III: 982)

> [it was seen that Michelangelo had not only excelled the masters who had worked there previously but had also striven to excel even the vaulting that he had made so famous; for the Last Judgement was finer by far, and in it Michelangelo outstripped himself.] (Bull, I: 380)

Once the description of the awe-inspiring work is finished, Vasari returns to the initial image, which compares its visual effect on the spectators to the way conquered nations were made to march in front of the victor's chariot.[42] The important difference is that Michelangelo conducts prisoners persuaded by his art, not conquered by arms. Thus Vasari transforms and introduces into the text a topos from the contemporary literary genre of the triumph.

The two cycles are connected in the *Life* by means of a similar narrative device. Just as Vasari specifically refers to the earlier work in the passage that introduces the Judgment frescoes, he concludes this account with an apostrophe to his age, exactly as he had done in the earlier work:

> Età veramente felice chiamar si puote e felicità della memoria di chi ha visto veramente stupenda maraviglia del secol nostro. (III: 985)

> [How fortunate they are, and what happy memories they have stored up, who have seen this truly stupendous marvel of our times!] (Bull, I: 383)

The implication here seems to be that Michelangelo has brought back the Golden Age and so made happy all who have experienced the revival. In the structure of the *Life* as a whole, however, this apostrophe links the descriptions located at its center and its end, thus making it clear that Vasari positions them as he would the verbal lights in a highly wrought rhetorical period. By thus positioning his descriptions of the works he believes have the greatest merit, he makes the textual center coincide with the completion of the ceiling of the Sistina and with the year at the center of Michelangelo's age span till then. This structure appears to be coincidental, but it is entirely in keeping with Vasari's conspicuous desire to give meaningful form to his celebration of the artist. How, then, did the death of Michelangelo in 1564 impinge upon the this artful pattern? Is Vasari content to be a mere reporter of additional events and works, or did he invent a new structure for the *Life?*

Let us consider the additions. Vasari had to include the impact of Michelangelo's death on the narrative and provide an account of his last fourteen years. The topos of the end was as important to sixteenth-century writers as it is to modern literary critics.[43] One need only recall the words of the Forestiero Napolitano, a disguise for Tasso himself, in *La Cavaletta, ovvero de la Toscana Poesia:*

> Dunque il fine, in quanto egli è finito, è certo. . ... E questa certezza egli prende dal fine o dal termine: laonde io direi ch'il termine, in quanto egli è termine, fosse certo sempre, o che le cose terminate, in

quanto terminate, fossero certe. La forma dunque de l'arte, determinando la materia, le dà qualche certezza.[44]

[Thus the end, in so far as it is the end is certain. . . . And this certainty it takes from the end or the conclusion: therefore I would say that the conclusion, in so far as it is a conclusion, always would be certain, or that things concluded, is given a degree of certainty. Hence the form of art, in determining the matter, gives it a degree of certainty.]

In the case of Vasari there is of course the question of a competition in critical authority, because Vasari had published the Giuntina in response to the *Vita di Michelangelo* by Ascanio Condivi (1553). The expanded *Life* openly engages with Condivi's book,[45] but in the present context this conflict is less interesting than the new design Vasari invents. The evidence of a new design appears already in the opening sentence of the 1568 *Life*, a sentence that, as we shall observe, has been expanded and revised.

It was to be expected that the imagery chosen to describe Michelangelo's peak performance as an artist would remain much the same, but there are nevertheless a number of changes, all of which reveal increasing emphasis on design. Although these revisions have been recorded in Barocchi (1987: 3–4), they have not been adequately explained. They include the omission of the word *altri* in the phrase "Giotto e de' altri seguaci suoi," but more important is the rewriting of the final phrase, "le difficultà nella scienza delle linee, nella pittura, nel giudizio della scultura e nella invenzione della veramente garbata architettura," as:

la perfezzione dell'arte del disegno nel lineare, dintornare, ombrare e lumeggiare, per dare rilèvo alle cose della pittura, e con retto giudizio operare nella scultura, e rendere le abitazioni commode e sicure, sane, allegre, proporzionate e riche di varii ornamenti nell'architettura.

[the perfection of the art of design in executing the lines, contours, shadows, and high lights, so as to give relief to works of painting, and what it is to work with correct judgment in sculpture, and how in architecture it is well-proportioned, and rich with varied ornaments.] (de Vere III: 1832)

We note, first, that by dropping the reference to *altri* the focus falls more squarely on Giotto as Michelangelo's unique precursor, a first Adam as it were.[46] In the second place, the resulting change in emphasis offers an excellent illustration of developments in Late Renaissance style, because such crucial terms as *disegno, lumeggiare, retto,* and *ornamenti* are new to the passage. These form a nexus of ideas in aesthetic theory, and when seen as such they draw attention to the need to have a preconceived plan and the means to make that plan visible. In addition, there is an increased emphasis on "correctness" ("retto guidizio") and proportion ("abitazioni . . . proporzionate"). All this shows a notable movement away from the preferences that are typical of early cinquecento art, particularly when we note that terms like difficultà, invenzione, and garbata architettura, found in the 1550 version, have been omitted or replaced. The reason Vasari drops "garbata architettura" in favor of an architecture characterized by perfect design ("la perfezzione dell'arte del disegno nel lineare") may be explained with reference to the stylistic development toward greater emphasis on order in the mannered art and literature after the Council of Trent.[47]

Vasari is not entirely consistent in the way he uses the terms *luce* and *lume,* both of which basically translate as "light." Roland Le Mollé has attempted a systematic survey of the usage, according to which Vasari uses *lume* to counterbalance *luce* just as he balances *licenza, ornamento, giudizio, facilità,* and *leggiadria* against the five precepts of *regola, ordine, misura, disegno,* and *maniera.*[48] This analysis is largely correct in most instances of Vasari's use of the terms in the *Lives* on the whole, but definitely not so in this particular period. I believe, instead, that what we witness here is the inception of a corrective movement in the opposite direction. Thus ornament would not counterbalance order but should be seen to strengthen it, as in the phrase "ordine . . . con più ornamento." Hence we note that when *lume, luce,* and *lumeggiare* occur in this sentence, it is *luce* that carries the greatest symbolic import by being more natural and divine than "the light of Giotto and his followers" or Michelangelo's practice of *lumeggiare* ("highlighting"). But terms like *luce, lumeggiare,* and *ornamenti* do not have one plain meaning only. In fact, one of their several meanings—*lumen,* or *lux* as rhetorical ornament—helps us to see how this stylistic shift is manifested in the arrangement of the rhetorical design.

Indeed, the verbal change from "le difficultà nella scienza delle linee" to "la perfezzione . . . nel lineare" reverts to, and puns on, the *lineamenta* that had controlled Early and High Renaissance compositions. Typically, the focus on utility and practice emerges clearly in the professed purpose of rendering habitations comfortable and secure, healthy ("rendere le abitazioni commode e sicure, sane"; II: 717). *This* desire is visible in the new and grander plan of the *Life of Michelangelo*, where the cupola of San Pietro, God's highly proportioned habitation, is given an important position within the redesigned totality. Another likely explanation, and one relevant to the increased emphasis on design in the 1568 *Lives*, is Vasari's actual preoccupation with and practice of architecture in the period after the completion of the first edition of the *Lives* in 1550.[49] By 1570 Vasari is already mentioned by Palladio as an "architetto raro" and ranked among the leading architects of his time.[50]

There is more to the revised opening sentence, however, than changes in terminology; the number of repetitions is greater. The few lines added introduce a number of words already found in the first part of the opening period, and for this reason they convey an element of redundancy or mere repetitiveness. This is especially true of words like *lumeggiare*, *retto*, and *proporzionate*, words that echo *lume*, *proporzionata*, and *Rettore* earlier in the passage. A semantic scanning of repetitions yields the following outline:

### 1568 Life of Michelangelo, Repetitions in the Initial Period

| | | | |
|---|---|---|---|
| (h) | *Rettore* | *spirito* | (a) |
| (g) | universalmente | universalmente | (g) |
| (f) | indarno | senza alcun frutto | (f) |
| (e) | si affaticavano | tante fatiche | (e) |
| (d) | arte | arte | (d) |
| (c) | proporzionata | lumeggiare | (b) |
| (b) | lume | *retto* | (h) |
| (a) | *spiriti* | proporzionate | (c) |

(The repetitions that constitute examples of *epanados*—that is, linkage between beginning and middle, or middle and end—are in italics.)

The listing above shows Vasari's careful distribution of verbal ornaments of essentially two kinds: *chiasmus* (or *antimetabole*) and *epanados*. In all, eight equivalent words or synonyms are repeated sequentially (d-e-f-g-g-f-e-d), while another four (*lume, proporzionata, lumeggiar,* and *proporzionate*) are repeated in a sequential pattern (b-c-b-c). This pattern is more sustained than the pattern found in the 1550 edition, shown in earlier in this chapter. In this later case too, the repetitions seem to be somewhat "disordered," but we note that the disorder is of a different kind. The apparent disorder in the 1568 *Life of Michelangelo* is due to the asymmetrical inclusion of *spiriti, Rettore, spirito,* and *retto,* but these words have been inserted knowingly and precisely, so as to forge a strong link between the beginning and the middle (spiriti— spirito) and the middle and the end (Rettore—retto). Furthermore, when we consult the *editio princeps* we notice that Vasari creates a pregnant pause in the sentence after having described how God, appropriately placed at the center of the period, surveys the earth ("volse clementemente gli occhi alla terra"). The pause is marked by a full stop and a capital letter ("E veduta . . ."). Barocchi, in her edition, obliterates this pause (1986: 3) by altering the full stop to a comma. Although the syntax shows the sentence to be one long syntactical construction, I believe Vasari placed the pause there to prepare for the climactic mention of the Ruler of Heaven ("il Rettore del Ciel") and before describing how he intervenes in human affairs ("si dispose di mandare in terra"). The pause, therefore, is aesthetically and theologically appropriate. Actually, the period has three well-defined parts. An initial part dwells on the shortcomings of the many artists who followed the example of Giotto, who labored to imitate "the greatness of nature" (1–7); the second and central part describes the clemency of God when he observes the earth from above (8–11); and while the third part describes his decision to send Michelangelo down to earth to redeem and perfect the arts through design (12–18). The notion of design introduced at this point assumes the function of spiritual *ordo* at the same time that it seems natural to relate the order created by these verbal and syntactical manipulations to Vasari's idea about a new architecture endowed with more ornaments.

In my opinion, it is impossible to overstate the importance of this sentence as a key to understanding the *Life* or Vasari's design for the *Lives* as a whole, for it summarizes the entire work, the ascent of art from Giotto to Buonarroti, at the same time that it provides an excellent example of the technique of shaping the text by distributing repeated "lights"—a kind of *dintornare* in narrative form. If we step back for a moment to survey the entire 1568 *Life* as one vast sentence on a par with the opening one, we find that the macro-period must be said metaphorically to be studded with three lights or ornaments of particular luster: the Capella Sistina ceiling, the *Last Judgment,* and the Cupola of San Pietro. Because the first of these works has been restored to a state approximating its former glory and luminosity, it is easier to understand Vasari's exalted praise of them as "lights," but in this context "lights" refer to ornaments deployed to signal the plot of Vasari's *Lives.*

When we consider the placement of the descriptions of these works in the 1568 *Life* in relation to the structure of the 1550 *Life,* we cannot avoid noticing that radical changes have taken place (Fig. 10). The Sistine ceiling no longer holds the center of the narrative, because so much material has been added after the description of the *Last Judgment.* In terms of placement, however, the three great works are evenly distributed within the body of the text. Thus, the description of the Sistine ceiling frescoes comes about one-third into the text, at II: 733–36; the *Last Judgment* (the last of Michelangelo's major works to be described in the 1550 edition) is now at the midpoint in the text; the narrative account of the San Pietro model is about one-third from the end (II: 765–69). The central position of honor thus is given to the work in which the artist surpassed even himself ("superò se medesimo"). I take these placements to be the product of a clear sense of proportion.

Vasari's description of the projected dome does not make for smooth reading. Its mass of technical detail compels us to slow down our reading and to concentrate intensely on seeing the dome erected in our inner eye. The difficulty of visualizing may well be the reason George Bull omitted the description in his translation of the *Life of Michelangelo.* Instead he adds the following note: "Vasari now goes on to describe in considerable and some-what confused detail Michelangelo's model for the dome of St. Peter's" (1966: 409). In so doing, Bull not only chooses the easy way out, he completely disregards the integrity and the design of Vasari's most important *Life,* where the model of the dome receives ample treatment. As I see it, there are two principal reasons that Vasari should have chosen to interpolate this long, detailed description.

The first and obvious reason is provided by history itself. When Vasari revised the *Vita of Michelangelo* he had to account for fourteen years of addi-tional artistic work, the *Last Judgment* no longer being the last great work on which posterity could base an assessment of Michelangelo's art. The master had gone on to a new and greater task of terrifying proportions: designing and constructing San Pietro. The design for the dome is indeed Michelan-gelo's crowning achievement, but the architect unfortunately did not live to see it completed. It is here that Vasari sees his mission and seizes the oppor-tunity. He enters into the debate about the dome and describes the model Michelangelo had had made, with the obvious intention of letting the model serve to prevent possible attempts to alter Michelangelo's grand de-

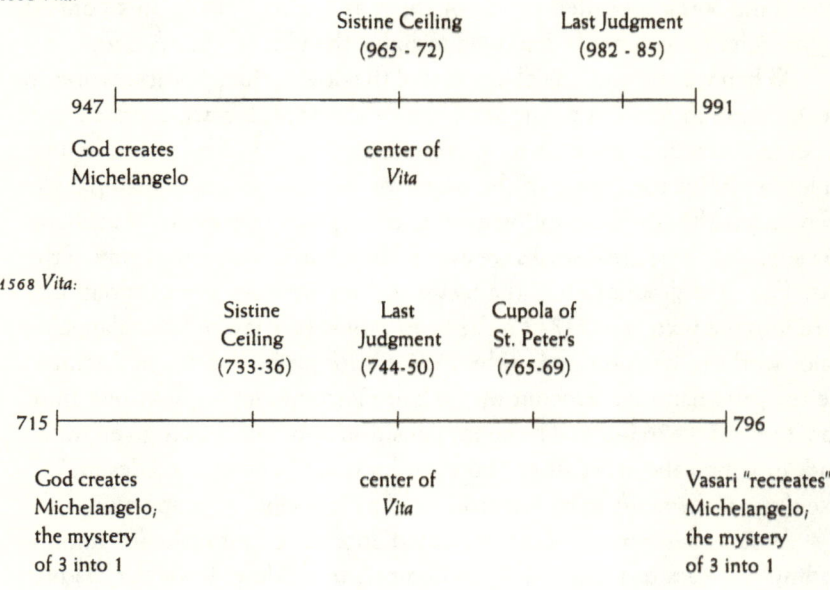

FIG. 10

The placement of Michelangelo's major works ("lumi") in the 1550 and 1568 editions

sign. In this manner he ingeniously allows himself, and us, to participate in the creative process by completing and re-creating in our minds the "disegno interno" of Michelangelo's work.

A second reason, I propose, is purely aesthetic, although it is linked with Vasari's attempt to "complete" and fix the design of St. Peter's. What we witness in this sentence is the artist's quest for a new aesthetic form for the expanded *Life of Michelangelo*. Because it no longer formed the conclusion, the *Life* needed a more comprehensive design in order to integrate the new materials and underscore the argument that the oeuvre of Michelangelo epitomized the highest degree of perfection. As shown above, this new design did not restrict itself to the addition of a new finale; it also entailed small but important adjustments in its opening period and its first paragraph, adjustments that on the whole are typical of the revisions in the expanded *Lives*, where Vasari essentially preserves and strengthens his earlier emphases.[51] One significant new element is the description of the dome, but this description too develops the themes introduced in the 1550 *Life*. The description is spiritually edifying, so as to inspire not only Michelangelo's faithful friends ("fedeli") who were to complete the San Pietro, but also readers of the *Life*. The description is a remarkable manifestation of Vasari's well-proportioned textual architecture, as we see from its place within the *Life* itself. By deliberately shaping his narrative in a particular way, Vasari builds on and inventively extends "Michelangelo's pauline image of himself . . . as a 'wise master builder' " who gives purpose and direction to his own work.[52] Let us go on to consider how his architectural thinking is realized in the ekphrastic description of the model of the dome.

The account at first seems difficult to follow because Vasari bombards the reader with volleys of measurements, but this initial impression cannot conceal the fact that it consists of fairly well defined blocks of text. True enough, in view of the repeated references to order we would perhaps have expected an even higher degree of order, for the description seems essentially to consist of series of numerical ratios produced in swift sequence, interrupted at one point by an exalted apostrophe to the building and its creator. In fact, the description presents a broad symmetrical outline consisting of six parts. Thus the narrative proper, which occupies three and a half pages in the *editio princeps* (II: 765–69), is introduced by what may suitably be termed a narrative frame where the author states his intention:

> con quella brevità che potrò, ne faremo una semplice narrazione, acciò che, se mai accadessi (che non consenta Dio), come s' è visto fino a ora essere stata questa opera travagliata in vita di Michelangelo, così possino questi miei scritti, qualunque e' si sieno, giovare ai fedeli che saranno esecutori della mente di questo raro uomo, et ancora raffrenare la volontà de' maligni che volessino alterarle; e così in un medesimo tempo si giovi e diletti et apra la mente a' begl ingegni che sono amici e si dilettano di questa professione. (II: 765)

> [wherefore with such brevity as we may we will give a simple description of it, to the end that, if it should ever be the fate of this work, which God forbid, to the disturbed by the envy and malice of presumptuous persons after the death of Michelangelo, even as we have seen it disturbed up to the present during his lifetime, these my writings, such as they may be, may be able to assist the faithful who are to be the executors of the mind of that rare man, and also to restrain the malignant desires of those who may seek to alter it, and so at one and

the same time assist, delight, and open the minds of those beautiful intellects that are the friends of this profession and regard it as their joy.]
(de Vere, II: 1911)

In addition to serving as the point of departure, this passage makes it clear
that Vasari is not exclusively a historian, for he is also conducting a campaign of moral edification and building a memorial. Shortly after this passage, the narrative proper begins with another clear initial marker: "E per dar
principio, dico che questo modello, fatto con ordine di Michelangelo, trovo
che sarà . . ."; 96.30–31 ("I must begin by saying that according to this
model, I find that it will be . . ."). Then he goes on to give a series of measurements for the foundations of the dome, the four great pilasters, the
arches, the pillars, and the cornices, until he reaches the level from which
the cupola is to be vaulted. At this point he erupts into a passionate apostrophe on the greatness of the cupola, stressing the judgment, strength, eternity, and perfection with which it has been conceived:

> non si può vedere, agli occhi di chi sa e di chi intende, cosa più vaga,
> più bella e più artifiziosa: e per le legature e commettiture delle pietre,
> e per avere in sé in ogni parte e fortezza et eternità, e con tanto
> giudizio aver cavatone l'acque che piovono per molti condotti segreti,
> e finalmente riddottotola a quella perfezione. (98.28–33)

> [to the eyes of who can see and understand, one cannot see a thing
> more pleasing, more beautiful and more highly wrought with art: and
> both with regard to the joining and placing of the stones, because
> they everywhere contain strength and eternity, and for the judgement
> displayed in the carving of many secret water conduits, and finally be-
> cause it was all compacted with such perfection.]

The excursus ends with an expression of regret that Michelangelo died before "sì bella e terribil machina" was completed.

The next step in the account is to turn to the incomplete part of the
building. Again Vasari marks this transition as a new beginning: "solamente
restaci a dar principio al voltare della tribuna"; 98.38–39 ("it only remains to
make a beginning with the vaulting of the tribune"; de Vere, III: 1913). Hence
he goes on to explain the ratios that inform the dome itself and its supporting arches and vaults. First he singles out the three crucial points in the de-

sign for the dome, points marked graphically in the text by capital letters arranged to form a triangle in this manner ("tre punti che fanno triangolo in questo modo"):

A.   B.

C.

These three points may be said to hold the entire secret of the dome; they should be seen, I suggest, not only as parts of a technical design but also as functioning on a symbolic level as an analogue to the operation of the Trinity in the universe.[53] The alignment between the tectonic and the theological is suggested also by the declared purpose of the construction: "perché possa eternamente aver vita" ("so that the structure may have eternal life" [III: 1914]). The phrase highlights the obvious spiritual dimension of the building. The fact that these graphically marked points occupy the exact numerical center of Vasari's "brief description" is indicative of the author's sense of shape and of his perfect control of his materials. These aspects, though, cannot be perceived by anyone admiring the wooden model of the dome—but only by reading Vasari's text.

The outline of the various points and stages in Vasari's textual model reveals the logic of its basic design, whose parts are distributed symmetrically within the body of the text: sections *a* to *c* occupies approximately the first half of the text, *d* to *f* the second half. The textual center is located at the beginning of section *d*.

(*a*) narrative frame
   (*b*) the description of the foundations of the cupola
      (*c*) Vasari's interpolated praise of the *terribile machina*
      (*d*) the description of the vaults of dome
   (*e*) description of the staircases and the cupola's ornaments
(*f*) narrative frame

The verbal texture of these segments binds the various parts together by means of verbal repetitions. Thus the phrase "con *brevità* . . . faremo una semplice narrazione" ("we shall *briefly* make a simple narration") at the beginning of section *a* is echoed in the phrase "*brevemente* fatto uno schizzo" ("having *briefly* made a sketch") at the end of this section, thus marking a circular return. The phrase "*per aver* in sé in ogni parte e fortezza ed *eternità*" is inverted so as to read "*perché* possa *eternamente aver* vita." Likewise a sequence of three identical words links the beginning to the middle of the segment: the words "dar principio . . . modello . . . ordine" found at the beginning of the narrative proper (in segment *a*), reappear (in segment *d*) immediately before the description of the "tre punti" used for designing the vaults ("dar principio . . . modello . . . in ordine").

Then too, the end of the "narrazione" (in segment *f*) is clearly marked by a final punning reference to the completion and purpose of the model: "Fu la fine di queste modello . . . il fermamento e stabilimento di questa fabbrica" (II: 768). In my opinion, this phrase solicits a greater attention than De Vere gives to it when he translates "the completion of this model, . . .the form of the fabric having been thus settled and established" (III: 1915), a phrase that excludes the play on *fine* ("end") in the sense of "purpose," for the model was indeed completed with the purpose of ensuring the completion of the projected building. The model therefore has the same function that has been attributed to Vasari's *Life of Leonardo*, where his "intention was to create an instrument of judgment by giving models for appraisal and action."[54]

If we consider the description of the model as a piece of metaphoric architecture, as I believe we should, the three points outlined (A.B.C.) mark the lowest (C) and the highest positions (A B) on a curve, which would correspond to a section of the cupola, or—put differently—the beginning, the middle, and the end of the diameter in a circular representation of the curve. The various verbal repetitions, as it were, sketch in these contours as a kind of "dintornare" or a tracing of contours in the text. It is a fact that Vasari loved puns. Indeed, on this occasion he seems punningly to refer both to the cupola's curve and to the fact that we have reached the exact halfway point in his narrative. Then he wraps his description of the central principles of the dome in phrases like "[h]a girato il sesto con tre punti" ("he turned the curve of the vault on three points") and "con quale egli ha girato il primo mezzo tondo della tribuna, col quale e' da la forma e l'altezza" ("wherewith he turned the first half-circle of the tribune, with which he gave the form, height and breadth of this vault"; 1913). The references to the turning of the curve, the halfway point of its span, and the height of the vault all seem to indicate that we are at the center and the halfway point of the narrative account of the vault.

This compositional technique is of course no invention of Vasari's, although his application is unique and impressive. He draws on ideals of rhetorical composition dating back to antiquity, as we find the basic implied metaphor of text as architecture already in Demetrius's *De elocutione* when the periodic style is said to combine "the part of a sentence together in flowing regularity and may be compared to stones, supporting and keeping together a dome-shaped vault." In Chapter 3 we saw how Leon Battista Alberti created a similar but simpler "textual dome" in the first paragraph of the moral dialogue *Profugiorum ab aerumna* (1441), when he describes the quality and impact of Brunelleschi's cupola. This link between Alberti and Vasari becomes particularly significant when we realize that behind Alberti's description looms the example set by Manuel Chrysoloras's description of the Hagia Sophia in *Comparison Between Old and New Rome* (1411). In Alberti's text too, rhetorical repetitions, which appropriately belong within the textual microcosm of a single perfect period, are employed to mark the inherent *lineamenta* of both *narratio* and cupola, but there is a major difference between Alberti and Vasari. Alberti's description embodies the aesthetic principles that had gone into the building of the cupola, whereas Vasari to a greater extent describes the technical specifications and actual architectonic shape of a planned edifice. Still, we should not miss the point that the 1568 *Life* offers Vasari the opportunity to do for Michelangelo what Alberti had done for Brunelleschi. His commemorative description of Michelangelo's unfinished cupola emulates the example set by Alberti's description of Brunelleschi's cupola in the *Profugiorum ab aerumna*: both invest the cupola with a specific moral purpose.

Returning to Buonarroti's dome, or rather to Vasari's textual emplotment of it, we notice that it becomes the vehicle by means of which we may recreate the inner design of Michelangelo's "tribuna." The "tribuna" enables us to judge the artist's work before the fact. In this context it becomes meaningful to remember the various connotations of the word Vasari uses about the cupola *tribuna*, derived from the Latin noun *tribunal*. The word not only signifies the most spacious part of a large edifice such as a church, but also has been used to describe the platform from which in classical Rome the tribune addressed the people, and about that part of the apse in a civic basilica where the judge was seated. In his metaphoric use of *tribuna*, so it seems, Vasari lets all these meanings work together, for the cupola of San Pietro is both the place where Michelangelo's genius speaks most eloquently and the place where we can form the most complete judgment of his art. And Vasari himself is the tribune proclaiming the true character of the dome to all the people.

The *Last Judgment* was the final major work in the *Vita di Michelangelo* in the 1550 edition. There it was followed by references to a few minor works, some anecdotes that reveal artist's character, plus a final peroration on the subject of Michelangelo's genius. In the 1568 *Life* a substantial number of documents is amassed to provide detail in order to verify Vasari's account of Michelangelo, rather like a realistic or documentary novelist who includes lots of facts to strengthen the impression of the fiction's truthfulness. My own approach does not entirely coincide with the scholarly view that Vasari's "orientation as a writer shifted from the mythical towards the factual, from the rhetorical to the narrative and discursive."[55] In the 1568 edition of the *Vite*, 80 lines and three and a half words precede the line that contains the printed capital letters, just as eighty lines and four words follow it. The segment containing the description, however, is not marked typographically in any particular way. The textual parts accurately proportioned around the compass points (A. B. C.) indicate that Vasari must have had complete control of the shape of his presentation when he penned it. When writing, Vasari probably used the placement and length of the inserted apostrophe, and possibly also the final section on ornament, as variable elements to balance the structure.

It can be argued that the 1568 *Life* is open-ended because Vasari opens his narrative to other living artists, but in the 1550 version too the work ends is non-finito because Michelangelo is still alive. If we consider only the *Life of Michelangelo*, however, the element of closure is stronger in the 1568 version since the author plays a more active role in the narrative. With the placement of the *Last Judgment* in the middle of the *Life*, the symbolically important, final position is now reserved for Vasari himself—his own monument to Michelangelo. However, even this concluding self-congratulatory section accords well with the conventions of closure, when the monument is seen as a realization in stone of the *Life's* opening period. Although he is only one man, Michelangelo excels in three arts, and so by implication does Vasari, who designed the sculptural personifications of the same arts, each to be made by a different artist:

> la quale col disegno da Giorgio Vasari fu allogata a Battista Lorenzi, . . .e perchè vi hanno essere tre statue, La Pittura, la Scultura e l'Architettura, una di queste fu allogata a Battista sopradetto, una a Giovanni dell'Opera, l'ultima a Valerio Cioli, scultori fiorentini.

> [which (that is, the tomb) was allotted to Battista Lorenzi . . . to execute after the design of Giorgio Vasari, . . .And since there are to be three statues there, Painting, Sculpture, and Architecture, one of these

was allotted to the above-named Battista, one to Giovanni dell'Opera, and the last to Valerio Cioli, Florentine sculptors.] (III: 1954)

The text of the opening period has been metamorphosed into stone and then transformed back to text again. In this sense Vasari's desire to be the authoritative and official chronicler of Michelangelo's life and works is realized when the essence of the recorded life is eternalized in stone through the metamorphoses of his pen. Like the *Life*'s opening period and the description of the cupola, Vasari's monument to Michelangelo embodies both the essence of his commemorative praise and his own desire to win glory. This intention is clear from the very beginning of the *Life* in the 1550 and 1568 versions: the differences found in rhetoric and plot design in the two versions are consistent with the development toward greater reliance on conspicuous verbal artifice and order in late cinquecento art. The theme of Chapter 5 is the climatic point in this development as seen in Tasso's epic poetry and Monteverdi's subsequent revision of Tasso's elaborate art.

# "Una fabrica di non tanta grandezza"

## The Architecture of Tasso's *Paragone*

In the previous chapter we saw how Vasari crowns his tripartite epic biography on the rise of art with the *Life of Michelangelo*, to turn this the final biography (in the 1550 version) or the culminating one (in the 1568 version) into a carefully designed whole. Moreover, we observed how the biographer-artist had shaped particularly significant moments or places in that whole, such as the ekphrasis of the dome, by an ingenious deployment of tectonic oratory, establishing as he puts it, "ordine con più ornamento." Torquato Tasso (1544–96) was faced with a problem of composition of similar proportions when designing the vast whole and the individual parts of *La Gerusalemme liberata* (1581). Because Tasso appears at various points in this book, I here want to explore how the poet rhetorically shapes a celebrated episode in Book Twelve, the nocturnal duel between Clorinda and Tancredi, and I do so in the context of cinquecento poetics and notions of dramatic structure. Then, as a test case, I shall briefly consider how in 1624 Claudio Monteverdi adapts the text for his proto-opera *Il Combattimento di Tancredi e Clorinda*.[1]

For my purpose in this chapter, I do not carry out a detailed and potentially tedious analysis of Tasso's rich fabric of musical poetry, but rather limit myself to outlining the principal points of the episode's design in keep-

ing with the theme of this book. I therefore refer readers with special interests to the close philological analysis published in my article "Posta in musica: Tasso's *Paragone* and Monteverdi's *Combattimento*."[2] Tasso is the poet most
favored by Monteverdi and other composers who belonged to the *seconda
practica*.[3] There are several reasons for their choice. In the dialogue *La Cavaletta overo de la Toscana Poesia*, Tasso presents himself as proficient in the art of
and in his practice of using "the words like cells of sound to be framed, like
musical elements to combine."[4] In this respect he relates to the *seconda pratica*
as Bembo does to the *prima pratica*.

Tasso's arguably new poetic style and use of Aristotelian concepts of
dramatic structure and unity in general have been studied in some detail, but
the crucial role of rhetorical composition in relation to the key concept of
*enargia* still remains obscure, despite some important recent contributions.[5]
His discourses on poetics and on heroic poetry draw on Aristotle and also
on the treatises of his teacher Sperone Speroni, on Giorgio Trissino, on
Castelvetro, and on others who focus on unity and "the Unities." Throughout his career, Tasso advocates what he terms a mixed unity ("unità mista") in
the choice and distribution of subjects, themes, and modes of style.[6] The
phrase "io parlo di quell'unità ch'é mistà" occurs in the *Discorsi dell'arte poetica*,[7]
a work that rightly has been called "the primer" for his epic,[8] but the central
notion is further developed in the *Discorsi del poema eroico*, where the relationship between music and poetry is strongly stressed. Only recent critics have
begun to study what this musical coupling of unity and multiplicity actually
implies in terms of epic construction.[9]

We must not put too much emphasis on the increasing imitation by
means of sound in Tasso's poetry, for Tasso is a great admirer of Dante and
sonneteers like Della Casa and not given to facile word-painting. His use of
the term "musical" then is not merely metaphorical. Unfortunately, as a rule
he does not put his technique openly on display in his theoretical works, or
explicitly disclose his tricks. This reserve is stressed in the dialogue *La Cavaletta*, where the Forestiero Napolitano argues that "to hide the deceit and,
so to speak, the dissimulation of art, is therefore the highest artifice."[10] A
master in the use of devices of repetition, Tasso characteristically warns
against excessive repetition, particularly with regard to rhyme—warnings
that serve merely to conceal his own artifice.[11]

In the *Discorsi del poema eroico*, Tasso gives the following famous definition: "l'arte del comporre il poema sarebbe simile a la ragion de l'universo, la
qual è composta de' contrari, come la ragion musica" ("the art of composing

a poem could be said to be similar to the proportion of the universe, which is composed of contraries, like musical harmony").[12] Later in the treatise he broadens the basis for grasping what he understands by "musical proportion" in a surprisingly abstract arithmetico-musical explanation of his choice of the ottava.[13] Such references to "musica specolativa," an abstract music perceived only by the mind, seem dated when compared with the compositional habits of the *seconda pratica*.[14] These allusions may be a bit confusing when we recall what has been said of Tasso as the poet of the *seconda pratica* and of mimesis, but we should keep in mind that mimesis does not necessarily refer to a vivid and truthful representation of events—that is, that it is not a technique only to produce representational verisimilitude. Mimesis can be more abstract, reflecting the principles inherent in all creations whether made by God or man. The universal system capable of providing these principles was of course rhetoric, for "the analytical vocabulary of rhetoric and art is one entity."[15] In terms of composition, then, we can analyze the music of Tasso's poetry as realized in his use of *dispositio* and *elocutio*—in the way he shapes and distributes textual units devoted to particular events and how the words on the page serve to indicate and integrate these units. This abstract form of mimesis inevitably produces an *enargia* totally different in kind from the effect created by vivid description alone (*ekphrasis*) alone. It is an *enargia* where the distribution of words as signs creates its own luster and "music." Without disregarding the role of vivid description of physical action or the passions, I want to focus here on the global aspects of this more abstract kind of mimesis, by examining in detail how Tasso shapes his text into "una sola attione."

Tasso's *La Cavaletta* may serve as a good point of departure in the present context. Aristotle's definition of unity—a whole is that which has a beginning, a middle, and an end—is an important subtext, as when Tasso discusses patterns of sound and rhyme with reference to *la testura* ("the texture or web") of sonnets that have "a tempered form" (*forma temperata*). It does not suffice to enchant the reader only at the beginning and the middle of the sonnet, Tasso reminds us, because attention and consistency must be retained right to the end. His model sonnet is Giovanni Della Casa's "Questa vita mortal, ch'in una o in due," which he praises because the poet

> molto l'avanza nel fine del sonetto con la scelta de le parole e con lumi e con gli ornamenti, e particolarmente con la pienezza de le consonanti e co 'l numero e co 'l suono de' versi.[16]

[(h)e considerably enhances the grandeur of the ending of the sonnet in his choice of words and lights and ornaments, and particularly with the richness of the consonants, the number and the sound of the lines.]

These words may evoke his sound-painting alone, an aspect that surely would not have made Tasso's poetry less appealing to Monteverdi, but inclusion of the phrase "with lights and ornaments" (that is, "rhetorical figures") alerts us to the importance of ornament in the artifice of the sonnet. Let us first consider the text:

1 Questa vita mortal, che 'n una o 'n due
 brevi e notturne or trapassa, oscura
 e fredda, involto avea fin qui la pura
 parte di me ne l'atre nubi sue.
5 Or a mirar le grazie tante tue
 prendo che frutti e fior, gielo et arsura
 e sì dolce del ciel legge e misura,
 eterno Dio, tuo magisterio fue.
 Anzi il dolce aer puro e questa luce
10 chiara, che 'l mondo agli occhi nostri scuopre,
 traesti tu d'abissi oscuri e misti.
 E tutto quel che 'n terra o 'n ciel riluce
 di tenebre era chiuso, e tu l'apristi;
14 e 'l giorno e 'l sol de la tua man sono opre.

1 [This mortal life that passes by in one or two
 brief nocturnal hours, dark and cold,
 had till now wrapped the pure
 part of me in its gloomy clouds.
5 Now that I see your many graces
 among which I number fruit and flower, ice and heat,
 and the so merciful law and measure of Heaven,
 that they were, eternal God, part of your design.
 Even the sweet pure air and this light,
10 that reveals the world to our eyes
 did you draw from the dark and confused abysses.
 And everything that yields light on earth or in the sky
 was closed by darkness did you open;
14 And the day and the sun are works of your hand.]

Tasso brings to this sonnet the awareness that Dante defines poetry as "a rhetorical fiction set according to the laws of music" (*De vulgari eloquentia doctrina* II.iv.2).[17] This involves a conception of poetry as a spatial art, where the words are distributed and held together by means of a unifying design. Fortunately Tasso's textual analysis of this very sonnet in his early "Lezione" helps us to understand what additional "lights and ornaments" he has in mind in *La Cavaletta*: I quote what I take to be a most remarkable but brief glimpse into the poet's workshop:

> Volle con nobile negligenza, per dissimular l'arte, queste tre voci nel Sonetto due volte replicare: . . . TRAPASSA OSCURA . . . ABISSI OSCURI, E MISTI . . . E SÌ DOLCE DEL CIEL . . . DOLCE AER PURO . . . INVOLTO AVEA LA PURA. . . . Queste cose sì brevemente passo, e molte in tutto ne taccio, poichè questa prima, e lunga parte del mio raggionamento veggio esser più oltre, che al convenevole termine, arrivata.[18] (Tasso's capitalization)

> [He wanted with noble negligence, to hide his art, and repeat three words in the sonnet twice: . . . PASS(ES) DARK . . . ABYSSES DARK, AND CONFUSED . . . AND SO SWEET OF HEAVEN . . . SWEET PURE AIR . . . WRAPPED HAD THE PURE. . . . I pass these things briefly, and keep silent about many others, because I see this first and long part of my discourse has exceeded by far a suitable end.]

The crucial moment passes quickly, and Tasso fails to tell it all even here ("I pass these things briefly"), but in this rare passage, he pinpoints part of Della Casa's artifice. Some words are repeated as if by negligence, in the sense of a failed avoidance of repetition, but instead of vulgar "negligenza" these words constitute a noble compositional feature that strengthens the texture of the sonnet. Once we scan the text panoramically we see that these and other repetitions in fact embrace and "frame" the entire sonnet in a striking manner. Beginning with the words singled out by Tasso, we notice that they are repeated in inverse order around the central lines: *oscura-pura-dolce // dolce-puro-oscuri*. When we see that the word "ciel" (lines 7 and 12) also occurs twice, we discover the following configuration:

| a | b | c | d | c¹ | b¹ | a¹ | d¹ |
|---|---|---|---|----|----|----|----|
| *oscura* | *pura* | *dolce* | *ciel* | *dolce* | *puro* | *oscuri* | *ciel* |

The pattern created by these recurrences is marked by other finesses as well. We note the significant move from "vita mortale" and "notturne ore" in the first lines to the concluding reference to " 'l giorno e 'l sol" in line 14, implying an ascent from earth to heaven, which originally was the spiritual subtext of the quatorzain or the sonnet form.[19] Moreover, the words "oscura" and "oscuro" appear within sound patterns that reinforce the basic repetition; thus the sounds in "trapassa, oscura" recur in "traesti tu d'abissi oscuri." Furthermore, the principle of inequality favored by Tasso is found within pairs of iterated words when singular forms balance plural forms just as the male gender balances the female gender. Then too, the repeated concepts— one for each division—reinforce the pattern. Thus the idea of being "involto . . . ne l'atre nubi" corresponds to "di tenebre . . . chiuso," and the idea of seeing ("a mirar le grazie tue") anticipates the notion of the revealed world (" 'l mondo agli occhi nostri scuopre"). To complete the analysis, these various repetitions converge on the statement in the two central lines: "e sì dolce del ciel legge e misura, / eterno dio, tuo magisterio fue" (7–8). The specific mention of the words *legge, misura,* and *magisterio* ("law," "measure," and "mastery") and the idea of order they embody have been realized in the sonnet's artificial texture. Not only are they present in the proportions inherent in the sonnet form itself (8 : 6; 8 : 2; and 6 : 3), but even in the added sequences of repetitions *per proportionem* (3 : 1 plus 3 : 1). In such a context it is hardly coincidental that Della Casa attributes three properties to God when seen as a Trinity, a device Tasso later was to use for his topos of God enthroned in the *Liberata* III.55–59.[20]

Tasso was not the only one to appreciate Della Casa's achievement, nor is the present writer the only critic to savor the qualities praised by Tasso. In another "Lezione" dating from "Verona il dì 11. Marzo 1602," Francesco India, "Dottor medico e filosofo veronese," presents an analysis of the sonnet. His analysis differs from that of Tasso, he argues, because he does not restrict his analysis to form, because it also focuses on the sonnet's deep doctrine; "the skill and praise due to Monsignore della Casa concern not only the exterior form, and the lineaments of his poetic painting, and in its simple web and the order of the selected words and grave cadences and intersected verses, it also comprises his profound doctrine, the high sentiments and mysteries therein contained."[21] Dottor India nevertheless commends Tasso's analysis, and he summarizes it in terms that underline the sonnet's design (*lineamenti . . . poetica pittura . . . tessitura e ordine delle scielte parole*) and visible form, its *enargia.* He fully realizes that Tasso's artful deployment of rhetorical figures ("l'artificio de' colori") is not accessible to all and therefore requires an explication: "these are not open to all eyes, and understood and grasped by the ears of all" (p.379; my translation).

The elaborate verbal surface is a tour de force. Of course, we cannot expect such finesse in all Tasso's poems. The young poet chooses to comment on the phenomenon because it illustrates a number of techniques that became crucial in his own poetry and that he continually draws attention to in his use of metaphors of space and shape. He compares his own "Lezione" to the work of a painter who sketches distant buildings on a small canvas: "and I shall proceed like a painter, who is constrained by the narrow borders of a canvas, solely to indicate distant buildings, villages with brief lines, leaving the rest to the spectators' imagination."[22] When we apply our imagination to and take our bearings from sketched "lines," we can perceive the shapes of those edifices and their proportions. Like Della Casa, Tasso simultaneously writes music for both the ear and the eye. The *enargia* of their poetry stimulates the imagination through lively description at the same time that it produces visible shapes by means of a "novel use of rhetorical schemes."

Writing in 1584 from his "picciola villa in Fiesole," Camillo Pellegrino clearly saw this quality in Tasso's epic and praised it in a dialogue based on the metaphor of *ut architectura poësis*.[23] Let us consider some of his statements. The dialogue, which initiated the controversy between the supporters of Ariosto and Tasso, lauds the latter for having created "one unified action" (III.312) in having made a poem that can be surveyed in one mental effort ("in una sola speculazione"; III.317)—that is, an extensive text can be surveyed panoramically because it is ordered symmetrically. In fact, the plan of the *Gerusalemme* is similar to a palace: "imagine that Jerusalem Delivered were a building of not too large proportions, but well conceived with the measures and proportions of architecture; and suitably adorned with real friezes and colors."[24] Rhetorical *ornatus*, including verbal repetitions and figures of thought, obviously occurs in the *Orlando furioso* too. Pellegrino allows that Ariosto's poem is worthy of praise, but not for the same reasons as Tasso's. In his view, the *Orlando furioso* is similar to "a palace based on a faulty design" ("un palagio . . . falso di modello"; III.318). The statement recalls Vasari's similar *paragone* between Michelangelo and Tiziano, where the latter, despite his many good qualities, is censured because of his imperfect design ("disegno non perfetto").

Leaving behind these *paragoni* between painters and poets, we approach the more pressing questions of structure, segmentation, and verbal ornament, which are so crucial to the notion of global design. How do we identify an integrated design, or, more particularly, how do we isolate the various parts that when combined constitute the design? Sperone Speroni, Torquato Tasso's teacher of rhetoric, provides us with important clues to the spatial thinking that went into creating such a design. He puts the case bluntly but accurately when arguing that "solo il sito delle parole è tutta l'arte oratoria" (the entire art of rhetoric depends on the location of the words), and Tasso heeded that advice.[25] The architectural term *sito* is the equivalent of the Latin *area* or of the English Renaissance terms *ground-plot* and *platform*, so that it refers to the location on which buildings are to be erected (see above, Chapter 1). However, by extension it refers also to the plot of a literary work. Tasso's repeated alignment between poetry and architecture explains this usage,[26] *sito* being his chosen word for the place of an episode in the epic plot.[27] Here we may recall the passage by the English classicist Ben Jonson, already cited, to the effect that "in the constitution of a poem, the action . . . answers place in a building."[28]

Modern readers may find it difficult to perceive any unified design in the *Gerusalemme liberata* and be troubled by Tasso's often knotted syntax. His contemporaries noted that he chose "the novel, the unfamiliar, the unexpected, the admirable, both in ideas and in words: which [were] artificially interwoven more than is normal, and adorned with varied figures suitable for tempering that excessive clarity."[29] Ellipsis, inversions, antitheses, disruptions, chiasmuses, or figures of verbal repetition—everything that Tasso praised in Della Casa—tend to make critics forget that mixed unity does not preclude unity of design, "l'idea del poema eroico" in Tasso's own words. In the plainest architectural sense, the idea is a plan for the textual "building" executed according to the laws of symmetry. Underneath the multifarious seductive textual surface lies a controlling abstract design executed according to a music of shapes. How exactly is this expressed?

In general we observe today an increasing tendency to consider *ornatus* as an indication of the underlying symmetrical arrangement of episodes and themes in Tasso's oeuvre.[30] His conceptual or architectural model for the epic is traced in the verbal surface in the form of combinations of repeated signs, where the inner design and the poet's formal intention are reflected in verbal artifice as *enargia*. Tasso himself had observed about the poet that "it is necessary that the poet possesses *enargia* [*energia*] that by means of words puts a thing before the eyes in such a manner that one does not seem to hear those words, but rather sees them" (my translation).[31]

To decide where continuous narrative breaks into manageable and correlationable units is a vexing problem in the analysis of epic narrative. How can we delimit the building-blocks that constitute an episode like the *Paragone* of Tancredi and Clorinda? How can we be certain that a textual segment has reached its end so that it can be used convincingly in the structural analysis and interpretation of the text? The need for transitions and continuity makes it far too easy to "think" that an action begins or ends at a particular point. However, if we consider the segmentation from the poet's point of view the problem is reduced to the simple questions of disposition and elocution, whereas the task of the reader is to perceive, correlate, and interpret the visible signs on the page so as to trace their order and combination. Speroni's thoughtful observation on "il sito delle parole" may serve as a guideline.

Following the example set by Francesco Flora, Lodovico Magugliani (the editor of the BUR-edition of Tasso's poem) suggests that the *Paragone* comprises twenty stanzas running from ottava 50 to ottava 69. This is a fair delineation of the episode, although others have been proposed.[32] To solve this problem we must take into account the need to connect the *Paragone* to the preceding and ensuing action by means of transitional ottave (49 and 70), that will ensure the linear and progressive connectedness of the action. It is true that the particular action leading to Clorinda's death begins when she finds herself in the dark outside the walls of Jerusalem among her enemies, thinking herself dead ("morta allor si tenne"), and that it ends pathetically when she lifts up her arm and dies in ottava 69. Yet this oversimplifies the issue, as Tasso's very words indicate at this point. The phrasing suggests that ottava 70 is a stanza of transition serving several functions. It is an ottava that establishes continuity by harking back to the beginning of the entire sequence at the same time that it serves as its epilogue and as a "bridge" leading on to a new action in another sequence reporting the mental agony of Tancredi.

Let us take first things first. In ottava 50 Clorinda regains her calm after she has killed her opponent, Arimon, in lines marking the conclusion of the burst of activity witnessed in the preceding excursion-ottave. In a move that may be termed end-linking, the change from a state of agitation to control regained is inverted and echoed in ottava 70, where Tancredi, weakened after the combat, loses control over himself when he sees the slain Clorinda: "Come alma gentil uscita ei vede, / Rallenta quel vigor ch'avea raccolto; / E l'imperio di sé cede" ("Once he saw the gentle soul had left her, his gathered strength weakens; and he loses command of himself").

Then too, we recall that Clorinda in ottava 50 sees the closed gates and at first believes herself dead—"Vide *chiuse* le porte . . . *morta* allor si ritenne" ("she sees the closed gates . . . and accounted herself dead")—and we note that Tancredi's reaction in ottava 70 matches hers: *"chiusa* in breve sede / La vita, empie di *morte* i sensi e 'l volto" ("his life was enclosed in a narrow space, his face and senses filled with death").[33]

In Tancredi's case the feelings are entirely internalized, leaving him no means of escape, which is what Clorinda hoped for in ottava 50. This proleptic device functions on a par with the reference to blood ("sangue") in that ottava's second line, "sangue" being the pregnant word that in rhyme position seals off the sequence. These instances indicate how Tasso's web of words functions in the contingent parts of the *Paragone.* Let us now consider its dramatic structure.

Stanza 51 presents the beginning in an Aristotelian manner when the skulking Clorinda is spotted by Tancredi ("Only Tancredi chances to recognize her; . . . he saw and marked her and began pursuing her"; 51:5–8). Now the conflict becomes inevitable and irreversible, both antagonists being in place for the *paragone.* Tasso engenders suspense: will Clorinda manage to slip away under the cover of night, and what will be the outcome when Tancredi spots her and she hears him coming at her? Clorinda's acceptance of Tancredi's challenge opens the initial ritual part of the *Paragone* (52:7–8 and 53:1), but it is off to a slow start. First Tasso tells us that what we are about to witness befits "a crowded theater" and he asks permission of the Night to report the great deeds to posterity. Then, finally, the harsh action commences in ottava 55 when the first blows are struck. Contrary to what has been suggested, Tasso emphasizes his own presence in the narrative, thus guiding our interpretation of the generically mixed narrative.[34]

Where, then, does Tasso place the episode's peripety? It occurs at 67:6—"La vide, la conobbe, . . .ahi conoscenza!" ("he saw her, recognized her, alas what knowledge")—whereas Clorinda's conversion takes place at 68:5–8:

> As he uttered the sounds of sacred words.
> she transformed herself in joy, and smiled;
> and in the act of dying happily and vividly,
> seemed to say: Heaven opens itself; I depart in peace.[35]

Tancredi, on the other hand, does not change conclusively until after Clorinda's death. His transformation is reported in ottava 70: "e l'impero di sé libero cede . . ."; "empio di morte i sensi e 'l volto" (70:3; 7). This ottava is also the place where interest definitely shifts to Tancredi as the action turns from female to male, from spiritual to earthly, from movement to immobility. In tragic terms, the immobilized Tancredi becomes an epitome of the isolated hero, tragically locked within himself, but then again, this transformation takes place in the final stanza 70 or—if one so wishes—in the epilogue to the *Paragone.*

In terms of the structure of action, however, we cannot question the location of Tasso's *mutazione di fortuna;* he places it in the verbal exchange, which fully reveals the protagonists' flaws of character or ruling passions: wrath and pride.[36] The duel between conflicting wills occurs in stanzas 60 and 61, in the lull resulting from exhaustion. Here Tancredi confidently asks his opponent to disclose his identity:

> I beg you (if prayers have a place among arms)
> that you reveal your name to me,
> so I can know, when I have lost or won,
> to honor with death or victory.

> The ferocious woman replies: You ask in vain
> what I usually do not reveal.
> But whoever I am, you see before yourself
> one of the two who burned down the great tower.[37]

Tancredi desires to know her name primarily to feed his own pride, as Tasso makes evident at 58:7 ("superbisce") and 59:2 ("il vanto"), and the knight is furious when rebuffed. Through her irate and stubborn refusal Clorinda precipitates her own death when the combat is renewed. This is the decisive peripeteia in view of its being the last moment when death could have been averted had she chosen to reveal her identity.[38] The adversaries thus reveal their respective versions of *hamartìa,* by posing as embodiments of pride and rage *(superbia* and *ira).* From here onward the wheel of fortune turns, so to speak, and Tasso carefully prepares us for the imminent turning-point in another strategically situated authorial intrusion shortly before the change itself:

> Oh our foolish
> minds that are carried away by every whim of fortune!

> Wretch, what makes you enjoy? Oh how miserable
> will the triumphs be and unhappy your vaunt!

$$(58:7-8; 59:1-2)^{39}$$

To sum up, Tasso's *Paragone* episode has a clearly marked beginning, middle, and end, a unified Aristotelian plot indicated also by the inclusion of metatheatrical markers at strategic points in the narrative. We are here clearly on the track of the technique of rhetorical shaping that Tasso advocates. As we shall see from his distribution of subject matter and rhetorical pointers within the segment, the episode manifestly exhibits a tightly knit "testura."

Certain stanzas in the *Paragone* are paired or in other ways interlinked, as pointed out by earlier critics.[40] But if we read the sequence carefully with Tasso's formula for the entire epic in mind, we discover that the twenty ottave agree perfectly with this macrochiastic mold. Linkage between stanzas is achieved through an ingenious system of parallels and antitheses supported by verbal repetitions, the principle of organization essentially analogous to the one Tasso uncovered in Della Casa's "Di questa vita mortal 'n un o 'n due."

Consider the two central ottave: they match and "correspond" by means of a sequence of terse questions and answers, at the same time that a series of words and phrases ("silenzio" [silence], "degno" [worthy], and "pregoti . . . 'l tuo stato a me tu scopra" ["I beg thee . . . to reveal your state to me"]) find their counterparts in the inverted sequence of "tacer" ("be silent"), "sdegno" ("disdain"), and "quel c'ho per uso di non far palese" ("what I usually do not reveal"). The linkage is created by antitheses and parallels. At the midpoint of the entire episode (60:8 and 61:1) we characteristically find a structural pun marking the related topoi of honor and victory: "chi la mia morte o la *vittoria onore*" ("who will honor my death or victory"; 60:1). In this fashion Tancredi's rash anticipation of victory marks what Alastair Fowler has termed the point of triumph.[41] Also, the pivot is indicated by an unusual threefold repetition (*vinto . . . vittore . . . vittoria*) similar to the repetition marking the moment of *agnorisis* later in the episode (*vide . . . conobbe . . . vista . . . conoscenza!*). These are compositional moves that Tasso has been shown to employ elsewhere in the *Liberata*, at other points in the action.[42]

Stanzas 59 and 62 form a contrast because they describe a pause in the combat and its resumption, but this notable correspondence through contrast is in accord with the general pattern. Thus the phrases in stanza 59 "se in *vita resti*" ("if you remain alive"; 59:3), "sangue" ("blood"; 4), "i *sanguinosi guerrieri* cessaro alquanto" ("the bloody warriors ceased somewhat"; 6) are repeated in stanza 62 in inverse order as "debili in *guerra*" ("weak in combat"), "*sanguigna*" ("bloody"), and "se la *vita* non esce" ("if life does not leave"). Repetitions by themselves are not necessarily of structural intent, but their systematic distribution is.

On working our way outward from the centrally placed peripety, we see that ottave equidistant from the center are linked through a system of antithesis and parallelism. Thus ottave 58 and 63 are linked through the contrast between rest and action and the attention paid to natural phenomena and the antagonists' loss of vigor. Thus ottava 58 describes changes in the heavens, while ottava 63 focuses on the aftermath of a storm. In the former ottava Tancredi notes the greater loss of blood in his opponent ("in maggior copia il sangue"), a point echoed later in the observation that "manca in lor co 'l sangue vòto / quel vigor" ("vigor was lacking in them with the loss of blood").

The parallels between ottave 57 and 62 are perhaps more spectacular in view of the strong sexual symbolism. Three times during the combat the adversaries reach a deadlock during which the couple wrestle and engage in a way that suggests a merging of the Ariostian "dolce" and "fiero assalto." In other words, they seem to embrace rather than fight:

> Tre volte il cavalier la donna stringe
> con le robuste braccia, ed altrettante
> da que' nodi tenaci ella si scinge,
> nodi di fer nemico non d'amante.

> [Three times he presses the lady
> with his strong arms, and three times
> she undoes the hard knots,
> knots made by a fierce enemy, not by a lover.]

The poet's denial of amorous embrace ("non d'amante") is entirely disingenuous and no doubt intentionally so, as we must needs think of lovers. This motif is repeated when Clorinda is mortally wounded:

> Spinge egli il ferro nel bel sen di punta
> che vi s'immerge 'l sangue avido beve;
> e la veste, che d'or vago trapunta

le mammelle stringea tenera e leve,
l'empie d'un caldo fiume. Ella già sente
morirsi . . .

$$(64:3-8)$$

[He pushes the iron by the point into her beautiful breast,
where it once immersed drinks avidly;
and her light dress, which is embroidered with gold
pressed tenderly against her breasts, is filled by
a warm stream. She already felt herself dying. . . . ]

The grotesquely erotic symbolism of the climactic death wound suggests sexual penetration and consummation, thus evoking the language of love madrigals,[43] but this erotic aspect is merely part of the presentation of the complex "divine" Clorinda.[44] Two exact verbal repetitions link stanzas 57 and 64: *al fin* (57:7 and 64:2) and *stringe-stringea* (57:1; 64:6), and *spinge* (64:2) reinforces the parallel by echoing the rhyme sound of 57. Thus death in combat mimics the commonplace topos of death in love.

Similar relations exist between ottave 56 and 65 and 55 and 66. The act of giving described in the phrase "[n]on danno i colpi or finti, or pieni, or scarsi" (55:3) is utterly transformed in Clorinda's last requests: "io ti perdon . . . perdona / tu ancora" and "e dona battesmo a me ch'ogni mia colpa lave" ("I forgive you . . . forgive me too . . . and give me a baptism that will wash away my sin"; 66:1–4). Hate is converted to spiritual love, and forgiveness freely offered.

On surveying the outer perimeter of the episode, we note the metatheatrical references in stanzas 54 and 67. The invocation to Night is preceded by the statement that the heroic deeds about to be performed are worthy of a theater (54:1–2), and in 67 the poet indicates the moment and manner of *anagnorisis*: "Ahi vista! ahi conoscenza!" ("Oh sight! Oh knowledge!"). Also, in the earlier stanza (54) the poet-narrator asks permission to draw the great event ("fatto sì *grande*") from the bosom of the Night ("profondo scuro *seno*"), and this anthropomorphic image is repeated when Tancredi later fetches water from "the bosom of the hill" (*nel sen del monte;* 67:1) in order to perform the great and pious act, "*grande* ufficio pio" (67:4). Here, then, acts of heroism are surpassed by the sacrament of baptism.

The remaining paired stanzas, ottave 53 : 68, 52 : 69; and 51 : 70, complete this system of linkage. The fall into aggression is exchanged for ascent and transfiguration, when God's plan for Clorinda is completed in a stunning act of divine *meraviglia*.

We see, thus, that antithesis serves to link the first and the last stanza. When Clorinda attempts to circumvent the enemy ("Va girando colei l'alpestre cima" ["she circles around the rocky peak"]; 51:2) and is discovered by Tancredi, who takes her to be a man ("un uom la stima"), she triggers a violent reaction on both sides. Tancredi's furious pursuit causes his weapons to clatter, so that she turns and shouts at him ("si volge e grida"). Her initial irascible words to her opponent are strikingly different from the silent gesture of benediction with which she bids him farewell:

> e la man nuda e fredda alzando verso
> il cavaliero in vece di parole
> gli dà pegno di pace. In questa forma
> passa la bella donna, e par che dorma.
>
> (69:5–8)

> [and while raising her naked and cold hand
> towards the knight, instead of words,
> she gives him a token of peace. In this manner
> the beautiful lady passes away, and she appears to sleep.]

This is the only point in the episode when she is openly referred to as a woman, so the initial mistake has now been fully corrected.

As previously argued, the *Paragone* episode proper begins in the middle of ottava 51, when Tancredi spots Clorinda ("lei conosca / . . . vide e segnolla"). This is where all the necessary conditions for the *Paragone* are presented so that the armed conflict can begin; in other words, this is the stanza that constitutes a beginning in terms of plot structure. In regard to the verbal linkage, however, ottava 50 presents the clearest analogue to ottava 70, that—as I have explained—functions as the epilogue to the *Paragone* itself: "l'alma gentile uscita ei vede" (70:1). The initial lines of 51 serve as a prologue to the action proper and connect with ottava 70 on a symbolic level. Moreover, I think we are justified in seeing the elaborate epic simile in 51:1–4 on Clorinda'a sinful state as an example of the kind of artifice recommended by Tasso for the beginning of poems: "they should be full of grandeur, magnificence and splendor, like the facade of palaces."[45] The parallel drawn between Clorinda in her black armor and the wolf that tries to escape after its misdeed effectively foreshadows the coming tragedy.

Having surveyed the bilateral symmetries of the *Paragone*, we can conclude that its *dispositio* fully accords with the poet's comparison between stanzas in poetry and palaces in *La Cavaletta*: the ottave are arranged "sì come ne' palagi l'una stanza corrisponde a l'altra con bella proporzione" ("as when one stanza corresponds to another in terms of beautiful proportion"), and not only the stanzas but also the actions therein contained.[46]

The verbal repetitions recorded above will seem to most modern readers capable of influencing the reader on a subliminal level, but this may not have been the case in the Renaissance. An indication that rhymes have functions unknown to us today is found in such treatises of the period as those by Ruscelli and Daniel.[47] More important is that Tasso too has been shown to follow this advice when he distributed rhymes as compositional elements elsewhere in the *Liberata*.[48] In fact, the rhetorical techniques used to fashion and connect individual ottave are indebted to the rhetorical strategies deployed by Italian sonneteers from Petrarch onward. Already Dante had created textual symmetries built on distant rhymes, and, as argued in Chapter 2, models were readily available in classical poetry.

The interlocking patterns outlined above pull the narrative together by establishing a rich web of echoes and parallels, but from the point of view of linear progress they could perhaps also be taken to disrupt the forward thrust of the action. But this is not the case in Tasso, who saw to it that his stanzas would link and flow naturally one into another. Poets used this technique of verbal embroidery throughout their epics, especially when stitching separate episodes and actions together. We see this technique in XII.19–20, for example, but it is no less prominent at the conclusion of Solemano's and Clorinda's abortive charge in XII.48–49 or between individual stanzas in the ensuing *Paragone*.[49] Today such verbal patterns may seem tedious and pedantic, and they have been condemned by the venerable De Sanctis in his seminal *Storia della letteratura italiana*. De Sanctis states that Tasso's way of writing produces "an artificial form of showing things, in which the thing is less important than the way it is looked at."[50] However, this way of writing is part of Tasso's deft manipulation of surface structure to point the reader's attention in the desired direction. As a rule, such repetitions are akin to the measured placing of words and sounds in Latin poetry that every Renaissance writer had been drilled to copy in the classroom.[51] All these repetitions produce an ambiguous and restless verbal surface despite the narrative's clear forward thrust, and we may compare their mixed effect to what we perceive in the visual art of painting. Late *maniera* paintings are generally characterized by symmetrically balanced, crowded, but completely artificial or contrived compositions, and do not create a sense of emotional involvement. Some of these schemes find equivalent expression in poetry as well, although works concerned with such themes as love, death, and religious warfare hardly can escape inviting a sense of emotional involvement in any period. The enjoyment of the elaborately arranged words, however, is a question of acculturation and training, so that such arrangements hardly appeal to those unfamiliar with such contrived conventions. Monteverdi's sensibility would of course have matched that of Tasso in several respects, so it is particularly fascinating to follow his expert interpretation and rewriting of the latter's "superficie movimentata."

How, then, does Monteverdi's text compare with the tightly textured architecture of Tasso's *Paragone*, and how does his practice of taking command of a poetic text by cutting, adding to, and revising it affect the *Combattimento*? As we have seen, Tasso's composition is a graphic example of a text where removal of an element would, to paraphrase his words in the *Discorsi*, destroy the whole. Nevertheless, Monteverdi cuts four entire stanzas (51, 63, 69–70) from the fabric of symmetries here uncovered. Furthermore, he inventively rewrites two lines (1:1–2), changes the order of four lines (3:1–4), and alters a number of individual words, especially in the first half of the *Combattimento*. These are all significant and knowingly executed alterations.

By collapsing the *Paragone*'s introitus (51:5–8) into ottava 52:1–2 ("Tancredi, who thinks Clorinda is a man, / wishes to try her in combat") Monteverdi achieves three effects at once: the text begins *in medias res*, he identifies the antagonists, and he introduces the main action. The result is a strong and precise opening passage unconnected with the preceding action, but Monteverdi needed no such connection, because in 1624 he could rely on an audience familiar with the poem. He also pares away two stanzas from the conclusion so that the microdrama ends with Clorinda's last words: "S'apre il cielo; io vado in pace" (66:8; 68:8). He does not wait for her to die at 69:8, or for Tancredi to react to the departure of her soul (70:1). Thus he achieves a most effective ending that reinforces the theme of ascent, but at the cost of losing the contrasts and the verbal linkage between stanzas 51–52 and 69–70 (or those between the transitional XII.50 and XII.70).

By cutting unevenly, Monteverdi makes the dramatic curve steeper than the "rising" action in the episode's triangular story-line. In his version, linearity therefore is preferred to spatiality. He also disturbs the balance of the building by omitting XII.63, so that Tasso's stanza 58 loses its supporting artifice as an alternative center for the *dispositio*.[52] It is reasonable to conclude that what has to go is the structural artifice typical of the *prima pratica*. Because he favors the mimetic aspect of Tasso's poem, Monteverdi instead chooses to stress the progressive movement and cohesion of contingent stanzas.

This formal intention manifests itself clearly in Monteverdi's revisions in several other stanzas as well. The "purification" of Tasso's narrative is carried out by removing clashing sonorities by increasing the smooth flow of certain phrases to provide a greater forward thrust to the narrative. By ending where he does, Monteverdi concludes on a note of ascent, and on the highest pitch in the entire piece, rather than with a tempered circular return and a transition to the ensuing action, which of course was Tasso's preference by necessity.

The analysis of Tasso's *Paragone* presented here enables us to decode most of his metaphorical statements concerning poetic structure and to understand how unity and multiplicity can be reconciled. His poetic ideal finds structural and verbal expression in various ways, the most important one probably being the use of metaphor as a formal matrix when passing from *inventio* via *dispositio* to *elocutio*, or to the visual aspects of his art. His definition of poetry as a *discordante concordia*, or of a poem as a palace with neatly arranged rooms, can be traced in the actual arrangements in the *Paragone*. When Monteverdi turns to the complex patterns of the narrative, his revisions reveal an acute awareness of the inner design of Tasso's dramatic inset. He dismantles solely the structural elements that supported the more abstract proportioning of the text, lifting, as it were, the elements of the *seconda pratica* out of Tasso's contrived architecture of opposites.

In this chapter I have also argued that the sonnet as a genre and the refined verbal discriminations developed by Italian sonneteers were essential to the compositional techniques developed by Tasso and his use of dramatic structure in the *Paragone* between Trancredi and Clorinda. In the next and final chapter, Tasso's poetic technique is again the focus of attention when I analyze how three great epic writers of the Renaissance, Ariosto, Tasso, and Milton, design their versions of the biblical topos of God enthroned as "epic rooms."

# Designing Epic Rooms

## Ariosto, Tasso, and Milton

> Quia prospexit de excelso sancto suo,
> Dominus de caelo in terram adspexit,
> Ut audiret gemitus compeditorum,
> ut solveret filios intemperorum.
>
> —Psalmus 101:20–21

> For he hathe loked downe fro[m] the height of his Sanctuarie:
> out of the heauen did the Lord beholde the earth,
> That he might heare the mourning of the prisoner,
> and deliuer the children of death.
> —Psalme 101:19–20

The preceding chapters have shown that the same kind of textual patterning can be traced in different genres and art forms and that the same compositional principles are valid for all of them. Once the theory and the practice are known, interesting comparisons can be made between them. Artists will always emulate each other, or they will return to what they have written with a view to revising, as in the case of Vasari's two versions of his *Life of Michelangelo* (see Chapter 4). The study of different versions provides us with useful critical insights, especially when different writers employ the same topos. Divine intervention is one such topos also selected by Vasari to introduce his biography; from his throne, God surveys his creation and decides to assist humans by sending Michelangelo down to earth—an event he describes in order to make associations with the sending forth the Son to redeem humankind. This biblical topos,[1] was sufficiently popular to be featured in several epics, but of course with significant variations in treatment. To study such variations, I have selected epics from three different periods: Ariosto's *Orlando furioso* (1532), Tasso's *La Gerusalemme liberata* (1581), and Milton's *Paradise Lost* (1667).

It is impossible to conduct a proper discussion of style without at the same time showing, by close analysis, what the relevant critical terms actually entail in terms of formal patterns on the printed page. These patterns and their effect are therefore my chief concern, my purpose being to consider how the artifice of Italian Renaissance epics conditions the textual architecture of *Paradise Lost*. The rich Italian tradition in heroic poetry offered Milton many useful models of epic construction for the various levels of his epic.[2]

Leaving aside the complex issue of the structure of the entire poem, I want to carry out a topomorphical analysis of one of its an important microstructures: the topos of divine intervention as presented in Book III.55–59. I propose to read this textual segment against its possible antecedents in the epics of Ariosto and Tasso, and more particularly against *Orlando furioso* VIII.70 and *La Gerusalemme liberata* IX.55–58.[3] All these passages depict actions that have far-reaching structural implications, in the sense that each contains, or prepares for, an important peripeteia in the plot of its particular epic. In addition to this shared structural role, the passages also indicate that they have been executed according to a similar kind of balanced rhetorical design, which again suggests that all three poets patterned their texts rhetorically, to increase the impact of their plot reversals. In order to illustrate and broaden the basis of my argument, I shall adduce other patterned textual segments in these epics, segments that exhibit similar compositional characteristics.

Apart from the ironical echo in the line "Things unattempted yet in prose or rhyme" (*Paradise Lost* I.16), *Orlando furioso* has not frequently figured among the poem's principal models. The marked difference in scope and tone between *Orlando furioso* and *Paradise Lost* naturally explains this omission in discussions of Milton, but a range of possible intertextual dependencies may be found with regard to technique and minor themes. The dominant theme of Ariosto's witty poem is the romantic quest for honor and chivalrous love, the *fiero* and the *dolce assalto*. In comparison, the serious epic strand—the defense of Paris against the infidels and the implicit religious concern—is textually of minimal importance, although later theorists tried hard to interpret the poem according to the fourfold method of scriptural exegesis.[4] On the occasions that politico-religious strands appear, they are never allowed to dominate for long. We witness one brief but significant example of such intrusion in Canto VIII, where Ariosto interrupts his description of the fair Angelica, who is fettered Andromeda-like to a naked rock, deftly inserting some stanzas that focus on the epic's politico-religious overplot. The situation is critical: Paris is ablaze and about to fall into the hands of Agramante and the attacking Saracens. At this crucial point Charlemagne implores God to intervene and save "il santo Imperio e 'l gran nome di Francia" ("the sacred Empire and the great name of France"; VIII.69.8).[5] God turns his eyes on Paris and promptly sends a heavy rainfall that rapidly quenches the threatening fire:

> Il sommo Creator gli occhi rivolse
> al giusto lamentar del vecchio Carlo;
> e con subita pioggia il fuoco tolse:
> né forse uman saper potea smorzarlo.
> Savio chiunque a Dio sempre si volse;
> ch'altri non poté mai meglio aiutarlo.
> Ben dal devoto re fu conosciuto,
> che si salvò per lo divino aiuto.
>
> (70.1–8)

> [The highest Maker turned his eyes
> to the just lament of the old Charles;
> and with a sudden rainfall put out the fire:
> perhaps no human skill could have put it out.
> Wise is the man who always turned to God;
> because nobody could ever help him better,
> This the pious king knew well,
> who saved himself thanks to divine assistance.]

Ariosto's ottava describes the close, harmonious relationship between the devout old king and the enthroned deity, who allays his just wrath and extends grace to his loyal subject. We recognize immediately that this is the very same topos (Psalm 101:19–20) with which Vasari opens his *Life of Michelangelo* (see Chapter 4). In Ariosto the stanza has two parts. Lines 1–4 contain the entire action—Charlemagne's lament, God's survey of the situation, and God's intervention, whereas lines 5–8 comment on the wisdom of the man who in his hour of need addresses God like Charlemagne. Ariosto pulls these elements together in a balanced rhetorical structure hinging on lines 4 and 5, as indicated below. When the repetitions are isolated we observe that the concept of divine creation and assistance encircles the notion of human wisdom as in a protective enclosure:[6]

> a Il sommo Creator
> > b       il vecchio Carlo
> > > cd       uman saper
> > > dc       savio chiunque
> > b       devoto re
> a divino aiuto

This structure, then, repeats the balanced pattern of Psalm 101:20, where the Vulgate text has an a-b / b-a structure around the mention of God (*dominus*) *prospexit de excelso / de caelo adspexit*. We witness in VIII.70 a similar will to shape that recalls the poet's play on the "room" of the stanza in Canto III.7:

> La stanza, quadra e spaziosa, pare
> una devota e venerabile chiesa,
> che su colonne alabastrine e rare
> con *bella* architettura era *suspesa*.          a b
> *Surgea* nel mezzo un *bel locato* altare          b a c
> ch'avea dinanzi una lampada accesa;
> e quella di splendente e chiaro foco
> rendea gran lume all'uno e all'altro *loco*.          c

> [The room was square and spacious,
> solemn and sacred as a church,
> and supported by rare alabaster columns
> its beautiful architecture was suspended in the air.
> In the middle surged a beautiful altar
> with a lamp burning in front of it,

whose shining and clear light
illuminated its every part.]

Ariosto alludes both to the architectural properties of the ottava itself and
its well-placed ornaments (a b b a c c), as later explained by Tasso, and to
the central position of the altar ("nel mezzo"; 5) in the churchlike room.

Returning to Canto VIII.70, we find a change in the rhetorical pattern
that is highly appropriate because it signals a reversal in the action of the
epic's overplot. The fortune of war changes dramatically when God intervenes, so that what we actually witness at this point is one of the many
peripeteias found in single episodes. Dramatic reversals within individual
cantos or other textual segments of varying length is a familiar occurrence,
recognized by John Harington and employed by Tasso as well as Milton.[7] If
we turn briefly to Harington's rendering, which is by no means an attempt to
achieve a stanza-by-stanza fidelity, we note that his version lacks Ariosto's
balanced design altogether. Instead, Harington concentrates on underlining
the dramatic contrasts between the different strands of action described in
the contingent stanzas 61 and 63 (according to his numbering).[8] We shall
see later that in his version of this topos Milton favors a balanced design,
thus following Ariosto's practice.

The absence, in Harington's version, of the sort of rhetorical patterning found in Ariosto does not mean that Ariosto's stanza is a special case
found nowhere else. Ariosto's use of such carefully balanced phrases in
VIII.70 finds a clear parallel in the stanza that is at the mathematical center of
*Tasso's Gerusalemme liberata* XI. 10. Such repetitions are typical of literary *maniera*.
Tasso, in that stanza, underlines the sacramental centrality of Mount Olivet
within the Christian faith:

| | |
|---|---|
| Così cantando, il popolo devoto | |
| con larghi giri *si dispiega e stende,* | a b |
| e *drizza a* l'Oliveto il lento moto, | c |
| *monte* che da l'olive il nome prende, | d |
| *monte* per sacra fama al mondo noto, | d¹ |
| ch'oriental *contra* le mura *ascende,* | c¹ |
| e sol da quelle *il parte e ne 'l discosta* | b¹ a¹ |
| la cupa Giosafà ch'in mezzo è posta. | |

(XI. 10)

[Singing and saying thus the camp devout
spread forth her zealous squadron broad and wide,
Towards mount Olivet went all this rout,
So call'd of olive trees the hill which hide;
A Mountain known by fame the world throughout,
Which riseth on the city's eastern side,
From it divided by the valley green
Of Josaphat that fills the space between.]⁹

Elsewhere I have discussed the function of this ottava within the nineteen-stanza processional peripeteia in the epic as a whole (XI.1–19),¹⁰ so that here it will suffice to indicate the discrete convolutions of its rhetoric. Occupying as it does the exact midpoint of the poem's structure, the anaphoric repetition of "monte" in lines 4 and 5 further underlines the centrality of Mount Olivet as the symbol of Christ's redemptive sacrifice. Like Ariosto, Tasso groups synonymous verbs symmetrically around the references to the mountain: "si dispiega" and "drizza a" are balanced by "contra . . . ascende" and "discosta." The syntactical inversions strengthen the impression of the poet's firm control over his circular design of *contrapposti*, to which he also alludes in the phrase "con larghi giri" ("in wide circles").

The centrality of stanza XI.10 is indicated also by a self-referential phrase bearing on the deep gulf of Giosafà (Josaphat); this gulf is placed in the middle—"in mezzo è posta." The stanza on the mountain, then, is itself *in mezzo* in the most literal sense, because 949 stanzas precede and follow.¹¹ As in the case of Ariosto's structural compliment to a vigilant and benevolent deity, the rhetorical shape of Tasso's ottava should be seen as a conscious design aimed at reflecting the order of the creation and God's providential plan, at the same time that the device indicates the reversal of the fortune of the Christians in their campaign against the infidels. We note also that Mount Olivet and the valley of Josaphat symbolize the two opposite aspects of God: mercy and justice. Mount Olivet reminds us of the sacrifice of Christ for the benefit of humankind, while Josaphat, as Dante points out, figures as the future site of the Last Judgment.¹²

*Orlando furioso* VIII.70 and *La Gerusalemme liberata* XI.10 show how subtly Italian poets use their signs and that they do not readily employ rhymes as structural tokens. The particular technique found in individual stanzas should be related to the rhetorical strategies adopted by Italian sonneteers from Petrarch onward, from the point where they found their way to the more prestigious and elevated genre of heroic poetry.[13] Ariosto as well as Tasso sometimes turned to various sorts of concentric disposition in order to give added emphasis to reversals of fortune. In *La Gerusalemme liberata* XI this type of structure is extended to several ottave in order to encompass all the stanzas devoted to the topos of God enthroned.

Serious epic themes dominate the "unità mista" of Tasso's epic, so that the topos of divine intervention described by Ariosto in a single stanza is given full and serious attention. Yet in Canto IX Tasso clearly took his cue from Ariosto's swift thumbnail sketch in describing how God sends Michael to ward off an attack by the infernal powers:

Gli occhi fra tanto a la battaglia rea
dal suo gran seggio il Re del Ciel volgea.

[Then from his great seat the King of Heaven
to the wild battle turned his eyes.]

(55.7–8)

In lines that amplify Ariosto's "Il sommo Creator gli occhi rivolse" ("The highest Creator turned his eyes"), Tasso seizes the opportunity to elaborate upon the idea of the power God exerts over his creation from his "trono augusto" ("august throne"). Thus Tasso imagines that God sits in state looking down upon the arena of human action, as from a balcony in a palace, and to give the illusion of space he introduces an architectural metaphor. Tasso focuses on God's function as the giver of just laws and the creator of fair forms, and he pays homage to divine proportion in the chiastic form of his argument ("dà legge al tutto e 'l tutto orna e produce" ["gives laws to all things and everything adorns and creates"; 56.2]),[14] which recalls the familiar statement concerning the sweetness with which God orders his creation (Wisdom 8:1; "disponit omnia suaviter"). Chiasmus and antithesis, we recall, are rhetorical figures favored by Tasso.[15] Tasso's next concern is the presentation of the deity as a monarch. God sits in triumph on his throne, treading underfoot Fate, Nature, and Fortune, who distribute as well as subvert worldly riches and empires (56.7–57.4). The topos of God enthroned concludes with an almost Dantesque vision of the deity surrounded by light and innumerable immortals who make the celestial palace resound with joyful praise (57.7–58.2). It is only after Tasso has presented God as ruler of the universe that we learn how God intends to intervene at this critical moment in the history of the crusade (58.3ff.) by sending Michele to compel the infernal multitudes to return to hell (9.58.3–66). And the intervention itself is one of the most important peripeteias in Tasso's poem.

The structural similarity between *Orlando furioso* VIII.70 and *La Gerusalemme liberata* XI.10 is such that it comes as no surprise to discover that Tasso's expanded presentation of the topos of God enthroned displays the same rhetorical patterning throughout the twenty-line segment (55.7–58.2). These lines are arranged in the sequence 2 + 16 + 2. In the two introductory lines, Tasso locates the phrase "il Re del Ciel" ("the King of Heaven"; 55.8), later echoed in inverted order in the last two lines in "la celeste reggia" ("the royal palace of heaven"; 58.2). He draws attention to this linkage in a self-reflexive passage replete with musical imagery: We notice in particular the phrase "Al gran concento de' beati carmi / lieta risuona la celeste reggia" ("at the great harmony of holy songs the royal palace of heaven resounds with joy"), where "lieta" ("joyful") picks up "letizia" ("joy") from two lines above.[16] Together with the adjective "great" found in *"gran seggio"* ("great seat"; 55.8) and repeated in *"gran* concento" ("great harmony"; 58.1), these verbal recurrences consolidate the structure,

| | |
|---|---|
| *gran* seggio . . . il *Re* del *Ciel* | a b c |
| *letizia* | c |
| *lieta* | c |
| *gran* concento . . . la *celeste reggia* | a c b |

Such reiterations, which resemble examples of the musical figure of *circulatio,* or return to one note, often occur when a poet wants to draw attention to a prominent verbal sign. Good examples that come to mind are the points of transition between *La Gerusalemme liberata* X.78 and XI.1 and XI.19 and 20.[17] On these occasions the verbal reports help to mark the borders of the segment, thus indicating a desire to focus on the framed topos.

In his translation of Tasso's topos, Fairfax reveals that he is aware of its rhetorical structure, but he chooses—perhaps because of difficulties in translation—to locate the symmetry at the center of the segment rather than at its borders. His text thus represents an important intermediary stage between Tasso and Milton. Unlike Tasso, Fairfax does not link the concluding couplet of stanza XI.55 to the two first lines of stanza 58 by means of repetitions; instead, he locates his structural markers in the main body of the segment:

IX.56 From whence, *with grace and goodness compass'd round,*     a b
He ruleth, *blesseth,* keepeth all he wrought,     c
Above the air, the fire, the sea, and ground,
*Our* sense, *our* wit, *our* reason, and *our* thought;     d
Where persons three (with *power* and glory crown'd)     e
Are all one God, who made all things of nought,
Under whose feet (subjected to his grace)
Sit nature, fortune, motion, time, and *place:*     f

IX.57 This is the *place* from whence, like smoke and dust,     f
Of this frail world the wealth, the pomp, and *pow'r,*     e
He tosseth, tumbleth, turneth as he lust,
And guides *our* life, *our* death, *our* end, and hour:     d
No eye (however virtuous, pure and just)
Can view the brightness of that glorious bow'r;
*On every side* the *blessed* spirits be     b c
Equal in *joys,* though diff'ring in degree.     a

In keeping with Tasso's original version, Fairfax reinforces the idea of formal balance between the two stanzas. We note the rather heavy-handed and rigid effect created, for instance, by the catalog of "[o]ur sense, our wit, our reason, and our thought" (56.4) as counterbalanced by in the second ottava: "our life, our death, our end, and hour" (57.4).[18] The number 4 should here be taken to reflect the mortal world, in which time rules, just as "trinitarian" verb clusters (55.2 and 56.3) and noun clusters (56.2 and 52.4) confirm that he appreciated Tasso's structural art.

Although the two stanzas are continuous, Tasso contrasts the presentation of God's eternal reign in 56.5–6 ("e de l'Eternità nel trono augusto / risplendea con tre lumi in una luce" ["and of the Eternity in the august throne shone three lights in one"]) with the fickle power of earthly kings in 57.1–3 ("la gloria di qua giuso e l'oro e i regni" ["the glory of this world and its gold and kingdoms"]). At the textual center of the segment by line-count Tasso positions the humble servants of divine omnipotence, Fate, Nature, and Fortune[19] in chains at the feet of God in a posture well known from the iconography of the triumph. In a much more direct manner than witnessed in Ariosto's Fortune-sequence, Tasso makes Fortune subservient to divine control. Fairfax on the other hand, in the two central lines of his segment, refers to the abode of God's ministers and "the place" from which he controls them, repeating the word "place" at 56.8 and 57.1 to signpost his pivotal point. Tasso thus creates a celebration of heavenly triumph where the images of God enthroned enclose the passage cataloging the powers subjected to God's rule. We recall that Ariosto's stanza VIII.70 similarly lets God as creator and protector circumscribe the presentation of the two forms of human knowledge at the center.

Tasso, we remember, uses verbal repetitions in this segment more specifically than Fairfax. The obvious example is the repetition of the verb *risplendere* ("*risplendea* con tre lumi in una luce" ["shining with three lights in one"; 56.7]) in stanza 57, where it recurs in connection with the idea of enfolding: "Quivi ei così nel suo *splendor* s'involve" ("Where he so envelops himself in his own splendor"; 57.5).[20] Compared with Ariosto, what Tasso adds in his version of the topos, apart from increased length and wealth of descriptive detail, is a pronounced sense of movement; we are brought from the throne of God in heaven down to earth and to the fickle affairs of mankind, before soaring upward again to where God is seated in glory. We encounter such swift movement and compositional symmetry again when Milton, I argue, elaborates on Tasso's survey of God's works.

In *Paradise Lost* III.56–79 Milton describes God enthroned and surveying a situation when danger again is imminent: Satan is approaching the world, and the history of man rapidly approaches one of its decisive peripeteias. Like Tasso before him, Milton chooses to focus directly upon God seated in glory; but he also introduces Satan into the panoramic vision of God's works, just as he stresses divine prescience in relation to the threat posed to humankind. These are the opening lines of the twenty-four-line segment:

> Now had the almighty Father from above,
> From the pure empyrean where he sits
> High throned above all highth, bent down his eye.

> (III.56–58)

This passage reads like an inventive expansion of Tasso's biblical phrase "Gli occhi . . . / dal suo gran seggio il Re del Ciel volgea" ("from his great seat the Heavenly King turned his eyes"), where "*gli occhi . . . volgea*" matches Milton's "bent down his eye" as God directs his attention to the threatening situation developing on earth.[21] We note that Milton, too, introduces architectural metaphors, both explicit and implicit, that invite the reader to imagine a vast room where the events take place. In this way "a place of action" is established. Accompanying the architectural imagery we find also a number of rhetorical markers that define the outer perimeter of this dramatic space, and these markers bear a distinct resemblance to the markers used by Ariosto and Tasso.[22] The phrase that introduces the segment, "the Almighty Father from above, / *High* throned above all *highth*, bent down his eye," is summarized in its conclusion: "Him God beholding from his prospect *high*" (77). Thus the images of God surveying the world from his throne define the borders of and circumscribe the main body of this segment of the poem.

Turning to the organization of the segment itself, we note that the description that follows of "all the Sanctities of Heaven" recalls Tasso's image of the innumerable blessed spirits surrounding God (IX.57.7–8), but also Psalm 101:19, where God "loked downe fro[m] the height of his Sanctuarie." Apart from this similarity, Milton treats the topos freely and in accordance with his particular thematic concerns. He substantially reinforces the triumphal motif by a "strong central accent,"[23] a device of the kind already encountered in Ariosto's Fortune sequence.[24] In Milton's text too the pivot is located in the lines at the textual center in a passage on Adam and Eve:

> On Earth he first beheld
> Our two Parents, yet the onely two
> Of mankind, in the happie Garden plac't,
> immortal fruits of *joy* and *love*,
> Uninterrupted *joy*, unrivald love
> in blissful solitude.

> (64–69)

This implies not that the center of this vision "merely" celebrates Adam and Eve but that the more important theme is the principle of divine love at work in the universe: "l'amor che move il sole e l'altre stelle" ("the love that moves the sun and the other stars"; *Paradiso* 33.145). Indeed, the unusual rhyme effect created by the repetition of "love" at the end of lines 67 and 68 helps to single out the thematic and structural centrality of the concept, as does the repetition of "joy" (67; 68) and of "onely two" (65) and "solitude" (69). Reduplication of rhetorical markers, we recall, is a distinguishing feature also in the passages at the center of *Orlando furioso* VIII.70 and *La Gerusalemme liberata* IX.10.

In *Paradise Lost* III.56–79 Milton may in fact be adding a theological finesse, because the repetition of "love" possibly alludes to the diapason, the harmonious principle of two into one, that Augustine traced in God's two works of creation and redemption.[25] Similarly, the nexus of three co-equal terms—*immortal, uninterrupted, unrivald*—may be taken to allude to the Trinity, as these epithets reflect the three chief aspects of divine bliss.[26] Such formal jeux d'esprit were introduced into English at least as early as Gascoigne and Spenser and are well known in Jonson, Vaughan, and Herbert;[27] and we have already noted that Fairfax plays similar games. As for the reduplication of thematic and rhetorical markers in Milton, it would not be inappropriate to claim that its function within the segment is analogous to that of the double center within the poem as a whole.[28] Such finessing of the center can be combined with a recessed symmetrical structure and graded arrangements.[29]

That Milton's topos of God enthroned can be shown to possess a clearly marked beginning, middle, and end is no unique phenomenon, as we see from his further distribution of subject matter and rhetorical markers within this segment, and also from comparable examples of the same technique elsewhere in the poem. On both sides of the exact textual center, balanced passages are linked by means of antithesis. To one side of the center is the Son and to the other side is Satan, so that God's vision of Adam and Eve in bliss is bracketed by these conflicting powers. These passages (III.62–64 on the Son, and III.69–71 on Satan) are linked by means of rhyme. On God's "right, / The radiant image of his glory sat, / His onely Son" (62–64), while Satan, his antagonist, is seen "[c]oasting the wall of Heav'n on this side Night / In the dun Air sublime" (71–72). The rhyme "right" / "Night" strengthens the link through antithesis. A similar link through rhyme connects the lines that are third from the beginning and the end (III.58 and III.77), for God "High Thron'd above all highth, bent down his *eye*" is echoed by "Him God beholding from his prospect *high*." These similar actions, then, placed so precisely within the textual body of this segment, are therefore linked also by means of rhyme. The balanced pattern is created in part by means of antithesis and in part by parallelisms. If one believes that such rhymes are placed too far apart to function as such, it must be recalled that a rhetorician like Hermogenes explicitly recommended this rhetorical finesse.[30] The overall structure of this segment may be referred to as chiastic or symmetrical. The effect of chiasmus is connected with rhyme—for example, in *Paradise Lost* III.138–42:

> Beyond compare the Son of God was seen
> Most glorious, in him in all his Father shon
> Substantially express'd, and in his *face*
> Divine compassion visibly appeer'd,
> Love without end, and without measure *Grace*.[31]

Examples of this kind are legion in *Paradise Lost;* another example is the rhyme "own"/"known" in Book VIII.103–6, which may not be quite as elegant as the example quoted above, but its architectural image agrees with the rhetorical constructivism it exhibits and with the theme of Book VIII (that is, the proper order of God's creation):

> That man may know he dwells not in his *own,*
> An edifice too large for him to fill,
> Lodged in a small partition, and the rest
> Ordained for uses to his Lord best *known*.

> (8.103–6; italics added)

In addition to the rhyme that encloses this segment on the construction of an "edifice," we find an *epanalepsis* (know versus known), two *antitheses* (man versus God, and small versus large), and a central *chiasmus* (*edifice-large-fill* versus *lodged-small-partition*). A passage like this, then, refers to its own structure in a way that would have been appreciated by contemporary readers, and this too should perhaps be seen as a remnant of Italian artifice.

Milton employs masked rhymes and rhetorical recurrences fairly frequently in order to provide a symmetrical and hence perfect structure for important topoi. An additional rhyme adorns the segment on God enthroned: the last word in its first line—*above*—rhymes with the twice-replaced word *love* at the textual center. The rhymes occur in the following sequence:

> *above   eye   right   love   love   night   high*

We observe the familiar *epanados* linkage (c-cc) between the beginning and the middle, and the symmetrical a-b-c-c-b-a linkage of the six other rhymes—rhetorical devices that serve to unify and adorn this significant passage. Milton clearly treats the topos as one place or room of action in the way outlined by Heinsius and Jonson thus expanding the period so as to include the segment as a whole (see Chapter 1). An even greater large-scale variant of this figure encloses the first half of Book III, beginning when God is hailed as "Light" in the first line and concluding with a similar address in the hymn located at the midpoint of the book (III.372ff.).

In fact, the entire book could be said to be embraced by this structure, because its very last words on Satan's descent into the world, "Nor stayed, till on Niphates' top he lights" (741), punningly picks up the same sound. Such repetitions are not normally used to structure an entire book, but they will often be used to shape textual segments within a canto. In a 113-line paragraph in Book VIII repetition occurs in combination with a second rhyme scheme embedded in the flow of blank verse. In this paragraph (VIII.66–178), it has been observed, "the word sun is placed in the center of the paragraph."[32] However, we need also to recognize the prominent rhetorical structure that supports his observation. The beginning, middle, and end of the paragraph are linked by the symmetrical distribution of the word "heaven" at verses 66, 123, and 178.[33] The lines at the textual center anticipate the conclusion by the iteration of the words "earth" and "high[est]." In lines 120–21 we learn that God has "placed *heaven* from *earth* so far, that *earthly* sight, / If it presume, might err in things too *high*" (italics added), where the key words are echoed in the final line: "not of *earth* only but of *highest heaven*" (178; italics added). Milton does not stop here; he also reinforces the structure by implementing a partially imperfect rhyme-scheme:

| *heaven* | *moved/seem* | *seem/move* | *heaven* |
|----------|--------------|-------------|----------|
| (66) | (116/117) | (129/130) | (178) |

What such patterned textual segments of varying length demonstrate is that the compositional formulas employed in Milton's presentation of the topos of divine intervention are essential to his art of composition. If we consider symmetrical structures as bipartite they may be related to the metaphor of the divine logos as a two-edged sword, a principle of division that is a principal component of Milton's divine universe.[34] Like a double-edged sword, the divine word cuts through and shapes the narrative of human history.

Comparing Milton's topos of divine intervention with those of Ariosto and Tasso, we observe that some elements remain more or less constant: the emphasis on God as creator, his place in initial and final position, and the balanced rhetorical structure. Moreover, these chiastic or symmetrical structures are found in segments depicting dramatic changes in action and scene, and I believe that the textual structure is intended to reinforce the impact of these passages as instances of peripeteia. In *Paradise Lost*, however, we witness a double peripeteia: within the segment itself a negative reversal is announced when Satan enters the world, whereas Christ's decision to intervene and counter that attack follows immediately upon the topos analyzed here. In this way Milton skillfully delays the decisive intervention in order to create dramatic suspense. Christ's act of redemption will be fully achieved, not Satan's.[35] In this sense, my examination of these microstructures bears directly on what has been called the "epic and tragic structures" of *Paradise Lost*—that is, on the poem's macrostructure of plot. Also, I would claim that Milton continues the English practice of using rhymes as structural markers, a technique established by Gascoigne and perfected by Spenser, and one that Milton availed himself of in "Il Penseroso" and "L'Allegro."[36] This technique is well adapted to blank verse, and the way in which it is deployed by Milton here recalls its similar use in long speeches in the blank verse dramas of Marlowe and Shakespeare.[37] But it should be pointed out that in *Paradise Lost* this technique is also used in passages other than those presenting instances of peripeteia. Such structures do not always bear directly on the meaning of their respective passages, but rather operate on a verbal-structural level to unify the particular paragraph. In such cases they function simply as a compositional tool, reflecting an ingrained compositional habit. The rhetorical pattern of the segments analyzed here, however, transcends such purely compositional functions by bearing directly on the theme presented.

Milton's most important addition to the topos as presented by Tasso is no doubt the strongly emphasized triumphal center , where prominence is given not to God's "ministri umili" ("humble ministers") but to the principle of divine love, a love expressed during the Council in Heaven when the Son freely declares his willingness to die for humankind. Milton also introduces a more prominent dramatic element into the episode: the paragraph (3.56–79) comprises four periods of unequal length (8 1/2, 5, 7 1/2, and 3 lines of verse). These divisions create a notable asymmetry, because two of the constituent periods end in mid-verse by means of enjambment and hiatus. It has been observed that in seventeenth-century prose style the *cola* and *semicola* have been replaced by commas and periods, at the same time that sentences have been added either without the use of conjunctions or by "loose" present continuous forms. In this way the periods no longer are circular in the sense favored by Cicero, and an effect of continuity is created. Yet in spite of this syntactic looseness, Milton gives the segment a clear, logical structure so that the reader is conducted vigorously toward its conclusion. This he achieved by giving the segment a progressive structure by distributing temporal markers like "now," "first," and "then": "*Now* had the almighty Father. . . ," "On earth he *first* beheld. . . ," "*Then* he surveyed. . ." An illusion is created that we, the readers, follow his glance in one continuous take of the camera. We look, as it were, over God's shoulder down upon the creation. The illusion of unlimited expansion is captured in these lines:

> On the bare outside of this world, that seemed
> Firm land imbosomed without firmament,
> Uncertain which in ocean or in air.

The description calls to mind the claim that "infinity is the boldest baroque spatial illusion."[38] Gone are the continually shifting points of view that characterize Tasso's *maestas* topos; Milton creates mobility and dynamism by compelling our attention in one direction and by stringing together a series of progressive verb forms ("reaping . . . coasting . . . beholding . . . foreseeing"). We witness similar effects in painting and architecture in what is termed "Hochgedrang." The spiraling figures in the frescoes by Pozzo in Sant'Ignazio in Rome (Fig. 11) create the striking illusion that they and we ascend into the heavens together. Milton inverts the direction of the movement by placing the reader in the privileged position next to God on his throne and letting him too observe Satan from above.

If my attention to textual details seems tedious, I want to adduce the words of E. A. Armstrong in my defense: "Why should . . . the study of the relationship of the bricks and buttresses, foundations and finials . . . diminish our delight in the building itself or our appreciation of the skill with which it was designed and constructed?"[39] By undertaking a careful analysis of Milton's art of construction and comparing it with the techniques of his predecessors, we discover new aspects of his indebtedness to a tradition of structural aesthetics whose roots should be traced in classical and Renaissance notions of architecture and edification.

FIG. 11
Andrea del Pozzo, *Ingresso di S. Ignazio in Paradiso*, Church of S. Ignazio, Rome

Leave the goodly fabric of houses, for beauty only, to the enchanted palaces of the poets, who build them with small cost.

—Francis Bacon, "Of Building"

In this book I have argued that architecture and literature share a common theoretical basis in rhetorical theory and practice and that this is evident in the tectonics of Renaissance literature and writings on art. Moreover, I have traced the origin and history of this synthesis primarily in relation to works written by such Italian Renaissance figures as Alberti, Ariosto, Della Casa, Vasari, and Tasso, but I have also devoted space to analyses of classical writers, specifically Catullus, Propertius, Ovid, and Augustine, as well as the early thirteenth-century theorist Geoffrey de Vinsauf.

Although my main focus is on the Italian Renaissance, some of my analytical examples are drawn from English Renaissance writers: Shakespeare, Daniel, and Milton. I have chosen to do this partly because, like Renaissance artists, Renaissance poets in different languages rely on the same rules and habits of composition rooted in rhetorical doctrine. In addition to showing the influence of Italian culture in England, English Renaissance intellectuals and poets have been included, as more readers are comfortable with English. In so doing I have traced the idea behind Bacon's view that costly ornaments better befit "the enchanted palaces of poets" than buildings proper, a statement that reflects the pervasive use in the Renaissance of architectural imagery to describe "literary architecture" while at the same time commenting on the central issue of the relationship between structure and ornament in late sixteenth- and early seventeenth-century architectural theory and practice.

The relationship between abstract design on the one hand, and its material and textual realization on the other hand, is crucial to an investigation of the impact of architecture on the shapes of Renaissance texts and vice versa, and it is important for the influence of rhetoric on Renaissance art and architecture. "Topomorphology" is a useful term in such analyses, because the concept of a topomorphical structure draws attention to the distribution of ornaments that highlight the inner design of a work. The term therefore refers to both the *dispositio* and the *elocutio* aspects of a text. We have thus seen that theorists like de Vinsauf, Alberti, and Tasso advocate and use rhetorical repetitions in their compositions, employing repeated words as building blocks in an almost architectural sense. An implicit materiality of words *(verba* as *res)* lies at the core of this practice involving the combination and distribution of verbal signs according to a preconceived plan, the *innatus spiritus* that Alberti describes in the *De re aedificatoria*. Then too, a preconceived plan often reflects the theme and purpose of a work, that it is edifying not only in a compositional and aesthetic sense but also ethically in being part of a strategy of persuasion to make people shun evil and seek what is good and useful. The emphasis on shared design and the usefulness of such designs is one of the main points in Vasari's *Life of Alberti*.

Comparing the biography of Alberti in the Torrentiniana of 1568 with that in the 1550 Giuntina edition, we cannot avoid noting the marked change in the biographer's attitude to his great predecessor. While the first life is surprisingly brief and even critical of Alberti, the second is much fuller and more appreciative of his remarkable versatility and genius, although Vasari still finds him less than perfect for want of *disegno* and sufficient practice. However, the openings of both *Lives* are identical in making a general statement on the value of writing and publication in ensuring the fame of men, stressing the ease with which books appear everywhere and gain credibility, when truthful: "i libri agevolmente vanno per tutto e per tutto si acquistano fede, pure che siano veritieri e senza menzogne" (III.284). Although his comments on books serve as an introduction to the remarkable success of Alberti as a writer, Vasari also seems here to meditate on books in general, including his own work. In the substantial additions that follow in the 1568 *Life*, there is a puzzling passage that Vasari scholars pass over without further comment but that makes sense in said "bookish" context. I refer to Vasari's comparison of Alberti to Gutenberg:

> L'anno poi 1457 che fu trovato l'utilissimo modo di stampare i libri da Giovanni Guittembergh germano, trovò Leon Battista, a quella similitudine, per via d'uno strumento il modo di lucidare le prospettive naturali e diminuire le figure, et il modo parimente da poter ridurre le cose piccole in maggior forma e ringrandirle: tutte cose capricciose, utile all'arte e belle affatto. (III.286)

> [Then in the year 1457, when the most useful method of printing books was discovered by the German Johannes Gutenberg, Leon Bat-

tista, in similar fashion, by means of an instrument discovered the method for elucidating natural perspectives and diminishing figures, and likewise the method to reproduce small things in larger format and to magnify them: these are all wonderful things, useful to art and on the whole beautiful.]

Vasari is here so intent on aligning the methods of the two innovators that he deliberately dates their discoveries to the same year. In keeping with Vasari's synthetic mind and his eye for the critically relevant parallel, he sees the shared formal properties of the two inventions.

Why does Vasari align the methods of the two innovators and even wrongly dates their discoveries to the same year?[1] What does he see in their achievements that justifies the surprising appearance of "Giovanni Guittembergh germano" in the life of the Florentine *uomo universale*? Surely the answer is found not in the comparison of their respective influence and fame but in the phrase "a quella similitudine per via d'uno strumento." I shall suggest that the answer is simple but nonetheless characteristic of Vasari's synthetic mind and eye for the critically relevant parallel.

At the root of the Vasari's simile is his appreciation of what Alberti and Gutenberg, although working in different media, achieved by providing a related method for representing the world. As we all know, Gutenberg perfected the art of printing by inventing reusable lead characters to be combined and fixed within a frame for the purpose of description and communication. In theory the same characters can be combined ad infinitum to represent all kinds of phenomena, to print compositions on any imaginable topic, which then may be repeated as many times as one would like. The secret of Gutenberg's art, then, resides in how movable characters are combined within a frame before being transferred to an empty planar surface, a blank sheet of paper.

This procedure, Vasari suggests, is not unrelated to Alberti's invention of perspective by the use of a fixed frame, or a window, which is also instrumental by "uno strumento." A set of geometrical operations developed from Euclid are here combined to represent all kinds of objects, real or imaginary, to be projected onto a blank planar surface regardless of their shape and size. The similarity between the printer composing his page within a rectangular frame and the artist plotting and composing his *pictura* by means of Alberti's *fenestra* and the mechanical device of the *velo* is indeed striking,[2] suggesting how the German's revolutionary invention came to be aligned with Alberti's conquest of pictorial space. But Vasari does not stop here. He also suggests a kinship between the two that extends to himself, when describing Gutenberg with a latinate and literary term as a *germano*, derived from the Latin noun *germanu(m)*, which replaces the more common *alemanno* or *tedesco*. In fact, in Italian *germano* can also mean "born from the same parents,"[3] and hence Vasari punningly proposes that there exists a brotherhood to which both Gutenberg and Alberti belong.

The concepts of *fratellanza* and the extended family, it has been pointed out, inform the entire *Lives*.[4] Vasari poetically embellishes the lives of many artists, including his own, by creating new family ties between artists who were not related in real life, strengthening and magnifying such ties that did in fact exist. These bonds not only weave together the lives and achievements of numerous artists with the power of the Medici and the genius of Michelangelo, they also have significance for Vasari himself. Being both a painter and the writer of the lives of artists, Vasari relied on the mechanical art, or *techne*, of Gutenberg, and the perspective art of Alberti. By using the charmingly alliterative version of Gutenberg's name in his text, "Giovanni Guittembergh germano," he implicitly reminds us that like, Alberti and Gutenberg, "brothers" in art, he is part of the same *fratellanza*, or brotherhood, of those who use the kindred techniques of printing and perspective to both frame and represent the world.

Composition in the various arts, then, depends on similar ideas of formal organization, design, or *lineamento*, which are equally important for Vasari "in architecture and sculpture as in painting; but particularly so in architecture."[5] Indeed, as Vasari's *Lives* and the other types of writing analyzed in this book amply illustrate, this shared aesthetic also extends beyond the visual arts to Renaissance poetry and to the very theory of art.

## INTRODUCTION

1. Demetrius, *On Style* I.12.307.

2. Ingrid D. Rowland, "Raphael, Angelo Colocci, and the Genesis of the Architectural Orders," *The Art Bulletin* 76 (March 1994): 82.

3. I refer to such figures of repetition as *antithesis, parallelismus, epanalepsis* (that is, repetition between beginning and end of a textual segment), *epanados* (repetition between the beginning and the middle, or the middle and the end), and *antimetabole* (chiasmus or inversion), among others.

4. *Enarrationes in psalmos*, ed. D. E. Dekkers and I. Fraipont (Turholti, 1956), *Corpus Christianorum, Series Latina*, XL.iii (1891–92). Translation from *Expositions on the Book of Psalms*, 6 vols., trans. Members of the English Church (Oxford, 1847–57), 6:64.

5. Cristoforo Landino, "Che sia poesia et poeta, e la sua origine divina et antichissima," preface to *La Divina Commedia* (1481) (Venice: Marchiò Sessa e fratelli, 1564). Trans. Roy Eriksen, "What Constitutes Poetry and a Poet, and About Its Divine and Most Ancient Origin" (unpublished manuscript, 1976).

6. Brian Vickers, "On the Practicalities of Renaissance Rhetoric," in Brian Vickers, ed., *Rhetoric Revalued* (Binghamton, N.Y.: MRTS, 1982), 135. My translation.

7. See my discussion of topomorphology in relation to dramatic speech in *The Forme of Faustus Fortunes: A Study of "The Tragedie of Doctor Faustus" (1616)* (Atlantic Highlands, N.J.: Humanities Press, 1987), chap. 7; and Maren-Sofie Røstvig's entry on "The Topomorphical Approach," in *The Spenser Encyclopedia*, ed A. C. Hamilton et al. (Toronto and Buffalo: Toronto University Press; London: Routledge, 1990), 693.

8. Architectural and literary compositions therefore seem to display relationships similar to those between painting and the humanists' notions of rhetorical composition. See, for instance, Michael Baxandall, *Giotto and the Orators: Humanist Observers of Painting in Italy and the Discovery of Pictorial Composition, 1350–1450* (Oxford: Clarendon, 1971); and Edward Wright, "Alberti's *De pictura*: Its Literary Structure and Purpose," *Journal of the Warburg and Courtauld Institutes* 47 (1985): 52–71.

9. Aristotle, *The Art of Rhetoric*, trans. W. Rhys Roberts (Cambridge, Mass.: Harvard University Press; London: Heinemann, 1926), 3:9.

10. *The Forme of Faustus Fortunes: A Study of The Tragedie of Doctor Faustus (1616)* (Atlantic Highlands, N.J.: Humanities Press, 1987), chap. 7, 207–8, esp. n. 45.

11. *A Treatise of Humane Learning*, stanza I, from Arthur Kinney, *Humanist Poetics: Thought, Rhetoric, and Fiction in Sixteenth-Century England* (Amherst, Mass.: University of Massachusetts Press, 1986), 3.

12. Tasso, *Discorsi*, 21.

13. Renaissance commentators on plot structure in *The Poetics* often gloss the definition of a unified plot with Aristotle's definition of the period in *The Rhetoric*. See Francesco Robortello, ed., *In librum Aristotelis de arte poetica explicationes* (Florence, 1558): "Aristotelis libro Rhetoricorum tertio, vbi loquitur de periodo in oratione, habet quiddam, quod simillimum est his verbis, quibus vtitur nunc in declarando" (72). In English the passage reads as follows: "The third book of *The Rhetoric*, where the period in a speech is discussed, has something very similar in its phrasing to what is now used to explain here [that is, in *The Poetics*]" (my translation).

14. For the essential facts about the sonnet, see "The Origin of the Sonnet: Form as Optimism," in S. K. Heninger Jr., *The Subtext of Form in the English Renaissance: Proportion Poetical* (University Park: The Pennsylvania State University Press, 1994), 69–118.

15. Sonnets that display verbal linkage between either the poem's beginning and its middle, or between its middle and its end, or that link all three positions, are, for example, *Il Canzoniere* 4, 25, 42, 75, 82, 140, 144, 175, 333, and 334.

16. In this sonnet Petrarch links the beginning of the octave to the beginning and end of the sestet by repeating the words *Amor/amando* and *cor[e]* ("Love/loving," and "heart"). In addition, the sonnet's first and last lines are contrasted in their emphasis on life and death (*vive* and *more*).

17. Michelangelo, Buonarroti, *Rime*, ed. Enzo Noé Girardi (Bari: Laterza, 1960), 60. The translation is Saslow's in *The Poetry of Michelangelo* (New Haven: Yale University Press, 1991).

18. Further examples are offered in my discussion of sonnets by Samuel Daniel and Della Casa. See Chapters 2 and 4.

19. I refer to the the following repetitions: *extreme . . . enjoyed . . . had . . . mad // Mad . . . Had . . . extreme . . . joy*. We see another "conventional" circular pattern in the repeated rhyme sounds *shame/blame* versus *extreme/dream*, which in Shakespeare's time would be close in pronunciation.

20. Thomas P. Roche Jr., *Petrarch and the English Sonnet Sequences* (New York: AMS Press, 1989), chap. 7.

21. Contrary to Mary Jane Doherty, *The Mistress-Knowledge: Sir Philip Sidney's "Defence of Poesie" and Literary Architectonics in the English Renaissance* (Nashville, Tenn.: Vanderbilt University Press, 1991), who thinks that "Sidney's case for poesie resists the architectural interpretation of architectonic form that twentieth-century readings of Renaissance texts have observed in a modern obsession with structure and technique" (6), I believe that we cannot get around the simple fact that poetry is a verbal art and that the poet is a builder with words.

22. Paul Ricoeur, *Time and Narrative*, trans. Kathleen McLaughlin and David Pellauer (Chicago: University of Chicago Press, 1984), 1:41. See also Karol Berger, "Narrative and Lyric," in *Musical Humanism and Its Legacy: Essays in Honor of Claude V. Palisca*, ed. Nancy Kovaleff Baker and Barbara Russano Hanning (Stuyvesant, N.Y.: Pedigree Press, 1992), 457.

23. See Aldo Scaglione, *The Theory of Composition* (Chapel Hill: University of North Carolina Press, 1972); and M. S. Røstvig, *Configurations: A Topomorphical Approach to Renaissance Poetry* (Oslo: Scandinavian University Press, 1994).

24. See Lorna Hutson's discussions of the relationship between textual plotting and social and economic planning by means of projects, in *Thomas Nashe in Context* (Oxford: Oxford University Press, 1989), particularly the chapters "Literature in an Economic Context" and "The Profitable Discourse of the Elizabethans."

25. See the valuable contributions by, for example, Alan T. Bradford, "Drama and Architecture Under Elizabeth I: The 'Regular' Phase," *English Literary Renaissance* 14, no. 1 (1984): 3–28; John Onians, *Bearers of Meaning: The Classical Orders in Antiquity, the Middle Ages, and the Renaissance* (Princeton: Princeton University Press, 1988); Elisabeth Jordan, "Inigo Jones: The Architecture of Poetry," *Renaissance Quarterly* (1991): 2; and A. W. Johnson, *Ben Jonson: Poetry and Architecture* (Oxford: Clarendon Press, 1994).

## CHAPTER 1

1. Joel Altman reminds us that "foundation" also is a common English rendering of *firmamentum*, "the chief argument of the defense in the judicial case." Joel B. Altman, *The Tudor Play of Mind: Rhetorical Inquiry and the Development of Elizabethan Drama* (Berkeley and Los Angeles: University of California Press, 1978), 19.

2. Peter Brooks, *Reading for the Plot: Design and Intention in Narrative* (New York: Vintage Books, 1985), 11–12.

3. See, for example, Thomas Nashe in *The Unfortunate Traveller* (Harmondsworth: Penguin, 1972), where the terms "complotment" and "plot" are used in this sense.

4. For a different reading of the passage I analyze here, see the stimulating article by Elisabeth

Jordan, "Inigo Jones: The Architecture of Poetry"(1991), 2. The article does not cover the same ground as the present chapter.

5. As pointed out by Mathias A. Schaaber in his edition of Shakespeare's *The Second Part of King Henry the Fourth* (Philadelphia: J. B. Lippincott, 1940), the source is Luke 14:28–30.

6. To mark the central part of a text segment by means of an image of transition should be considered a conventional structural topos ("up to heaven . . . down to hell"), a structural pun ("high, raise," etc.), or a triumphal image ("king," "crown," "victory," etc). See my *Forme of Faustus Fortunes* (1987), chap. 7.

7. The *Nosce teipsum* theme also appears thinly disguised in the phrase "to know your own estate."

8. The Latin thus presents a denser texture, as in the parallel phrases "ne posteaquam posuerit fundamentum et non potuerit perficere" and "quia hic homo coepit aedificare et non potuit consumare." These devices are common in New Testament proverbial wisdom, reflecting the "most basic form of poetic expression in Hebrew literature, *parallelismus membrorum,*" as pointed out by David Jasper, *The New Testament and the Literary Imagination* (London: Macmillan, 1987), 80.

9. Ibid., 81.

10. Ernest Gallo, *The Poetria Nova and Its Sources in Early Rhetorical Doctrine* (The Hague and Paris: Mouton, 1971). Gallo provides a translation with copious notes to this useful text.

11. See Chapter 3.

12. At the time he wrote *2 Henry IV,* Shakespeare was preoccupied with the building of New Place at Stratford, a practical task that possibly made him turn to foreign pattern books for ideas, although the finished product seems to have been thoroughly traditional. See Schaaber in *The Second Part of King Henry the Fourth,* 95.

13. Federico Zuccari discusses inner design in *L'Idea de' pittori, scultori e architetti* (Rome, 1607), in which he summarizes a debate on aesthetics that had lasted for more than half a century and that, for example, had given birth to the Academia del dissegno. One of the writers whose treatise contributed to giving the concept of design such a prominent role was Benedetto Varchi, who gives "model" as one of several alternative terms for design: "idea, . . .essemplare . . . esempio, e più volgarmente modello." Benedetto Varchi, "Lezione sul sonetto 'Non ha l'ottimo artista alcun concetto,' " in *Scritti d'arte del cinquecento,* ed. Paola Barocchi (Milan, 1973), 2:1323.

14. John Dee, *The Mathematicall Praeface to the Elements of Geometrie of Euclid of Megara* (London, 1570), Sig. d.iiij.

15. Other repetitions link the beginning of the speech to the end (for example, "cost" and "house"), but they are not part of the inverted pattern.

16. De Vinsauf writes about this type of arrangement (verses 118–120): "Primus apex operis non solum fulget ab ipso / Fine, sed ipsius duplex est gloria, finis / Thematis et medium" ("The high point of the work does not radiate only from the very end, but has a double glory: the end of the work and the middle"). (*The Poetry Nova and Its Sources in Early Rhetorical Doctrine,* 21)

17. This way of providing a major structured speech with a frame is not uncommon elsewhere in Shakespeare, and examples abound in Tasso, Spenser, and Marlowe. In the case of drama such designs are realized in space and given body in performance, on a par with the spatial realization of a building.

18. Mark Rose, *Shakespearean Design* (Cambridge, Mass.: Harvard University Press, 1972).

19. Hanno-Walter Kruft, *A History of Architectural Theory from Vitruvius to the Present* (Princeton: Princeton Architectural Press, 1994), 42.

20. But see John Summerson on Elizabethan architectural style as "mannerist," mentioning Wollaston Hall, in his *The Classical Language of Architecture* (1963; London: Thames and Hudson, 1991), 66. For Longleat House, see Alan T. Bradford, "Drama and Architecture Under Elizabeth I: The 'Regular' Phase." For the importance of the architectural treatise in the period, see Alina Payne's 1999 study.

21. See, for example, Rudolf Wittkower, *Architecture in the Age of Humanism* (1949; London: Academy Editions, 1988); and Mario Praz, *Mnemosyne: The Parallel Between Literature and the Visual Arts* (Princeton: Princeton University Press, 1970).

22. See, for example, Wotton's regurgitation of the commonplace: "This led me to contemplate the Fabrique of our own Bodies, wherein the High Architect of the world, had displaied such skill, as did stupifie, all humane reason" (*The Elements of Architecture* (London: John Bill, 1624), 7 (the pagination in this source is confusing, because both Arabic numerals and signatures are used, and often incorrectly).

23. Plato, *Timaeus*, trans. R. G. Bury (1921; reprint, London: Heinemann, 1966), 53.

24. On this point, see, for example, the classic studies by Maren-Sofie Røstvig, "The Hidden Sense," in *The Hidden Sense and Other Essays* (Oslo: Oslo University Press, 1963) 3–112; E. K. Heninger, *Touches of Sweet Harmony: Pythagorean Cosmology and Renaissance Poetics* (San Marino, Calif.: Huntington Library, 1974); and Alastair Fowler, *Triumphal Forms: Structural Patterns in Elizabethan Poetry* (Cambridge: Cambridge University Press, 1970).

25. Leon Battista Alberti, *L'Architettura (De re aedificatoria)*, 2 vols., ed. Giovanni Orlandi and Paolo Portoghesi (1485; reprint, Milan: Edizioni il Polifilo, 1966).

26. See Baxandall, *Giotto and the Orators*, 129–32; and Jaap Bolten, "Ut Grammatica Pictura: A Method of Learning," *Ars auro prior* (1981): 71–74.

27. Anthony Blunt, *Artistic Theory in Italy, 1450–1600* (Oxford: Oxford University Press, 1962), 20. See also Portoghesi's introduction to his and Orlandi's edition.

28. Ibid., 21.

29. *L'Architettura (De re aedificatoria)* IX.v.812.

30. *L'Architettura di Leon Battista Alberti*, trans. Cosimo Bartoli (Venice: Francesco Franceschi, 1565), 337.

31. James Leoni, *The Ten Books of Architecture by Leone Battista Alberti* (1726; reprint, London: Alec Tiranti, 1965), 194.

32. See the observation by Portoghesi in his edition *of L'Architettura (De re aedificatoria)*, I: xxxiv: "L'Alberti però tende a forzarne il significato facendone una categoria convenzionale, connessa con la *unitas* e con la simmetria come è intesa nel *De vera religione* di S. Agostino" (VI.32).

33. *L'Architettura (De re aedificatoria)*, ed. Portoghesi, I.i.19n.

34. Alberti's phrase "tota aedificii forma et figura ipsis in lineamentis conquiescat" displays similarities with de Vinsauf's phrasing "intrinseca linea cordis / Praemetitur opus, . . .totamque figurat," which may be explained in terms of a common source.

35. Rudolf Wittkower, *Architecture in the Age of Humanism* (London: Academy Editions, 1988), 110.

36. Praz, *Mnemosyne*, 89.

37. Ben Jonson, *Timber; or, Discoveries* (Syracuse, N.Y.: Syracuse University Press, 1976), 92–93.

38. See, for example, studies by Neville Davies, Alastair Fowler, S. K. Heninger Jr., Kent A. Hieatt, Gunnar Quamström, Thomas P. Roche Jr., Maren-Sofie Røstvig, and the present author.

39. *Timber; or, Discoveries*, 44.

40. Cited by Jaap Bolten. "Ut Grammatica Pictura: A Method of Learning," *Ars auro prior* 72.

41. Central figures on the Elizabethan literary scene, such as Gascoigne, Sidney, Puttenham, and Daniel, obviously did think in this manner. See my "Two into One: The Unity of Gascoigne's Companion Poems," *Studies in Philology* 813 (Summer 1984): 275–99; and Christina Sandhaug, "The Poetics of the Sidney Circle" (unpublished thesis, University of Tromsø, 1999).

42. Varchi, "Lezione sul sonetto 'Non ha l'ottimo artista alcun concetto,' " 2:1323.

43. See Annabel M. Patterson's study *Hermogenes and the Renaissance: The Seven Ideas of Style* (Princeton: Princeton University Press, 1972).

44. Julius Caesar Scaliger, *Poetices libri septem*, ed. August Buck (1561; reprint, Stuttgart-Bad Cannstatt: Friederich Frommann Verlag, 1964), 80–173.

45. Sir Philip Sidney, *An Apology for Poetry*, ed. Geoffrey Shepherd (1965; reprint, Manchester: Manchester University Press, 1973). Sidney compares "the house well in model" to the learned philosopher's "many infallible grounds of wisdom," which must be "figured forth by the speaking picture of poesy"(107).

46. The sources of these ideas are found in Aristotle's discrimination between theoretical and practical knowledge in *Nichomachean Ethics*, trans. M. Rackham (1926; reprint, London: Heinemann, 1956), I.i–iv.3–5 and VI.vi.3.

47. *An Apology for Poetry*, 104.

48. Wotton uses, for example, *seate, place*, and *s(c)ituation* for Alberti's *area* and *situs* (Italian: *sito*), while *lineamenta* is variously rendered as *idea, designement*, and *plot*.

49. *An Apology for Poetry*, 101.

50. Per Palme notes that "[t]he Vitruvian principle of organic wholeness [was] first publicly applied to a work of architecture," when Ben Jonson in 1604 described Stephen Harrison's triumphal arch at Fenchurch Street. "Ut Architectura Poesis," in *Idea and Form*, ed. Nils Gösta Sandblad, *Figura* n.s. 1 (Stockholm: Almquist and Wicksell, 1959), 104.

51. Peter J. French, *John Dee: The World of an Elizabethan Magus* (London: Routledge and Kegan Paul, 1972), 40.

52. Frances A. Yates, *The Theatre of the World* (London: Penguin, 1966), 12.

53. Dee, *The Mathematicall Praeface*, d.iiij.

54. *John Dee: The World of an Elizabethan Magus*, 58.

55. Richard Wills, *De re poetica*, ed. A. D. S. Fowler (Oxford: Blackwell, 1958): "haec prima virtus orationis fuit, cuius mox amplificatus est usus, additis rudi atq; inchoato corpori quibusdam quasi dimensionibus ac lineamentis, unde certa lex dicendi orta est." Fowler's translation is highly illuminating: "This was the first power of language, and soon its use was enlarged by the additions of certain dimensions and lineaments (as it were) to its unformed and shapeless body" (51).

56. Shute, *The First and Chief Groundes of Architecture*, ed. Laurence Weaver (London: Country Life, 1912).

57. Anthony Blunt, "Des origines de la critique et de l'histoire de l'art en Angleterre," *Revue de l'art* 30, no. 3 (1975): 316.

58. Peter Kidson, Peter Murray, and Paul Thompson, *A History of English Architecture* (1962; reprint, Harmondsworth: Penguin, 1979), 161.

59. Bradford, "Drama and Architecture Under Elizabeth I," 7.

60. *History of English Architecture*, 161.

61. See Weaver's introduction to *The First and Chief Groundes of Architecture*, 15.

62. See the OED for the three meanings of plot relevant to the context of this chapter: 1. (a) A small piece of ground, generally used for a specific purpose. (b) A measured area of land; a lot. 2. A ground plan, as for a building; chart; diagram. 3. The series of events consisting of an outline of the action of a narrative or drama.

63. *History of English Architecture*, 161.

64. Compare also Shute's comment on "the south windes which are . . . great wasters of . . . buildings" (Sig. B.iii.v.) and the "inditia . . . ventorum" in *De re aedificatoria*, I.v.44.

65. An example of such artifice is nevertheless found in a prefatory poem dedicated to Shute. In it the anonymous poet employs a method of verbal ornamentation that Gascoigne was to advocate in *Certaine notes concerning the making of uerse in English*, ed. G. Gregory Smith, 2 vols. (Oxford: Oxford University Press, 1904), 1:46–57. The method entails distributing rhyme-words (and other key words) to emphasize the poem's inner design, or what Gascoigne terms the poem's "platforme of inuention."

66. See Lorna Hutson, *Thomas Nashe in Context* (Oxford: Oxford University Press, 1989), 38–54.

67. See Joan Thirsk, *Economic Policy and Projects* (Oxford: Clarendon, 1978), 1–50.

68. "Iohn Shute Painter and Architecte: vnto the Louing and freindly R[e]aders," Aiij.v.

69. *An Apology for Poetry*, 64–66.

70. Gascoigne similarly relates "rime" (an ornament) to "the platforme of inuention" (1.469) and thus parallels Alberti on architectural ornament and the underlying design. See *L'Architettura (De re aedificatoria)* VI.v. 472: "It is in every way necessary to distribute all materials so that the construction is not begun without a precise idea of what one wants to accomplish and of how to accomplish it, and that it is carried out in keeping with the same principles according to which it was initiated and that it is not abandoned before the work has been completed in every detail and with utmost care" (my translation).

71. *Francisci Robortelli . . . De Arte Poetica Explicationes*, 72.

## CHAPTER 2

1. See S. K. Heninger Jr., *Sidney and Spenser: The Poet as Maker* (University Park: The Pennsylvania State University Press, 1989) for a concise introduction to the topic.

2. Mary Jane Doherty, *The Mistress-Knowledge: Sir Philip Sidney's "Defence of Poesie" and Literary Architectonics in the English Renaissance* (Nashville, Tenn.: Vanderbilt University Press, 1991), 154.

3. James Mirollo, *Mannerism and Renaissance Poetry: Concept, Mode, Inner Design* (New Haven and London: Yale University Press, 1984), 167.

4. Clyde Murley, "The Structure and Proportion of Catullus LXIV," *Transactions of the Americal Philological Association* 68 (1937): 316.

5. Ian Worthington, *A Historical Commentary on Dinarchus: Rhetoric and Conspiracy in Later Fourth-Century Athens* (Chicago: University of Chicago Press, 1992), 27ff. See also Brooks Otis, *Virgil: A Study of Civilized Poetry* (Oxford: Clarendon, 1964) and *Ovid as an Epic Poet* (Cambridge: Cambridge University Press, 1966); and André Hurst, *Apollonius de Rhodes. Manière e cohérence*, Biblioteca Helvetica, vol. VIII (Rome: Swiss Academy, 1967).

6. See Worthington, *Historical Commentary on Dinarchus;* and Helena Dettmer, *Love by the Numbers: Form and Meaning in the Poetry of Catullus* (New York: Peter Lang, 1997).

7. Francis Cairns, *Tibullus: A Hellenistic Poet at Rome* (Cambridge: Cambridge University Press, 1979), 193.

8. T. P. Wise, *Cinna the Poet and Other Rome Essays* (Leicester: Leicester University Press, 1974), 64ff.

9. See the stimulating discussion by Røstvig, *Configurations*, 3–74.

10. Augustine's examples of sentences with antithesis and contraposita are taken from 2 Corinthians 6:7–10 and Ecclesiasticus 33:14–15: "With the weapons of righteousness for the right hand and for the left; in honor and dishonor, in ill repute and in good repute; treated as impostors, and yet truthful; as unknown, and yet well known; as dying, and behold we live; as punished, and yet not killed; as sorrowful, and yet always rejoicing; as poor, yet making many rich; as having nothing, and yet possessing everything" (495, 497).

11. George A. Kennedy discusses Aristotle's conservative view in "Aristotle on the Period," *Harvard Studies on Classical Philology* 63 (1958): 283–84. Aristotle defines the period in *The Art of Rhetoric* III.ix.6–9. Quintilian becomes more representative for Latin practice; see *Institutio oratoria* IX.iv.124.

12. Cairns, *Tibullus: A Hellenistic Poet at Rome*, 193. See also Wise, *Cinna the Poet and Other Rome Essays*, 64ff.

13. See, for instance, his description of the mystery of unity between God and man, when two become one in *Enarrationes in psalmos*, psalms LVIII and CXXIX.

14. The words "pulchritudo" and "pulchritudinem" link the period's middle and end, while the phrases "contraria contrariis opposita" and "contrarium oppositione" link its beginning and to the end.

15. See later in this chapter.

16. "Ita coelestibus terrena subjecta, orbes temporum suorum numerosa successione quasi carmini universitatis associant," *De musica* VI.xi.29, in *Sancti Aurelii Augustini Opera omnia*, vol. I, ed. J. P. Migne (Paris, 1841).

17. See Røstvig, *Configurations*, 10ff.

18. Augustine, *De vera religione* XXX.55 and 56: "lex omnium artium cum sit omnino incommutabilis." We may see a simple example of graded arrangement in the discussed sentence in the way two related lexical items oppose another of the same kind in the distribution of *contraria contrariis* versus *contrarium*. For an interesting Renaissance analysis and comment on Augustine's *carmen pulcherrimum* metaphor, see Luis Vida (Vives), *D. Augustini . . . De Civitate Dei libri XXII* (Basil, 1570), 630–31.

19. See Røstvig, *Configurations*, 75–130.

20. See the account by Ovid in *Fasti* I.63–294, ed. James George Frazer (London: Heinemann, 1967).

21. See later in this chapter.

22. "Everyone has a single doorkeeper for his house, and since he is a man, that is quite sufficient. But they [the pagans] put three gods there: Forculus for the doors *(fores)*, Cardea for the hinges *(cardo)*, and Limentinus for the threshold *(limen)*. Thus Forculus was not competent to guard both the hinge and the threshold along with the door." *The City of God Against the Pagans*, 7 vols., trans. William M. Green (London: Heinemann, 1963), IV.viii.33. It is interesting that the Renaissance mythographer Vincenzo Cartari comments upon this particular passage in *Le Imagini de i dei de gli antichi* (Venice, 1556 and 1571) and on the implicit alignment between the Trinity and the trinitarian symbolism attributed to Janus: "Santo Agostino beffandosi di loro dice che un portinaio solo huomo fa tutto quello, che essi fanno fare à tre Dei insieme, quali sono la Dea Cardinea, Forculo, e Limentino" (48–49).

23. *On Freedom of the Will*, ed. Ann S. Benjamin and L. H. Hackstaff (Indianapolis: Bobbs Merrill, 1964), 89.

24. Ibid., 89.

25. Smith, *Architecture in the Culture of Early Humanism: Ethics, Aesthetics, and Eloquence, 1400–1470* (New York: Oxford University Press, 1992), 83. Augustine's description of his desired knowledge of God is in *Soliloquies* I.iv-viii.

26. The whole passage describes the transition from the sensible and sensuous to the intelligible and spiritual.

27. L. Richardson Jr., "Catullus 67: Interpretation and Form," *American Journal of Philology* 93 (1972): 425.

28. Richardson, ibid., proposes that the poem draws on "a Fescennine playlet [recited] at the climactic moment of the wedding procession" (433).

29. J. P. Postgate simply states that "the idea of [*Elegy* I.xvi] is taken from Catullus 67." See *Propertius, Select Elegies*, ed. J. P. Postgate (London: Macmillan, 1962), 81.

30. Cited by Postgate in ibid., 89.

31. For a particularly informative and challenging interpretation of the Janus cult, see Louise Adams Holland, *Janus and the Bridge*, American Academy in Rome Papers and Monographs 21 (Rome: American Academy in Rome, 1961): esp. 265–309. She gives one possible etymology of *ianus* as "open door through which the light entered the windowless huts of prehistoric Rome" (302).

32. Augustine asks: "Therefore, since Janus is the world, and Jupiter is the world, and there is one world, why are there two gods, Janus and Jupiter?" (*City of God* VII.x.413).

33. "Whatever you see anywhere—sky, sea, clouds, earth—all things are closed and opened by my hand" (*Fasti* I.117–118.11).

34. In the case of Tibullus too there is a reference to sound at the crucial point of transition—that is, Tibullus transforms the line, using the verb *vocare* to refer to the "silent" finger ("et vocet ad

digiti me taciturna sonum"; 32), wittily developing and reworking the metaphor of the sound to one of silence. In the extant text this verse is number 32, but it ought to have been 33,because a verse has been lost after verse 25, making the relevant line of verse line 33 of a total of ninety-nine verses. As in *Propertius* I.xvi, this "musical" and structural division of the text is linked to the poem's opening and concluding verses by a veritable barrage of verbal repetitions.

35. See several examples analyzed by me in *The Forme of Faustus Fortunes*, 103–67.

36. See Fowler on Ovid and on triumphal centers in Renaissance literature, *Triumphal Forms*, 41 and 52 (*Amores* I.ii); 34–54 ("Fictional Triumphs").

37. The main *tesserae* of this "verbal mosaic" are as follows:

> "dura . . . fores" (1–2)
>> "amor . . . nocte" (13)
>>> "in media pace" (30)
>>>> "amantem" (31)
>>>>> "tempora . . . seram" (32)

**Center:**                    "corona" (37)

>>>>> "tempora . . . seram" (40)
>>>> "amantis" (41)
>>> "in mediae sidera" (44)
>> "Nox et Amor" (59)
> "duraque . . . fores" (74).

38. Aemilius Baehrens, *Fragmenta Poetarum Romanorum* (Lipsia: Teubner, 1886), 29–33.

39. *Theodosii Macrobii . . . Opera*, ed. Isach Pontanii et al. (Lipsia: Teubner, 1670), chap.ix. "Qui deus Janus, deque variis nominibus et potestate," 226.

40. For further information, see Baehrens's notes and C. M. Zander, *Versus Italici antiqui* (Lund, 1880).

41. *Bild als Figur* (Wolfenbüttel, 1976).

42. The cycle has recently been discussed in relation to Augustinian structural aesthetics by Røstvig, who reprints some of the poems; see *Configurations*, 169–87.

43. Ed. Sir Israel Gollanz, *Pearl, Cleanness, Patience, and Sir Gawain: Reproduced in Facsimile from the Unique MS. Cotton Nero A.x in the British Museum*, Early English Text Society, old series, 162 (London: Oxford University Press, 1923).

44. In a recent analysis, Donna Crawford, "The Architectonics of Cleanness," *Studies in Philology* 90, no. 4 (1993): 29–45, is able to show that the intriguing placement of the large decorated capital letters at irregular intervals in the poem coincides with "simple geometrical constructions" (37).

45. Ibid., 37.

46. S. L. Clark and Julian Wasserman, "The Significance of Thresholds in the *Pearl*-poet's Purity," *Interpretations* 12 (1980): 114–27.

47. "Ars amandi, Ars Legendi," *Exemplaria* 1 (March 1989): 181–205. Allen concludes that "the *Ars amatoria* and its medieval analogues teach their readers not how to behave, but how to understand love poetry—how, in short, to read" (195). This is a reading strategy I would also extend to the *Poetria nova*.

48. Another poet who exploited this number is Bonaventura, whose *Laudismus de Sancra Cruce* contains thirty-nine stanzas. See Røstvig, *Configurations*, 188.

49. The emphatic personal pronoun *ego* occurs only twice in the poem, in verses 1 and 19, thus forming a link between the beginning and the middle (*epanados*).

50. See Røstvig, *Configurations*, 188.

51. Torquato Tasso, *Discourses on the Heroic Poem*, trans. M. Cavalchini and I. Samuel (Oxford: Oxford University Press, 1973), 78.

52. See Heinrich Lausberg's treatment of the *periodos* "die vollkommenste Vereiningung

mehrerer Gedanken in einem Satz" in *Handbuch der Literarischen Rhetorik*, 2 vols. (Munich: Hueber, 1973), 1:458. Useful classical and Renaissance accounts are: Aristotle, *The Art of Rhetoric* III.ix.386–95; and Julius Caesar Scaliger, *Poetices libri septem* (Lyon, 1561), IIII.xxv.197a–8a.

53. *Francisci Robortelli . . . in librum Aristotelis de arte poetica explicationes*, 72; and Lodovico Castelvetro, *Poetica d'Aristotile vulgarizzzata e sposta* (Vienna, 1570), 87. See also Daniel Heinsius, *Aristotelis "De Poetica" liber* (Leyden, 1611), 76. Heinsius applies a common term for period, *ambitus*, to the plot of tragedy when he discusses the shape and magnitude of plot in terms of a building: "Quemadmodum de aedificio qui cogitat, primo ei locum designare solet; quem mox certa magnitudine ac *ambitu* definit: ita in Tragoedia" ("In the same way as one who thinks about a building, first marks off a place; which he delimits with respect to magnitude and circumference; so it is in tragedy"), IV.28; italics added.

54. *In librum Aristotelis de arte poetica explicationes*, 72.

55. See my discussion of this passage in *The Forme of Faustus Fortunes*, 208ff.

56. J. J. Keaney, "Ring Composition in Aristotle's *Athenaion Politeia*," *American Journal of Philology* 90 (1969): 406–23.

57. *The Forme of Faustus Fortunes*, chap. 7.

58. That twenty-four lines of verse may constitute an important unit within Ovid's integrated system can be seen in lines 24–25 ("Tempora noctis eunt; excute poste seram. Excute; sic umquam longa relevere catena"), where the internal refrain occurs for the first time. In the reference to the chain (*catena*), also here used in final position, we find a conspicuous link to the poem's first and forty-seventh lines.

59. See, for example, his preface to *A Defence of Ryme* (1603) in *Elizabethan and Jacobean Quartoes*, ed. G. B. Harrison (Edinburgh: Edinburgh University Press, 1966), 14.

60. Ibid., 16.

61. *The Arte of English Poesie* (London, 1589), ed. Gladys D. Willcock and Alice Walker (Cambridge: Cambridge University Press, 1970).

62. *Discorsi dell'arte poetica* III.31.

63. In her discussion of rhyme in relation to the Augustinian *mirabilis ordo*, Røstvig, *Configurations*, observes that in Daniel "[t]he appeal to the ear is intellectualized and so lifted to a higher level when structural patterns are created by repeating identical rhyme words," (66–67). See also Røstvig, "A Frame of Words," *English Studies* 60 (1979): 122–37.

64. Terence Cave, *The Cornucopian Text: Problems of Writing in the French Renaissance* (Oxford: Clarendon, 1979), 29.

65. *A Defence of Ryme*, 16. Daniel's terms recall Ficino's rhetorical description of the creation: "although in the beginning the matter of this world lay a formless chaos without the ornament of forms, attracted by innate love, it turned toward the Soul and offered itself submissively to it and by the mediation of this love it found ornament, from the Soul, of all the forms which are seen in this world; and thus out of a chaos was made a world." *Commentary on Plato's Symposium*, trans. S. R. Jayne (Columbia: University of Missouri Press, 1944), 129.

66. For the more uncommon term *girum*, see, for example, Pietro Vittorini, *Commentarii in tres libros Aristotelis de arte dicendi* (Florence, 1579), 631 ("angustiore gyro").

67. For a more detailed analysis, see Sandhaug, "The Poetics of the Sidney Circle," chap. 2.

68. See also Gascoigne's use of the architectural metaphor "the platforme of . . . invention" (*Works*, I: 469) and William Webbe's discussion of "the roomes" occupied by the feet of verse, *A Discourse of English Poetrie* (London, 1586), 69.

69. Scamozzi aligns the orator and the architect: "E sì come l'Oratore và narrando il tutto ordinatamente à tempo, e luogo . . . così parimente l'Architetto," *L'Idea dell'architettura universale* (Venice, 1615), 43. He also explains how the application of design provides a miniature version of the world: "per mezo del disegno si riduce in picciolissima forma il Mondo terrestre, & anco il celeste: intanto,

che e l'uno, e l'altro dimostra chiaramente sotto al senso, quasi tutte le cose nella sua vera somiglianza, e manca solo di corporeità, la quale si aspetta al Modello (XIV: 46).

70. Diana Poulton, *John Dowland* (Berkeley and Los Angeles: University of California Press, 1982), 195.

## CHAPTER 3

1. *Aedificatio* was used quite early in the extended sense of being spiritually edifying, as we see especially in the *Vulgata:* see 2 Corinthians 5:1, "aedificationem ex deo habemus, domum non manufactam, aeternam in coelis" ("For we knowe that if our earthlie of this tabernacle be destroied, we haue a buylding, *giuen* of God, *that is*, an house not made with hands, *but* eternal in the heauens"), and Ephesians 2:20, "superaedficati estis super fundamentum apostolorum et prophetarum ipso summo angulari lapide Christo Iesu, in quo omnis aedificatio constructa crescit in templum sanctum in domino" ("And are buylt vpon the fundacion of the Apostles and Prophetes, Iesus Christ him selfe, being the chief corner stone, In whome all the buylding coupled together, groweth vnto an holie Temple in the Lord"). I quote the translation of *The Geneva Bible* (ed. Lloyd E. Barry, 1969).

2. Giorgio Vasari, "Vita di Michelagnolo," ed. Ragghianti, *Le vite* IV: 384: "Rispose Michelagnolo che di quelle [that is, la scultura e la pittura] ne sapeva poco, anche del fortificare, col pensiero che lungo tempo ci aveva avuto sopra, con la sperienzia di quel che aveva fatto, gli pareva sapere più che non aveva saputo né egli né tutti que' di casa sua."

3. John Onians, "Alberti and Filarete," *Journal of the Warburg and Courtauld Institutes* 35 (1971): 97–114; and Richard Tobin, "Leon Battista Alberti: Ancient Sources and Structure in the *Treatises on Art*" (Ph.D. diss., Bryn Mawr College, 1979).

4. *Profugiorum ab aerumna*, ed. Cecil Grayson, in *Opere volgari*, vol. II (Bari: Laterza, 1966), 105–83. The largely neglected work has recently been discussed in context by Christine Smith, *Architecture in the Culture of Early Humanism: Ethics, Aesthetics, and Eloquence, 1400–1470* (New York: Oxford University Press, 1992).

5. Smith, *Architecture in the Culture of Early Humanism*, 3–18.

6. Ingrid D. Rowland, "Raphael, Angelo Colocci, and the Genesis of the Architectural Orders," *The Art Bulletin* 81 (March 1994): 81–104. Rowland explains that the term "Orders" did not acquire its standard meaning until 1519–20, when it was fixed by Raphael and Colocci. Smith translates *ordini* as "Orders" in her reference to the same passage (27). See also Rowland's recent book *The Culture of the High Renaissance: Ancients and Moderns in Sixteenth-Century Rome* (Cambridge: Cambridge University Press, 1998), 230–39. For a comprehensive view, see the discussion by John Onians, *Bearers of Meaning: The Classical Orders in Antiquity, the Middle Ages, and the Renaissance* (Princeton: Princeton University Press, 1988).

7. Cf. *Profugiorum ab aerumna* III.159–60, 170, 182.

8. Smith, *Architecture in the Culture of Early Humanism*, 7.

9. Smith's discussion titled "Variety and the Design of Pienza," in ibid., 98–129, provides an excellent illustration of the compositional ideal expressed in the passage.

10. Smith, *Architecture in the Culture of Early Humanism*, 7.

11. Julius Caesar Scaliger, *Poetices libri septem*, and Sir Philip Sidney, *Apology for Poetry*.

12. See the discussion by Claudia Lazzaro, *The Italian Renaissance Garden: From the Conventions of Planting, Design, and Ornament to the Grand Gardens of Sixteenth-Century Central Italy* (New Haven and London: Yale University Press, 1990, which cites several cinquecento examples (9). Lazzaro specifically mentions the garden as a third nature that grew out of established notions of art and nature, and recalled specifically a related concept of a second, or another, nature.

13. Cicero, *De natura deorum* II.lx.152. The Latin passage reads: "Terrenorum item commodum omnis est in homine dominatus; nos campis, nostri lacus, nos fruges serimur, nos arbores; nos

aquarum inductionibus terris fecunditatem damus, nostra flumina arcemus, dirigimus, avertimus; nostris denique manibus in rerum natura quasi alteram naturam efficere conamur."

14. *De Officiis* I.xxxv.129: [N]atura ipsa magistra et duce" and also"[n]os autem naturam sequamur" (130).

15. *De natura deorum* II.lx.150.

16. Onians, "Alberti and Filarete," 97–114.

17. Ibid., 100. For a comparable passage, see *Profugiorum ab aerumna* III.164.

18. "Alberti and Filareth," 103.

19. Tobin, "Leon Battista Alberti," 149.

20. Leoni, *The Ten Books of Architecture* VI.ii.113.

21. Hanno-Walter Kruft, *A History of Architectual Theory,* 48.

22. Christine Smith, "Leon Battista Alberti e l'ornamento: rivestimenti parietali e pavimentazioni," in *Leon Battista Alberti,* ed. Joseph Rykwert and Robert Tavernor, 196–215 (Milan: Electa, 1994). Smith remarks that "l'Alberti applica la definizione classica della bellezza (rapporto armonioso tra le parti più la gradevolezza del colore) non alla struttura del tempio [di Efeso] ma soltanto alla finitura" (198). In this respect he appears to follow Isidor of Sevilla rather than Vitruvius.

23. *De poetria nova* 53. The Latin text reads: "Se nisi conformet color intimus exteriori, / Sordet ibi ratio" (746–47).

24. For a discussion of Vinsauf's application of classical rhetoric, see Baldwin, *Medieval Rhetoric and Poetic (to 1400)* (New York: Macmillan, 1928), 187–88.

25. *De Officiis* I.xxxix.

26. *De Officiis* I.xl.144: "Itaque, ut eandem nos modestiam appellemus, sic definitur a Stoicis, ut modestia sit scientia rerum earum, quae agentur aut dicentur, loco suo collocandarum."

27. See the application of this phrase in Jonson, *Timber; or, Discoveries,* where Cicero's term *locus actionis* ("place of action") is used to align a building and a poem (46).

28. The original reads: "Talis sit igitur ordo actionum adhibiendus, ut, quem ad modum in oratione constanti, sic in vita omnia sint apta inter se et convenientia" (I.xl.144; p. 146).

29. Cicero notes that "[a] similar definition can be given for prudence" ("Sed potest eadem esse prudentiae definitio") (I.xl.143).

30. "Collocata autem verba habent ornatum, si aliquid concinnitatis efficiunt, quod verbis mutatis non maneat manente sententia; nam sententiarum ornamenta quae permulta, sed emineant pauciora" (XX.81.364).

31. Tobin, "Leon Battista Alberti," 149.

32. Mary Hollingsworth, "The Architect in Fifteenth-Century Florence," *The Art Bulletin* 7, no. 4 (1984): 396. Hollingsworth cogently analyzes the various aspects of the architect's role, arguing that, by emulating classical models, theorists like Alberti and Filarete showed "that a patron could enhance his own image by employing one of them" (406).

33. Scamozzi, *L'Idea dell'architettura universale,* 43.

34. Cf. Cicero, *De natura deorum* II.lx.150.

35. *L'Architettura (De re aedificatoria)* IX.v.812. Cf. Roy Eriksen, "The Lineaments of Influence: Alberti and the Elizabethans," 43–59.

36. For an illuminating discussion of the alignment between sketching a text and a building, see Cecil Grayson on Alberti's use of the verb *congettare,* "Leon Battista and Italian Grammar, " in *Art and Politics in Renaissance Italy,* ed. George Holmes (Oxford: Clarendon Press, 1993), 98.

37. Salvatore I. Camporeale, "Lorenzo Valla tra Medioevo e Rinascimento: Encomion s. Thomae (1457)," *Memorie Domenicane,* n.s. 7 (1976): 120.

38. Camporeale (ibid., 120 n. 54) notes: "One cannot avoid noticing Valla's analogy and its concomitant implications, which are determined with respect to parallel operations, between the 'restauration' of an authentic reading of Scripture and that of the 'Temple' as a sacred monument: in

both cases one activates a similar act of 'reconstruction,' that is, reconstruction of the proper origins, be it redactional (with respect to the text) or architectonic (with respect to the edifice)" (my translation).

39. Camporeale has kindly pointed out to me that Roberto Cardini made a similar observation regarding this passage in *Mosaici. Il "nemico" dell'Alberti* (Rome: Bulzoni Editore, 1990), an analysis I was not aware of when I wrote this chapter. It is interesting that Cardini argues that the quotations in Alberti's *Intercenales* are consciously deployed by the author like the *tesserae* in a mosaic (4–7), and that he quotes the same passage from the *Profugiorum* analyzed by me.

40. See Cecil Grayson, ed., *The Art of Painting*, 2:30–34. Alberti's terminology throughout is in accord with rhetorical terminology, thus showing how the formal properties of the period are evoked as a compositional ideal. The analogy originates in Cicero, *Orator* L.169, trans. H. B. Hubbell, where Cicero compares the arrangement of a sentence to the lines of mosaic in a pavement.

41. See the discussion by Charles Hope, "The Early History of the Tempio Malatestiano," *Journal of the Warburg and Courtauld Institutes* 55 (1992): 51–154.

42. *Mosaici. Il "nemico" dell'Alberti*, 7 ("una lucida e direi geometrica strategia della pagina all'interno della quale ciascun 'rottame' trova senso e funzione").

43. See Creighton E. Gilbert's pioneering discussion of Alberti's reshaping of classical models in "Antique Frameworks for Renaissance Art Theory: Alberti and Pino," *Marsyas* 3 (1943–45): 87–106. Gilbert points out that although the *De pictura* is "the very first work on a theoretical science in any modern language" (93), Alberti worked within the framework of the isogogic treatise of which Horace's *Art of Poetry* is a prominent example.

44. *L'Architettura (De re aedificatoria)* IX.v.812.

45. *L'Architettura di Leon Battista Alberti*, trans. Cosimo Bartoli 337.

46. Leoni, *The Ten Books of Architecture*, 194.

47. *L'Architettura (De re aedificatoria)* I.xxxiv.

48. Smith, *Architecture in the Culture of Early Humanism*, 85. But on this point, see Camporeale's discussion of Valla's application of rhetoric as *perfecta sapientia* to theology, "Lorenzo Valla tra Medioevo e Rinascimento: Encomion s. Thomae (1457)," 117–29.

49. Smith, *Architecture in the Culture of Early Humanism*, 94.

50. Ibid., 241–42.

51. S. Lang, "De Lineamentis: L. B. Alberti's Use of a Technical Term," *Journal of the Warburg and Courtald Institutes* 28 (1965). Lang's argument is supported by J. S. Ackerman, "Architectural Practice in the Italian Renaissance," *Journal of the Society of Architectural Historians* 13 (1954), 3–11, who argues that fifteenth-century architects appear to have worked from plans, not measured elevations.

52. Smith, *Architecture in the Culture of Early Humanism*, 84–85, argues that Alberti's source for his description by antitheses is Chrysoloras's description of Hagia Sofia in *Comparison of Old and New Rome* (1411).

53. Smith, *Architecture in the Culture of Early Humanism*, 87–96.

54. See Kruft, *History of Architectual Theory*, 42–43.

55. Aristotle, *The "Art" of Rhetoric* III.ix.9.

56. See also Dee's translation of the period in *The Matemathicall Praeface*, d.iiij.

57. Cf. *Orator* XXIV. 81 (365).

58. *De re aedificatoria* VI.ii.113.

59. *L'Architettura (De re aedificatoria)*, ed. Borghesi, I.i.19n.

60. Alberti, *Opere volgari. Rime e trattati morali*, II: 107–8. The Italian text is given in the appendix to this chapter.

61. Tasso, *Discorsi*, 21.

62. Smith, *Architecture in the Culture of Early Humanism*, 85.

63. Translation in ibid., 106.

64. Maren-Sofie Røstvig discusses this poem and poems by Rhabanus Maurous and others in the chapter "From Exegesis to Composition," in *Configurations*, 169–88.

65. Grayson quotes Landino's praise of Alberti's contribution to the study and practice of the vernacular: "notice with what industry he has contrived to transfer to our tongue all the eloquence, composition and nobility which is found in Latin." Trans. Cecil Grayson, *Leon Battista Alberti: On Painting*, 19.

66. *On Style* II.56, 337.

67. The end of the first paragraph and the beginning of the second are equally connected by the same technique, but here two of the elements have been inverted *("ragionamenti . . . Niccola . . . cose non accomodate* versus *Niccola . . . ragionamenti . . . non accomodatissimi")*.

68. Cf. Kenneth Clark, "Architectural Backgrounds in Renaissance Pictures," *Journal of the Royal Institute of British Architects* 41 (1934): 326–30.

69. "[T]empio" is repeated five times in the first half of the paragraph.

70. See John Onians' discussion of architecture and music in "On How to Listen to High Renaissance Art," *The Art Bulletin* 7, no. 4 (1984): 413.

71. See David Kipp, "Alberti's 'Hidden' Theory of Visual Art," *British Journal of Aesthetics* 24 (Summer 1984): 231–40. Kipp observes that "in the entire visual-artistic field, and actual cosmological 'unity' (the 'divine mind') that unfolds itself into actual architecture, actual sculptures, and actual paintings would be mirrored, and symmetrically reversed, by a painted surface that 'infolds' itself into painted sculptures, painted architecture, and a painted cosmological 'unity' (the vanishing point). In a sense, the whole arrangement could be seen as a symbolic structure enabling the 'God' at the heart of the universe to contemplate itself through the 'God' at the heart of the vanishing point" (238).

72. Tobin, "Leon Battista Alberti," xxx and 101. The reference is to *De pictura* I.3.27–29 and I.5.26–29.

73. The repetitions conform to the following prescription: "First of all your Ornaments must be exactly regular, and be perfectly distinct, and without Confusion. . . . Let the Builder fix his richest Ornaments in the principal Places" (Leoni, *Ten Books of Architecture*, IX.ix.204).

74. Rudolf Arnheim, *The Power of the Center: A Study of Composition in the Visual Arts* (Berkeley and Los Angeles: University of California Press, 1988).

75. Smith *Architecture in the Culture of Early Humanism*, 83, argues that the aesthetic experience Alberti recommends for churches in *De re aedificatoria* (VII.iii.543–45) corresponds to, and was perhaps inspired by, Augustine's description of his desired knowledge of God in *Soliloquies* I.iv-viii.

76. Kipp, "Alberti's 'Hidden' Theory of Visual Art," 231.

77. Smith, *Architecture in the Culture of Early Humanism*, 150–70.

78. Here Demetrius's description of the period glosses the inherent metaphor: "the image being that of paths traversed in an orb or circle" *(On Style* I.11.305).

79. The editors of the Loeb edition add the phrase "without likeness" to the first list, as the Greek text obviously has a lacuna that appears on comparing the first list of six properties to the second one of eight; it is the antithesis to "likeness" that is missing from the former. On the other hand, the editors add the term ("correspondence") to the second list, which clearly does not belong there. I am grateful to Ingrid Rowland, who explained the details in the Greek text to me.

80. For the visionary aspect of Brunelleschi's domes and their relation to Scripture, see Paul Barolsky, "The Visionary Experience of Renaissance Art," *Word & Image* 11 (April-June 1995): 174–81.

81. Smith, *Architecture in the Culture of Early Humanism*, 83.

82. Alberti heeds the advice of Cicero, who says that "[w]e must be careful to employ our thoughts on themes as elevating as possible and to keep our impulses under the control of reason." *De Officiis* I.xxxvii.132.

83. Smith, *Architecture in the Culture of Early Humanism*, 14.

84. Praz, *Mnemosyne*, 89.

85. See Hollingsworth, "The Architect in Fifteenth-Century Florence."

86. "Ma che sarà sì fastidioso che non approvi e lodi costui quale in sì compostissima opera pose sua industria e diligenza?" *Opere volgari* II: 161–62.

87. Erwin Panofsky, "Die Perspektive als 'Symbolische Form,'" *Vorträge der Bibliothek Warburg, 1924–1925*, ed. Fritz Saxl (Leipzig: Teubner, 1927), 258–330. See also S. K. Heninger Jr., "Alberti's Window: The Rhetoric of Perspective," *The Subtext of Form*, 155–95.

## CHAPTER 4

1. T. S. R. Boase, *Giorgio Vasari: The Man and the Book* (Princeton: Princeton University Press, 1979), 3.

2. "It would be too easy to dismiss Vasari as merely a disciple celebrating his master, since it is likely that his imaginative conception of Michelangelo influenced the way in which Michelangelo imagined himself. The relationship between the two is probably far more complex than we can ever know. . . . As Michelangelo initially shaped the manner in which Vasari wrote about him, Vasari's formulations may well have determined the ways in which Michelangelo conceived of himself." Paul Barolsky, *Michelangelo's Nose: A Myth and Its Maker* (University Park: The Pennsylvania State University Press, 1990), 62.

3. Barolsky, an acute critic and connoisseur of the *Vite*, summarizes Vasari's mythopoeic achievement as follows: "Vasari's *Lives* is unequivocally a history, though not a history of the kind modern art historians would write today. Why not, we may ask? Because Vasari's history is one rooted in fiction, filled with imaginary artists, events, epitaphs, tombs, emblems, speeches, anecdotes, and interpretations of works of art that transform their meaning, giving them new significance." Paul Barolsky, *Why Mona Lisa Smiles and Other Tales by Vasari* (University Park: The Pennsylvania State University Press, 1991), 108.

4. Patricia Lee Rubin, *Giorgio Vasari: Art and History* (New Haven and London: Yale University Press, 1995), "In Another's Dress: Vasari and the Writers of Histories," 148–86.

5. Ibid., 7.

6. See, for example, the work of Paola Barocchi, *Studi vasariani* (Torino: Einaudi, 1984), and *Le Vite de' più eccellenti pittori, scultori e architettori nelle redazioni del 1550 e 1568* (Florence: Studio per edizioni scelte, 1987).

7. Rubin defiantly declares that "Vasari's honor needs no apologist. I am enthusiast. Vasari did not pretend to be detached about his subject. Nor do I" (*Giorgio Vasari: Art and History*, 7).

8. Giovanni Previtali in L. Bellosi and A. Rossi, eds., *Le Vite . . . 1550*, Presentazione, vii-viii.

9. On the alignment between profane and sacred history, see *Configurations*, 347–54.

10. Paul Barolsky, *The Faun in the Garden, Michelangelo and the Poetic Origins of Italian Renaissance* Art (University Park, Pa.: The Pennsylvania State University Press, 1994), 140. Barolsky suggests that the Introit is based on a verse in the *Book of Wisdom*: "While all things were in quiet and silence and the night was in the midst of her course, Thy Almighty Word, O Lord, came down from heaven, from Thy Royal Throne."

11. Proemio, 7: "In all their actions noble minds are ablaze with a desire for glory, and do not renounce any effort, however great, to bring their works to the perfection that will make these stupendous and marvellous to all the world."

12. Thus Vasari writes: "l'altissimo Dio, fatto il gran corpo del mondo et ornato il cielo de' suoi chiarissimi lumi, discese con l'intelletto giú nella limpidezza dell' aere e nella solidità della terra e, formando l'uomo, scoperse con la vaga invenzione delle cose la prima forma della scoltura e della pittura" ("Proemio delle *Vite*," 111). In translation this is: "when the Almighty God, having made the great body of the world and having adorned the heavens with their exceeding bright lights, de-

scended lower with His intellect into the clearness of the air and the solidity of the earth, and shaping man, discovered, together with the lovely creation of all things, the first form of sculpture and painting." Trans. Bull, *Preface to the Lives*, 25.

13. *L'Idea della architettura universale*, XIV: 46.

14. *Michelangelo's Nose*, 91. This typological dimension was first pointed out in greater detail by Laura Riccò, *Vasari scrittore. La prima edizione del libro delle "Vite"* who (Roma: Bulzoni, 1976), has greatly advanced our understanding of Vasari as a literary artist.

15. *George Vasari et la vocabulaire de la antique d'art dans les "Vite"* (Grenoble: Elug, 1988), 6. Le Mollé writes that "[f]our centuries of Vasari interpretation has had relatively little to contribute to a deepened understanding of the language of the *Lives*" (my translation)(1988, p. 66).

16. Julian Kliemann, *Gesta dipinte. La grande decorazione nelle dimore italiane dal Quattrocento al Seicento* (Milan: Silvana Editoriale, 1993), 46.

17. See above, Chapter 3.

18. The concept "disegno interno" does not appear until Gabriele Paleotti in 1582 (*Discorso intorno alle imagini*, in Trattati d'arte del Cinquecento, ed. Paola Barocchi, 3 vols. 9 (Bari: Laterza, 1960–62), II: 138), and later in Zuccaro (1607), but it must have been implicit for centuries in the general reasoning attached to the concept of design or *lineamenta*; Geoffrey de Vinsauf is a case in point (see above, Chapter 2). For Vasari's use of the term *lineamento*, see his "Introduzione . . . alle tre arti del disegno," cap. XV: "lineamenti . . . servono cosí all'architettura e scultura come alla pittura; ma all'architittura massimamente, perciò che i disegni di quella non son composta se non de linee, il che non è altro, quanto a l'architettore, ch' il principio e fine di quell'arte," ed. Bettarini, *Le vite*, I: 112.

19. In reality the period is even longer; it begins with the following phrase: "Così, dunque, il primo modello, onde uscì la prima imagine dell'uomo fu una massa di terra: e non senza ragione" ("Thus, then, the first model whence there issued the first image of man was a lump of clay, and not without reason"). It should be noticed that only the part that compares God as architect to sculptors and painters is included in the elaborate rhetorical design. In the complete sentence, however, the initial reference to God's clay "modello" is echoed in the sculptors' "modelli" (II: 4).

20. *Vasari Scrittore*, 14: Riccò describes his syntax as "una costruzione per aggiunte successive che obbedisce alla volontà di rapprendere le vicende in spazio breve e sfocia in una paratassi spogliata anche di una variata iride lessicale."

21. The opening paragraph consists of three periods, two long ones divided by a shorter central one.

22. Previtali, *Le Vite . . . 1550*, "Presentazione," viii.

23. For this aspect, see Lawrence Rhu, *The Genesis of Tasso's Narrative Theory* (Detroit, Mich.: Wayne State University Press, 1993).

24. See Magne Malmanger's account of the use of "design" among Florentine theorists about the middle of the sixteenth century, "Between Renaissance and Baroque: Attitudes to Nature and the Concept of Nature," in *Contexts of Baroque Representation: Theatre, Metamorphosis, and Design*, ed. Roy Eriksen (Oslo: Novus Press, 1997), 38–41.

25. The cycle has recently been presented well by Kliemann, *Gesta dipinte*, 35–51.

26. Andrew Fichter, *Poets Historical: Dynastic Epic in the Renaissnance* (New Haven and London: Yale University Press, 1982).

27. *The Elements of Architecture*, Sig. A2 v.

28. I do not agree with Riccò, who stresses the work's paratactical organization and uniformity of style (*Vasari scrittore*, 14). While rightly emphasizing the dominance of "un registro espressivo tanto uniforme" ("uniform expressive register"), she nevertheless underestimates the function of ornatus in conjunction with *dispositio* in Vasari's work.

29. *Le vite*, III: 556.

30. Barolsky, *Michelangelo's Nose*, 108, 110.

31. Jonson makes the same point (*Timber, or, Discoveries*, 93), and his phrasing is close enough to Delminio's to suggest influence.

32. *Difesa dell'Orlando Furioso dell'Ariosto contra'l dialogo dell'epica poesia di Cammillo Pellegrino* (Ferrara: V. Baldini, 1586), 29.

33. Vossius, *Rhetorica*, IV: 1, 2–3.

34. *Sperone Speroni*, ed. Camporosano (1920), 132 ("the entire art of rhetoric depends on the site of the words"). The young Tasso, in his "Lezione sopra un sonetto di monsignore Giovanni Della Casa," stressed that verbal repetitions add to the poetic texture and presented a close textual analysis to underline his argument. See below in Chapter 5.

35. Ben Jonson, *Timber, or, Discoveries* Syracuse, N.Y.: Syracuse University Press, 1976), 93.

36. Quintilian, *Institutio oratoria* (IX.iv.521): "ideoque ex loco trans-feruntur in locum [verba], ut iungantur, quo congruunt maxime, sicut in structura saxorum rudium." See Onians ("Alberti and Filareth," 97–114) for Alberti's extensive use of Cicero's *De Officiis* in *De re aedificatoria*.

37. Scamozzi says that the creations of the orators only lack "body" (*corporeità*), *L'Idea universale*, 46.

38. Kliemann, *Gesta dipinte*. The Italian reads: "interpretare gli affreschi in una cornice retorica non solo perché rammentano noti topoi, ma anche perché la loro stessa disposizione può essere collegata a un procedimento retorico noto come ars memoriae" (46).

39. In view of Michelangelo's work on San Pietro between 1547 and 1564 the reference now seems conspicuously low-key: "la morte di Anton San Gallo gli ha fatto pigliar la cura della fabrica di Farnese del palazzo di Campo di Fiore e di quella di San Pietro" (III: 989). This lack of attention will be completely redressed in the the 1568 *Life* (see later in this chapter).

40. Of course, Michelangelo was seventy-five, not seventy-three, in 1550, and he was nearly ninety when he died.

41. *Vite*, III: 991.

42. He writes: "Questa opera mena prigioni legati quegli che di sapere l'arte si persuadono" ("this work keeps those who believe themselves to understand art in chains"). *Vite*, III: 985.

43. See, for example, Frank Kermode, *The Sense of an Ending: Studies in the Theory of Fiction* (1966; reprint, New York and Oxford: Oxford University Press, 1977); and Peter Brooks, *Reading for the Plot*.

44. Torquato Tasso, *La Cavaletta ovvero de la Toscana Poesia*, ed. Maier (1965), V:134.

45. See *Le Vite*, ed. Ragghianti, IV: 312–13.

46. This is seen also in the omission of the names of other pioneering artists toward the end of the first paragraph, where the 1550 version mentions Giotto, Donato, Filippo Brunelleschi, and Leonardo (III: 948).

47. See Blunt, *Artistic Theory in Italy, 1450–1600*, for the basic elements in post-Tridentine aesthetics that agree with the change of emphasis in Vasari's revisions.

48. Le Mollé, "Significato di LUCE e di LUME nelle VITE del Vasari," 173.

49. I am grateful to Patricia Rubin, who suggested that the architectural practice of Vasari during the 1560s also may have a lot to do with his emphasis on utility and design in his writings, a change in interest that is notable in his revisions in the lives of several architects for the 1568 edition.

50. C. Conforti, *Giorgio Vasari architetto* (Milan: Electa, 1993), 39.

51. Patricia Lee Rubin, "'What Men Saw': Vasari's Life of Leonardo da Vinci and the Image of the Renaissance Artist," *Art History* 13 (1990): 33–45.

52. *Michelangelo's Nose*, 52.

53. This analogue also extends the opening period and the final mention of Vasari's monument to Michelangelo, both of which focus on the latter's embodiment of the three arts. Barolsky notes

the following regarding the funerary monument: "Vasari alludes to the mystery of the Trinity to suggest the aesthetic trinity of the arts, all mysteriously united in *disegno*. In the *Faun in the Garden*, 141.

54. Rubin, "What Men Saw," 43.

55. *Giorgio Vasari: Art and History*, 188.

## CHAPTER 5

1. *Il Combattimento* was not published until 1638 as a part *of Madrigali guerrieri ed amorosi*, ed. F. Malipiero, 8 (Milan: Treves, 1929). The first performance was in Venice in 1624.

2. "Posta in musica: Tasso's Paragone and Monteverdi's Combattimento," *EST* X: Stil og Maniera. Grunnlagsproblemer i estetisk forskning, ed. K. Gundersen and S. Wikshåland (Oslo, 1994), 83–108. The article is discussed by G. Careri, "Tancrède et Clorinde: surprise, pressentiment, répétition," *La Surprise, actes du 6 colloque du Cicada*, ed. B. Rougé (Paris, 1998), 201–6, and more recently by Stefano La Via, "Le Combat retrouvé. Les 'passions contraires' du 'divin Tasse' dans la représentation musicale de Monteverdi," in *La Jérusalem délivrée du Tasse. Poésie, peinture, musique, ballet*, ed. Giovanni Careri (Paris: Musée de Louvre, 1999), 109–57 (esp. 142–49).

3. Paolo Emilio, "Tasso e la seconda pratica," ed. Maria Antonella Balsano and Thomas Walker, in *Tasso, la musica, i musicisti* (Florence: Olschki, 1988), 1–15. See L. Bianconi, "I fasti musicali del Tasso nei secoli XVI e XVII," in *Torquato Tasso tra letteratura, musica, teatro e arti figurative*, ed. A. Buzzoni (Bologna: Nuova Alfa Editoriale, 1985), 143–50.

4. Paolo Emilio Carapezza, "Tasso e la seconda pratica" in *Tasso, la musica, i musicisti*, ed. Maria Antonella Balsano and Thomas Walker (Florence: Olschki, 1988), 1: "le parole come cellule sonore da comporre, come elementi musicali da combinare."

5. See Gerard LeCoat, *The Rhetoric of the Arts, 1550–1650* (Bern and Frankfurt: Lang, 1975), a work that—despite its obvious merits—has been overlooked by later critics. Paolo Emilio Carapezza, "Tasso e la Seconda Pratica"; Dean T. Mace, "Tasso, *La Gerusalemme liberata*, and Monteverdi," in *Studies in the History of Music 1, Music and Language* (New York: Broude Brothers, 1983), 137; and Gavriel Moses, "Tasso to Monteverdi: Intertextual Poetics," *Studies in the Italian Renaissance: Essays in Memory of Arnolfo B. Ferruolo*, ed. Gian Paolo Biasin, Albert N. Mancini, and Nicholas J. Perella (Naples: Società Editrice napoletana, 1986), 245–59. The most recent major study is by Stefano La Via, "Le Combat retrouvé. Les 'passions contraires' du 'divin Tasse' dans la représeentation musicale de Monteverdi" (see note 2).

6. Varese summarizes mixed unity as follows: "When defining the coexistence and relationship between a unified or multiple style, he confronts a problem typical in cinquecento history, the problem of the disruption of equilibrium, convenience, and Renaissance harmony, as these concepts had been summarized, established, and practiced by Bembo" (my translation); Claudio Varese, *Torquato Tasso: Epos, Parola, Scena* (Messina and Florence: G. D'Anna, 1976), 34.

7. For Tasso's poetics, see B. T. Sozzi, "La poetica del Tasso," *Studi Tassiani* 5 (1955): 3–58, and "Introduzione ai *Discorsi dell'arte poetica* del Tasso," *Studi Tassiani* 26 (1977): 5–38.

8. Judith A. Kates, *Tasso and Milton: The Problem of Christian Epic* (Lewisburg, Pa.: Bucknell University Press; London: Associated University Presses, 1983), 50–65.

9. Today we know how similar and contrasting episodes in the *Gerusalemme* are combined in an overall structure according to the compositional ideal expressed in *La Cavaletta* and the *Discorsi*. Tasso arranged the epic's twenty cantos according to a principle of mirror symmetry, an arrangement clearly inspired by classical precedent—*The Aeneid*, in particular. Fredi Chiapelli, "Struttura inventiva e struttura espressiva *nella Gerusalemme liberata*," *Studi Tassiani* 15 (1964–65): 15–18, referred to the "connessioni diametrali" in the poem, and Giovanni Getto, *Nel Mondo della Gerusalemme* (Florence: Olschki, 1967), commented on the symmetrical distribution of some ottave in the very *paragone* episode, while carrying out an in-depth analysis of verbal texture and mood. Claudio Varese,

*Torquato Tasso: Epos, Parola, Scena* (1976), observed that "[l]a ripetizione diventa nella *Gerusalemme* un'eco, una risonanza insieme una connessione, un attivo strumento dell'unità." Such observations are later paralleled and reinforced by Andrew Fichter, "Tasso's Epic of Deliverance," *PMLA* 93 (March 1978): 265–74; and Maren-Sofie Røstvig, "Canto Structure in Tasso and Spenser," *Spenser Studies: A Poetry Annual* 1 (1980): 177–200, and *Configurations: A Topomorphical Approach to Renaissance Poetry* (Oslo: Scandinavian University Press, 1994). Fichter pointed out that the *Liberata*'s "symmetry is . . . an expression in poetic form of the poem's concept of deliverance," while Røstvig studied Tasso's poetic practice in the *Gerusalemme* and *Il Mondo Creato*, proving the importance of Tasso's canto structure for Spenser's technique in *The Faerie Queene*. My previous work (1987, 1991, and so on) focuses on dramatic structure and elocutio in rhetorically patterned episodes in the *Liberata* (for example, in *The Forme of Faustus Fortunes*, chap. 3).

10. "Il nasconder dunque l'inganno e, per così dire, la dissimulazione de l'arte è sommo artificio, "*La Cavaletta, Opere,* V: 137. This is an important point of Mannerist poetics; see, for example, Giordano Bruno's "De vinculi in genere" (c. 1590), in *De magia, De vinculis in genere,* ed. Albano Biondi (Pordenone: Edizioni Bibliotheca dell'Immagine, 1986).

11. See the statement "[S]i dee schivare la repetizione, l'equivocazione e l'asperità de le rime" ("One should avoid repetitious, ambiguous, and harsh rhymes"), *La Cavaletta, Opere,* V: 121.

12. The English translation of M. Cavalchini and I. Samuel reads: "The art of composing a poem resembles the plan of the universe, which is composed of contraries, as that of music is" (*Discourses on the Heroic Poem,* III.76). Note also that the plot of a poem, which according to Aristotle is the soul of a tragedy, is therefore like the human soul composed "di numeri armonici, e di musiche proporzioni."

13. I cite the English translation in Torquato Tasso, *Discourses on the Heroic Poem,* trans. M. Cavalchini and I. Samuel (Oxford: University Press, 1973), 201–2: "apart from this the texture of eight verses is spacious, because the number eight, according to the arithmeticians, is the first among the solid and cubic numbers. It is also perfect and adapted to receiving action since it is composed of even and uneven numbers, from finite and non-finite ones, for this reason the number eight is also perfect, because what you compose with a doubled quaternion forms a most sold web, and that is so also with a quadrupled binary, and apart from that from the numbers three and five, being the first of the even numbers." For the Italian original, see *Prose,* ed. Francesco Flora (Milan and Rome: Rizzoli, 1935), 6:533–34.

14. For earlier treatises on proportion, see Fabrizio Della Seta, "Proportio," in *Cantu et Sermone: For Nino Pirrotta on His 80th Birthday,* ed. Fabrizio Della Seta and Franco Piperino (Florence: Olschki, 1985), 75–99.

15. Ingrid D. Rowland, "Raphael, Angelo Colocci, and the Genesis of the Architectural Orders," 82.

16. *La Cavaletta, Opere,* V: 110–11. An English translation would be "[h]e considerably enhances the grandeur of the ending of the sonnet in his choice of words and lights and ornaments, and particularly with the richness of the consonants, the number and the sound of the lines."

17. See *La Cavaletta,* V: 117. On Dante's various definitions, see Alfredo Schiaffini, "Poesis e poeta in Dante," in *Studia philologica et literaria in honorem Leo Spitzer* (Bern: Francke, 1958), 379–89.

18. *Opere di Monsignore Giovanni Della Casa,* I: 373.

19. See S. K. Heninger Jr., *The Subtext of Form in the English Renaissance: Proportion Poetical* (University Park: The Pennsylvania State University Press, 1994), 75ff.

20. See below, Chapter 6.

21. "[I]l valore e la lode di Mons. della Casa, non solo nella forma esteriore, e ne i lineamenti di questa sua poetica pittura, e nella semplice tessitura e ordine delle scielte parole, e cadenze gravi, e versi intercisi consiste, ma eziandio nella profonda dottrina, e negli alti sentimenti, e misterj che sotto questi rinchiude, è risposta." Cited in *Opere di Monsignore Giovanni Della Casa,* I: 379.

These are qualities Benedetto Varchi had praised in an earlier "Lettura" concerned with another Della Casa sonnet, "Cura, che di timor ti nutri, e cresci." Varchi comments directly on the repetition of the word *ivi* three times at the center of the sonnet ("non senza grazia, e giudicio sia stata replicata tre volte la particella") and on the manner in which the beginning, the middle, and the end correspond: "Questa quarta, e ultima parte confacendosi mirabilmente col principio, e col mezzo, secondo il precetto di Orazio: *primum ne medio, medium ne siscrepet imo." Lettura alle rime di M. Della Casa,* I: 334–35.

22. The Italian reads: "e farò a guisa di Pittore, che ristretto fra i termini d'una picciola tela, accenna con brevi linee solamente i lontani delli edifici, de' paesi, e il rimanente all' imaginazione de' riguardanti rimette." *Opere di Monsignore Giovanni Della Casa,* I: 361.

23. Tasso, *Il Carrafà o vero de la epica poesia,* vol. 3 of *Trattati di poetica e di retorica del 500,* ed. Bernard Weinberg, 309–44.

24. Pellegrino writes: "immaginatevi che la Gerusalemme liberata sia una fabrica di non tanta grandezza, ma bene intesa, con le misure, & proportioni di architettura; et adorna secondo il convenevole di veri fregi, & colori" (ibid., 318).

25. Speroni, *Opere,* ed. Camporosano (1920), 132. For Tasso's view, see *Discorsi del poema eroico,* IV: 452: "Io dico che l'elocuzione altro non è che un accoppiamento di parole" ("I say that elocution is nothing but a combination of words" [my translation]). He aligns this coupling with the world made by the four elements. The ultimate source is Quintilian, *Institutes* (IX.iv.521).

26. He states, for example, that "the beginning of poems should be full of grandeur, magnificence, and splendor, like the facade of palaces." *Discorsi del poema eroico,* 21. In the dialogue *Il Ficino overo de l'arte* he argues that " 'l fine di ciascuna [arte] è drizzato al fine de la sua principale, ch'è quasi architettonica" ("the purpose of every art is aimed at its principal end, that is almost architectonic"); *Opere,* V: 388.

27. *Prose,* 412.

28. Ben Jonson, *Timber; or, Discoveries,* 92–93.

29. Translated by John Shearman, *Mannerism* (Harmondsworth: Penguin, 1966), 161.

30. See Eriksen, "God Enthroned: Continuity and Change in Ariosto, Tasso, and Milton," 405–25.

31. *L'arte poetica,* "Discorso terzo," 47: "necessaria è in lui l'energia, la quale sì con parole pone inanzi a gli occhi la cosa che pare altrui non di udirla, ma vederla."

32. See the account in Dario Rastelli, "Tasso e Monteverdi: Il Combattimento di Tancredi e Clorinda," in *Monteverdi e il suo tempo,* ed. Raffaello Monterosso (Verona: Valdonega, 1969), 557–69.

33. At the same time, the violent ottava 49.7–8 links antithetically to the subdued mood of the transitional ottava by means of a web of repeated key words (70.5–6).

34. Rhu, *The Genesis of Tasso's Narrative Theory,* 35.

35. The Italian text reads: "Mentre egli il suon de' sacri detti sciolse, / colei di gioia tramutossi, e rise; / e in atto di morir lieto e vivace, / dir parea: 'S'apre il cielo; io vado in pace.' "

36. I here agree with the view presented by Getto and later repeated by Rastelli.

37. Tasso's text reads: "pregoti (se fra l'arme han loco i preghi) / ch 'l tuo nome 'l tuo stato a me tu scopra, / acciò ch'io sappia, o vinto o vincitore, / chi la morte o la vittoria onore. / Risponde la feroce:—Indarno chiedi / quel che per uso di non far palese. // Ma chiunque io mi sia, tu inanzi vedi / un di quei due che la gran torre accese" (60.4–8; 61.1–4).

38. Tasso invented a double peripety in the *Liberata* XI and XVIII. LeCoat suggests that the peripety coincides with the present episode (XII.64; "Ma ecco omai l'ora fatale è giunta"), but it can be seen as a secondary peripety. For double peripeties, see Eriksen, *The Forme of Faustus Fortunes,* 112–15.

39. The Italian reads: "Oh nostra folle / mente ch'ogn 'aura di *fortuna* estolle! / Misero, di che godi? oh quanto mesti / fiano i trionfi ed infelice il vanto!" (italics added).

40. Getto singled out the parallels between ottave 55 and 66, 57 and 64, 58 and 67–69, and ot-

tave 61 and 69, but he does not pursue his observation in a systematic fashion. See *Nel Mondo della Gerusalemme*, 148–53. For details, see my account in "Posta in musica."

41. Alastair Fowler, *Triumphal Forms*, 34–61.

42. See my *Forme of Faustus Fortunes*, 103ff.

43. See Maria Rika Maniates, *Mannerism in Italian Music and Culture, 1530–1630* (Manchester: Manchester University Press, 1979), 302–30.

44. Not only is she evocative of the Amazon queen killed by Herakles, she is also a divine agent; see Antonella Perelli, "La 'divina' Clorinda," *Studi Tassiani* 39 (1991): 45–76.

45. Tasso, *Discorsi*, 21.

46. Tasso also marks the lineaments of his mini-drama by a configuration of rhymes, tracing its triangular trajectory somewhat imprecisely. The repetitions are distributed as follows:

| Stanzas | | rhymes/rhyme words |
|---|---|---|
| 51 | a | uccise (line 7), mise (line 8) |
| 55 | b | moto (7), vòto (8) |
| 56 | c | vendetta (1), fretta (3), ristretta (5) |
| 58 | d | essangue (1), langue (3), sangue (5) |
| 61 | c¹ | m'alletta (7), vendetta (8) |
| 63 | b¹ | Noto (1), moto (3), vòto (5) |
| 68 | a¹ | mise (2), uccise (4), rise (6) |
| 70 | d¹ | langue (7), sangue (8) |

We note that the repetitions enclose the entire episode (51–70), reaching its peak in ottava 58 with rhymes *(langue-sangue)* that also conclude the episode.

47. Ruscelli, *Del modo di comporre in versi italiani* (Venice, 1558); and Daniel, *A Defence of Rome* (London, 1601).

48. Eriksen, *The Forme of Faustus Fortunes*, 103–32, and "'What resting place is this?': Time and Place in *Dr. Faustus (B)*," *Renaissance Drama* 16 (1985): 49–74. In general, Italian poetic practice differs on this point from English Renaissance practice. Italian poets distribute their signs much more subtly, often shying away from repeated rhyme words, preferring conceptual or verbal repetitions within lines to establish relationships between parts and to direct the reader's attention, as in Tasso's general practice. This difference is seen in Edward Fairfax's translation (1600) and in Spenser's *The Faerie Queene*, which both repeat identical rhymes more often than Tasso; see Røstvig, *Configurations*, 267–370.

49. These links are forged with chiastic patterns or sequential repetitions, an obvious instance being found in XII.52–53.

50. Francesco de Sanctis, *History of Italian Literature*, trans. Joan Redfern, 2 vols. (New York: Harcourt, Brace, and Company, 1931), 2:665.

51. On this general issue, see, for example, Paul Grendler, *Schooling in Renaissance Italy: Literacy and Learning, 1300–1600* (Baltimore: Johns Hopkins University Press, 1989).

52. Not only does the rhyme *moto-noto* disappear, but so also do *sangue-langue* and *uccise-mise*, leaving only one of Tasso's significant rhyme-repetitions *(vendetta)* intact in ottave 5:1 and 10:8.

## CHAPTER 6

1. For this topos, see Psalms 13, 33 and 101.

2. John Steadman's examination of the relationship between Milton's poem and an impressive

body of Renaissance critical theory has demonstrated once and for all Milton's response to, and interpretation of, the works of leading cinquecento theorists, among them influential poets like Torquato Tasso (*Epic and Tragic Structure in Paradise Lost* (Chicago: University of Chicago Press, 1976), 1–19). Tasso is discussed throughout. For an excellent introduction to Tasso's poetics, see Lawrence Rhu, *The Genesis of Tasso's Narrative Theory.*

3. The editions consulted are: John Milton, *Paradise Lost*, ed. Alastair Fowler (London: Longman Group, 1976); Lodovico Ariosto, *Orlando Furioso*, in *Opere*, ed. Adriano Seroni (Milan: University of Mursia, 1970); John Harington, *Orlando Furioso in English Heroical Verse* (London, 1591), The English Experience 259 (New York: Da Capo Press, 1972); Barbara Reynolds, trans., *Orlando Furioso (The Frenzy of Orlando): A Romantic Epic by Lodovico Ariosto* (Harmondsworth: Penguin, 1975); Torquato Tasso, *La Gerusalemme liberata*, ed. Lanfranco Caretti (Torino: Giulio Einaudi, 1971); and Edward Fairfax, *Jerusalem Delivered* (1600), ed. Robert Weiss (New York: Centaur Press, 1962).

4. See Reynolds, *Orlando Furioso*, 1.78–79.

5. Unless otherwise stated, the translation is my own.

6. Note that Ariosto connects the middle of the stanza with the end by means of the rhetorical figure *epanados* ("Dio," line 5, and "divino," line 8).

7. Relying on the authority of Aristotle and contemporary theorists, Harington claims that "an heroicall Poem (a well as a Tragedie) [should] be full of Peripet[e]ia." For multiple peripeteias in Tasso, see *The Forme of Faustus Fortunes*, 112–14. For *peripeteias* in Milton, see Steadman, *Epic and Tragic Structure*, 41–59.

8. Ariosto aligns the furious battle around the walls of Paris with the storm that rages within Orlando's mind. Harington foregrounds this alignment by beginning his stanza 61 ("Now in this time to Paris siege was layd") with words that link up with the first line of stanza 63 ("Now lay Orlando on his restlesse bed").

9. Translated by Fairfax, 275.

10. Eriksen, " 'What resting place is this?' Time and Place in *Doctor Faustus*," 51–54.

11. See *The Forme of Faustus Fortunes*, 112–14.

12. See *Inferno* 10.11, where Dante mentions "Iosafàt" as the place from which the souls return after the day of universal judgment; *La Divina Commedia*, ed. Alberto Chiari (Sesto San Giovanni: Bietti, 1974), 56.

13. The balanced rhyme-scheme of the octave in a sonnet invites such patterning, but rhetorical structures enclosing a sonnet as a whole may occasionally be found as early as in *Il Canzoniere*, ed. Marcazzan (494), where Sonetto 352 displays a chiasmus ("dolcemente" [1], " 'l sole" [2], " 'l sol" [13], and "dolce" [14]) and a central accent through a pun in verse 7 ("sole"). For further cinquecento examples, see above in Chapters 1, 2, and 5.

14. This line deserves a comment of its own. The three verbs—"dà legge," "orna," and "produce"—reflect on the shaping power of the Trinity: to create, adorn, and give laws. And we note that their distribution within the chiasmus itself forms the harmonious proportion 1 : 2. Fairfax too tries to play similar structural games in his rendering of this stanza, but without quite matching Tasso's art.

15. Chiappelli, "Struttura inventiva e struttura espressiva nella *Gerusalemme liberata*," 15–18.

16. This musical "report" also contributes to linking the last two lines of the topos more closely to its main textual body. Similarly, "seggio" in the segment's second line connects with, and is a variation of, "[s]edea" in the third.

17. Tasso joins the end of the epic's "first movement" (Cantos 1–10) to the beginning of its processional centerpiece with a set of seemingly insignificant repetitions. Yet they are not insignificant, for they work on the reader's memory and create coherence. Thus, the words underlined in the final line in Canto 10: "*ma i suoi pensieri* in lui [that is, Piero] dormir non ponno" ("but his thoughts in him could not sleep") turn up again in the two first lines of Canto 11, immediately before Piero enters the

scene again at 11.1.4: *"Ma 'l capitan de le cristiane genti, / vólto avendo a l'assalto ogni pensiero"* ("But the leader of the Christian peoples having turned his every thought to the attack").

18. Because the context involves the Trinity, it could be argued that Fairfax creates two "trinitarian" verb clusters: "He ruleth, blesseth, keepeth" (56.2) and "He tosseth, tumbleth, turneth" (57.3).

19. In accordance with Augustine's argument in the *De Trinitate* XV.xx.39, Tasso may here have intended Fate, Nature, and Fortune to be an analogue or a type of the Trinity, to whom he refers in the preceding line.

20. On the principle of enfolding in connection with the Trinity, see Edgar Wind, *Pagan Mysteries in the Renaissance* (Harmondsworth: Penguin, 1966), 120ff. The verb "s'involve" strengthens the suggestion that here we have an example of enfolding.

21. We also recall Fairfax's rendering of Tasso at this point: "The Lord of heaven meanwhile upon this fight / From his high throne bent down his gracious sight" (55.7–8).

22. We know that Milton echoes Tasso in connection with other topoi. Theodore M. Anderson, "Claudian, Tasso, and the Topography of Milton's Paradise," *MLN* 91 (December 1976): 1569–71, argues that Tasso's description of Armida's mountain (Canto 15.55–57) provides the source for Satan's first view of Eden in *Paradise Lost* 4.131–1435.

23. In *Triumphal Forms* (132) Fowler uses this term to describe the centralized temporal scheme of *Paradise Lost*. Fowler also discusses central emphasis in Book 11, lines 388–407 (118).

24. Eriksen, "God Enthroned," 411–14.

25. The phrase "onely two" (65) embodies the same play on the diapason. Augustine discusses this phenomenon on a number of occasions, for example, *De trinitate* 4.2 and *Enarrationes in psalmos*, "In psalmum LVIII" and "In psalmum CXXIX."

26. See Augustine, *De Trinitate* XV.xx.39, as quoted by Røstvig in *Configurations*, 79. Røstvig points out that Augustine has three groups of three verbs and one group of three nouns.

27. In "Gascoignes good morow," lines 28–29, the rhyme-word "face" surprisingly occurs twice, thus breaking the established rhyme-scheme in stanza 4 on divine revelation. Gascoigne makes an elaborate system of rhetorical markers center on this stanza, which divides the poem into a sequence of 3:1:6 stanzas. See Eriksen, "Two into One," 275–98. See also Røstvig on Spenser, "The Shepheardes Calender: A Structural Analysis," 49–75.

28. Fowler argues that *Paradise Lost* retains "some mannerist complexities of structure" (*Triumphal Forms*, 116–17); one instance is the double center containing the Raphael episode. For a recent discussion of the epic's double center, see Røstvig, *Configurations*, 461ff.

29. Røstvig, *Configurations*, 461–534.

30. Hermogenes, *Ars oratoria absolutissima*, uses this term about *epanalepsis* employed over a long distance (1.11.337).

31. Christopher Ricks, *Milton's Grand Style* (New York: Oxford University Press, 1972), 140.

32. Fowler, *Paradise Lost*, 820.

33. Note, though, that the word "heaven" also occurs at the end of lines 79, 113, and 160.

34. See Sanford Budick, *The Dividing Muse: Images of Divine Disjunction in Milton's Poetry* (New Haven and London: Yale University Press, 1986).

35. There are of course two redeemers: Satan and Christ. Satan's offer is presented at 2.465ff., where his offer points forward to Christ's offer in Book 3 and also to that at 6.801–23.

36. For Gascoigne, see Eriksen, "Two into One: The Unity of Gascoigne's Poems," and for Spenser, see Røstvig, "Canto Structure in Tasso and Spenser," and Eriksen, "Spenser's Mannerist Manoeuvres: *Prothalamion* (1595)," *Studies in Philology* 90 (Spring 1994): 143–75.

37. See Eriksen, *The Forme of Faustus Fortunes*, chap. 7, and "Ars Combinatoria: Marlowe's Humanist Poetics," passim.

38. *Four Stages of Renaissance Style*, 214.

39. E. A. Armstrong, *Shakespeare's Imagination*, 140.

## EPILOGUE

1. Alberti finished the Latin version of his treatise in 1435, so the manuscript tells us, and the Italian version probably followed the year after. A number of manuscripts exist, but it is surprising that the treatise did not appear in print before well into the next century, actually about the same time Vasari finished the second version of the *Lives*.

2. The *velo* is a frame to which is fixed "a thin veil, finely woven, dyed whatever colour pleases you and with larger threads [marking out] as many parallel as you prefer. . . . On panels or walls, divided into similar parallels, you will be able to put everything in its place." Quoted from Leon Battista Alberti, *On Painting*, trans. John R. Spencer (New Haven and London: Yale University Press, 1970), 68, 69.

3. *Il grande dizionario Garzanti della lingua italiana* (UTET: Torino, 1987) gives *germano* as "che e nato dagli stessi genitori: fratello germano" (803).

4. See, for example, Paul Barolsky, *Giotto's Father and the Family of Vasari's Lives* (University Park: The Pennsylvania State University Press, 1992), the final volume of his Vasari trilogy, and Patricia Lee Rubin, *Giorgio Vasari: Art and History* (New Haven and London: Yale University Press, 1995), who discusses the related Ciceronian concept of *amicitia* or friendship.

5. *Le vite*, ed. Bettarini, I: 112 ("servono così all'architettura e scultura come alla pittura: ma all'architettura massimamente").

Ackerman, J. S. "Architectural Practice in the Italian Renaissance." *Journal of the Society of Architectural Historians* 13 (1954): 3–11.

Alberti, Leon Battista. *L'Architettura (De re aedificatoria)*. 2 vols. Ed. Giovanni Orlandi and Paolo Portoghesi. 1485. Reprint, Milan: Edizioni il Polifilo, 1966.

———. *L'Architettura di Leon Battista Alberti*. Trans. Cosimo Bartoli. Venice: Francesco Franceschi, 1565.

———. *Opere volgari. Rime e trattati morali*. 3 vols. Ed. Cecil Grayson. Bari: Laterza, 1966.

———. *The Ten Books of Architecture by Leone Battista Alberti*. Trans. James Leoni. 1726. Reprint, London: Alec Tiranti, 1965.

Alighieri, Dante. *La Divina Commedia*. Ed. Alberto Chiari. Sesto San Giovanni: Bietti, 1974.

Allen, Peter L. "Ars amandi, Ars Legendi." *Exemplaria* 1 (March 1989): 181–205.

Altman, Joel B. *The Tudor Play of Mind: Rhetorical Inquiry and the Development of Elizabethan Drama*. Berkeley and Los Angeles: University of California Press, 1978.

Ariosto, Lodovico. *Orlando Furioso (The Frenzy of Orlando): A Romantic Epic by Lodovico Ariosto*. Trans. Barbara Reynolds. Harmondsworth: Penguin, 1975.

———. *Orlando Furioso. Opere*. Ed. Adriano Seroni. Milan: Mursia, 1970.

Ariosto, Orazio. *Difesa dell'Orlando Furioso dell'Ariosto contra 'l dialogo dell'epica poesia di Cammillo Pellegrino*. Ferrara: V. Baldini, 1586.

Aristotle. *The Art of Rhetoric*. Ed. J. H. Freese. Cambridge, Mass.: Harvard University Press; London: Heinemann, 1926.

———. *Nichomachean Ethics*. Trans. M. Rackham. 1926. Reprint, London: Heinemann, 1956.

Armstrong, E. A. *Shakespeare's Imagination*. Lincoln: University of Nebraska Press, 1983.

Arnheim, Rudolf. *The Power of the Center: A Study of Composition in the Visual Arts*. Berkeley and Los Angeles: University of California Press, 1988.

Augustinus, Aurelius. *The City of God Against the Pagans*. 7 vols. Trans. William M. Green. London: Heinemann, 1963.

———. *Enarrationes in psalmos*, 3 vols., ed. D. E. Dekkers and I. Fraipont (Turholti, 1956).

———. *La Foi Chretiénne*. Vol. 8 of *Oeuvres de Saint Augustin*. Ed. J. Pegon, S.J. Paris: Desclée de Brouwer, 1951.

———. *On Freedom of the Will*. Ed. Ann S. Benjamin and L. H. Hackstaff. Indianapolis: Bobbs-Merrill, 1964.

———. *De musica. Sancti Aurelii Augustini Opera omnia*. Ed. J. P. Migne. Paris, 1841.

———. *The Trinity*. Trans. Stephen McKenna. Washington, D.C.: Catholic University of America Press, 1970.

Baehrens, Aemilius, ed. *Fragmenta Poetrum Romanorum*. Leipzig Batavorum, 1886.

Baldwin, C. S. *Medieval Rhetoric and Poetic (to 1400)*. New York: Macmillan, 1928.

Barocchi, Paola, ed. *Le Vite de' più eccellenti pittori, scultori e architettori nelle redazioni del 1550 e 1568*. Florence: Studio per edizioni scelte, 1987.

———. *Studi vasariani*. Torino: Einaudi, 1984.

Barolsky, Paul. *The Faun in the Garden, Michelangelo and the Poetic Origins of Italian Renaissance Art.* University Park, Pa.: The Pennsylvania State University Press, 1994.

———. *Giotto's Father and the Family of Vasari's Lives.* University Park, Pa.: The Pennsylvania State University Press, 1992.

———. *Michelangelo's Nose: A Myth and Its Maker.* University Park: The Pennsylvania State University Press, 1990.

———. "The Visionary Experience of Renaissance Art." *Word & Image* 11 (April-June 1995): 174–81.

———. *Why Mona Lisa Smiles and Other Tales by Vasari.* University Park: The Pennsylvania State University Press, 1991.

Baxandall, Michael. *Giotto and the Orators: Humanist Observers of Painting in Italy and the Discovery of Pictorial Composition, 1350–1450.* Oxford: Clarendon, 1971.

Berger, Karol. "Narrative and Lyric." In *Musical Humanism and Its Legacy: Essays in Honor of Claude V. Palisca,* ed. Nancy Kovaleff Baker and Barbara Russano Hanning, 451–470. Stuyvesant, N.Y.: Pedigree Press, 1992.

Berry, Lloyd E., ed. *The Geneva Bible: A Facsimile of the 1560 Edition.* Madison, Milwaukee, and London: University of Milwaukee Press, 1969.

Bianconi, L. "I fasti musicali del Tasso nei secoli XVI e XVII." In *Torquato Tasso tra letteratura, musica, teatro e arti figurative,* ed. A. Buzzoni, 143–50. Bologna: Nuova Alfa Editoriale, 1985.

Blunt, Anthony. *Artistic Theory in Italy, 1450–1600.* New York: Oxford University Press, 1962.

———. "Des origines de la critique et de l'histoire de l'art en Angleterre." *Revue de l'art* 30, no. 3 (1975): 3–16.

Boase, T. S. R. *Giorgio Vasari: The Man and the Book.* Princeton: Princeton University Press, 1979.

Bolten, Jaap. "Ut Grammatica Pictura: A Method of Learning." *Ars auro prior* (1981): 71–74.

Bongo, Pietro. *Mysticae numerorum significatione liber.* Bergamo, 1591.

Bradford, Alan T. "Drama and Architecture Under Elizabeth I: The 'Regular' Phase." *English Literary Renaissance* 14, no. 1 (1984): 3–28.

Brooks, Peter. *Reading for the Plot: Design and Intention in Narrative.* New York: Vintage Books, 1985.

Budick, Sanford. *The Dividing Muse: Images of Divine Disjunction in Milton's Poetry.* New Haven and London: Yale University Press, 1986.

Buonarroti, Michelangelo. *The Poetry of Michelangelo: An Annotated Translation.* Trans. James M. Saslow. New Haven and London: Yale University Press, 1991.

Cairns, Francis. *Tibullus: A Hellenistic Poet at Rome.* Cambridge: Cambridge University Press, 1979.

Camporeale, Salvatore. *Lorenzo Valla tra Medioevo e Rinascimento. Encomion s. Thomae (1457).* Memorie Domenicane, n.s., 7 (1976).

Carapezza, Paolo Emilio. "Tasso e la seconda pratica." In *Tasso, la musica, i musicisti,* ed. Maria Antonella Balsano and Thomas Walker, 1–15. Florence: Olschki, 1988.

Cardini, Roberto. *Mosaici. Il "nemico" dell'Alberti.* Rome: Bulzoni Editore, 1990.

Careri, G. "Tancrède et Clorinde: surprise, pressentiment, répétition." In *La Surprise, actes du 6 colloque du Cicada,* ed. B. Rougé, 201–6. Paris, 1998.

Cartari, Vincentio. *Le Imagini de i dei de gli antichi* (Venice: Vincentio Valgrisi, 1556, 1571). New York: Garland Publishing, 1976.

Castelvetro, Lodovico. *Poetica d'Aristotile volgarizzata e sposta.* Vienna, 1570.

Cave, Terence. *The Cornucopian Text: Problems of Writing in the French Renaissance.* Oxford: Clarendon, 1979.

Chiappelli, Fredi. "Struttura inventiva e struttura espressiva *nella Gerusalemme liberata.*" *Studi Tassiani* 15 (1964–65): 15–18.

Cicero, Marcus Tullius. *De natura deorum.* Trans. H. C. P. McGregor. Harmondsworth: Penguin, 1972.

———. *De Officiis.* Trans. Walter Miller. 1913. Reprint, Cambridge, Mass.: Harvard University Press, 1990.

———. *Orator.* Trans. H. B. Hubbell. London: Heinemann, 1939.

Clark, Kenneth. "Architectural Backgrounds in Renaissance Pictures." *Journal of the Royal Institute of British Architects* 41 (1934): 326–30.

Clark, S. L., and Julian Wasserman. "The Significance of Thresholds in the Pearl Poet's *Purity.*" *Interpretation* 12 (1980): 114–27.

Conforti, C. *Giorgio Vasari architetto.* Milan: Electa, 1993.

Crawford, Donna. "The Architectonics of Cleanness." *Studies in Philology* 90, no. 4 (1993): 29–45.

Daniel, Samuel. *A Defence of Ryme* (1603). Elizabethan and Jacobean Quartoes 14. Ed. G. B. Harrison. Edinburgh: Edinburgh University Press, 1966.

———. *Delia.* London, 1592.

———. *A Panegyrike with a Defence of Ryme.* London, 1603.

Dee, John. *The Mathematicall Praeface to the Elements of Geometrie of Euclid of Megara* (1570). Ed. Allen G. Debus. New York: Science History Publications, 1975.

Della Casa, Giovanni. *Opere di Monsignore Giovanni Della Casa.* 4 vols. Ed. Carlo Maria Carlieri. Venice: Angiolo Pasinello, 1728–29.

Della Seta, Fabrizio. "Proportio." In *Cantu et Sermone: For Nino Pirrotta on His 80th Birthday,* ed. Fabrizio Della Seta and Franco Piperino, 75–99. Florence: Olschki, 1985.

Demetrius. *On Style.* Trans. W. Hamilton Fyfe. Cambridge, Mass.: Harvard University Press; London: Heinemann, 1927.

De Sanctis, Francesco. *History of Italian Literature.* 2 vols. Trans. Joan Redfern. New York: Harcourt, Brace, and Company, 1931.

Dettmer, Helena. *Love by the Numbers: Form and Meaning in the Poetry of Catullus.* Lang Classical Studies, ed. Daniel H. Garrison, vol. 10. New York: Peter Lang, 1997.

Doherty, Mary Jane. *The Mistress-Knowledge: Sir Philip Sidney's "Defence of Poesie" and Literary Architectonics in the English Renaissance.* Nashville, Tenn.: Vanderbilt University Press, 1991.

Emilio, Paolo. "Tasso e la seconda pratica." In *Tasso, la musica, i musicisti,* ed. Maria Antonella Balsano and Thomas Walker, 1–15. Florence: Olschki, 1988.

Eriksen, Roy. " 'Un Certo Amoroso Martire': Shakespeare's 'The Phoenix and the Turtle' and Bruno's *De gli eroici furori,* " ed. Patrick Cullen and Thomas P. Roche Jr. *Spenser Studies: A Renaissance Poetry Annual* 2 (1981): 193–216.

———. "Desire and Design: Vasari, Michelangelo, and the Birth of Baroque." In *Contexts of Baroque: Theatre, Metamorphosis, and Design,* ed. Roy Eriksen, 52–78. Oslo: Novus Press, 1997.

——. *The Forme of Faustus Fortunes: A Study of "The Tragedie of Doctor Faustus" (1616)*. Atlantic Highlands, N.J.: Humanities Press, 1987.

——. "God Enthroned: Continuity and Change in Ariosto, Tasso, and Milton." In *Milton in Italy: Contexts, Images, Contradictions*, ed. Mario A. di Cesare, 405–25. Binghamton, N.Y. MRTS, 1991.

——. "The Lineaments of Influence: Alberti and the Elizabethans." In *Cultural Exchange Between European Nations in the Renaissance*, ed. Gunnar Sorelius and Michael Srigley, 43–59. Stockholm: Almquist and Wicksell, 1994.

——. "Posta in musica: Tasso's *Paragone* and Monteverdi's *Combattimento.*" In *EST X: Stil og Maniera. Grunnlagsproblemer i estetisk forskning*, ed. K. Gundersen and S. Wikshåland, 83–108. Oslo, 1994.

——. "Spenser's Mannerist Manoeuvres: *Prothalamion* (1595)." *Studies in Philology* 90 (Spring 1993): 143–75.

——. "Two into One: The Unity of Gascoigne's Companion Poems." *Studies in Philology* 81 (Summer 1984): 275–99.

——. " 'What resting place is this?': Time and Place in *Dr. Faustus* (B)." *Renaissance Drama* 16 (1985): 49–74.

Fairfax, Edward. *Jerusalem Delivered (1600)*. Ed. Robert Weiss. New York: Centaur Press, 1962.

Fichter, Andrew. *Poets Historical: Dynastic Epic in the Renaissance*. New Haven and London: Yale University Press, 1982.

——. "Tasso's Epic of Deliverance." *PMLA* 93 (March 1978): 265–74.

Fowler, Alastair. *Conceitful Thought: The Interpretation of English Renaissance Poems*. Edinburgh: Edinburgh University Press, 1975.

——. *Triumphal Forms: Structural Patterns in Elizabethan Poetry*. Cambridge: Cambridge University Press, 1970.

Frédéric, Madeleine. *La répétition. Etude linguistique et rhétorique*. Tübingen: Max Niemeyer Verlag, 1985.

French, Peter J. *John Dee: The World of an Elizabethan Magus*. London: Routledge and Kegan Paul, 1972.

Gallo, Ernest. *The Poetria Nova and Its Sources in Early Rhetorical Doctrine*. The Hague and Paris: Mouton, 1971.

Gascoigne, George. "Certaine notes concerning the making of uerse in English." In *Elizabethan Critical Essays*, ed. G. Gregory Smith, 1:46–57. Oxford: Oxford University Press, 1904.

——. *A Hundred Sundry Flowers*. London, 1573.

Getto, Giovanni. *Nel Mondo della Gerusalemme*. Florence: Olschki, 1967.

Giazotto, Remo. "Pianto e poesia del Tasso in Morte di Maria Gesualdo." In *Musurgia Nova*, ed. Remo Giazotto, 157–67. Milan: Ricordi, 1959.

——. *Torquato Tasso tra letteratura, musica, teatro e arti figurative*. Ed. A. Buzzoni. Bologna: Nuova Alfa Editoriale, 1985.

Gilbert, Creighton E. "Antique Frameworks for Renaissance Art Theory: Alberti and Pino." *Marsyas* 3 (1943–45): 87–106.

Gollanz, Sir Israel, ed. *Pearl, Cleanness, Patience, and Sir Gawain: Reproduced in Facsimile from the Unique MS. Cotton Nero A.x in the British Museum*, Early English Text Society, old series, 162. New York: Oxford University Press, 1923.

Grayson, Cecil, ed. *Leon Battista Alberti: On Painting*. Harmondsworth: Penguin, 1972.

————. "Leon Battista and Italian Grammar." In *Art and Politics in Renaissance Italy*, ed. George Holmes. Oxford: Clarendon Press, 1993.

Grendler, Paul. *Schooling in Renaissance Italy: Literacy and Learning, 1300–1600*. Baltimore: Johns Hopkins University Press, 1989.

Harington, John, trans. *Orlando Furioso in English Heroical Verse* (1591). The English Experience 259. New York and Amsterdam: Da Capo Press, 1972.

Heinsius, Daniel, *Aristotelis "De Poetica" liber*. Leiden, 1611.

Heninger, S. K., Jr. *Sidney and Spenser: The Poet as Maker*. University Park: The Pennsylvania State University Press, 1989.

————. *The Subtext of Form in the English Renaissance: Proportion Poetical*. University Park: The Pennsylvania State University Press, 1994.

————. *Touches of Sweet Harmony: Pythagorean Cosmology and Renaissance Poetics*. San Marino, Calif.: Huntington Library, 1974.

Hermogenes. *Ars oratoria absolutissima*. Ed. G. Laurentius. Cologne, 1612.

Hieatt, Kent A. *Short Time's Endless Monument: The Symbolism of the Numbers in Edmund Spenser's "Epithalamion."* New York: Columbia University Press, 1960.

Holland, Louise Adams. *Janus and the Bridge*. American Academy in Rome Papers and Monographs 21. Rome: American Academy in Rome, 1961.

Hollingsworth, Mary. "The Architect in Fifteenth-Century Florence." *Art History* 7 (1984): 385–410.

Hope, Charles. "The Early History of the Tempio Malatestiano." *Journal of the Warburg and Courtauld Institutes* 55 (1992): 51–154.

Hurst, André. *Apollonius de Rhodes. Manière e cohérence*. Biblioteca Helvetica Romana, vol. 8. Rome: Swiss Academy, 1967.

Hutson, Lorna. "History Plays and Humanists' Arts of War: Calculation and the Character Effect." Manuscript.

————. *Thomas Nashe in Context*. New York: Oxford University Press, 1989.

Jakobson, Roman, and Lawrence G. Jones. *Shakespeare's Verbal Art in "The Expense of Spirit in a Waste of Shame."* The Hague: Mouton, 1972.

Jasper, David. *The New Testament and the Literary Imagination*. London: Macmillan, 1987.

Johnson, Anthony W. *Ben Jonson: Poetry and Architecture*. Oxford: Clarendon Press, 1994.

Jonson, Ben. *Poems*. Ed. Ian Donaldson. New York: Oxford University Press, 1975.

————. *Timber; or, Discoveries*. Syracuse, N.Y.: Syracuse University Press, 1976.

Jordan, Elisabeth. "Inigo Jones: The Architecture of Poetry." *Renaissance Quarterly* 54 (Summer 1991): 280–319.

Kates, Judith A. *Tasso and Milton: The Problem of Christian Epic*. Lewisburg, Pa.: Bucknell University Press; London: Associated University Presses, 1983.

Keaney, John J. "Ring Composition in Aristotle's *Athenaion Politeia*." *American Journal of Philology* 90, no. 4 (1969): 406–23.

Kennedy, George A. "Aristotle on the Period." *Harvard Studies on Classical Philology* 63 (1958): 283–88.

Kermode, Frank. *The Sense of an Ending: Studies in Theory of Fiction*. 1966. Reprint, New York and Oxford: Oxford University Press, 1977.

Kidson, Peter, Peter Murray, and Paul Thompson. *A History of English Architecture*. 1962. Reprint, Harmondsworth: Penguin, 1979.

References

Kinney, Arthur. *Humanist Poetics: Thought, Rhetoric, and Fiction in Sixteenth-Century England.* Amherst, Mass.: University of Massachusetts Press, 1986.

Kipp, David. "Alberti's 'Hidden' Theory of Visual Art." *British Journal of Aesthetics* 24 (Summer 1984): 231–40.

Kliemann, Julian. *Gesta dipinte. La grande decorazione nelle dimore italiane dal Quattrocento al Seicento.* Milan: Silvana Editoriale, 1993.

Kruft, Hanno-Walter. *A History of Architectural Theory from Vitruvius to the Present.* Princeton, N.J.: Princeton Architectural Press, 1994.

Landino, Cristoforo, ed. "Che cosa sia poesia et poeta et della origine sua divina et antichissma" ("What constitutes poetry and a poet, and on the most divine and ancient origin of the poet") *La divina commedia.* 1481; Venetia: Marchiò Sessa et fratelli, 1564.

Lang, S. "De Lineamentis: L. B. Alberti's Use of a Technical Term." *Journal of the Warburg and Courtauld Institutes* 28 (1965): 331–35.

Lausberg, Heinrich. *Handbuch der Literarischen Rhetorik. Eine Grundlegung der Litteraturwissenschaft.* 2 vols. Munich: Hueber, 1973.

La Via, Stefano. "Le Combat retrouvé. Les 'passions contraires' du 'divin Tasse' dans la représentation musicale de Monteverdi." In *La Jérusalem délivrée du Tasse. Poésie, peinture, musique, ballet,* ed. Giovanni Careri, 109–57. Paris: Musée de Louvre, 1999).

Lazzaro, Claudia. *The Italian Renaissance Garden: From the Conventions of Planting, Design, and Ornament to the Grand Gardens of Sixteenth-Century Central Italy.* New Haven and London: Yale University Press, 1990.

LeCoat, Gerard. *The Rhetoric of the Arts, 1550–1650.* Bern and Frankfurt: Lang, 1975.

Le Mollé, Roland. *George Vasari et la vocabulaire de la critique d'art dans les "Vite."* Grenoble: Elug, 1988.

———. "Significato di LUCE e di LUME nelle VITE del Vasari." In *Il Vasari storiografo e artista,* ed. Mario Salmi et al. Florence: Istituto nazionale degli studi, 1976.

Mace, Dean T. "Tasso, *La Gerusalemme liberata,* and Monteverdi." In *Music and Language,* 118–56. Studies in the History of Music, vol. 1. New York: Broude Brothers, 1983.

Macrobius, Ambrosius Thedosius. *Ambrosii Theodosii Macrobii . . . Opera.* Ed. Isach Pontanii et al. Leipzig Batavorum, 1670.

Malmanger, Magne. "Between Renaissance and Baroque: Attitudes to Nature and the Concept of Nature." In *Contexts of Baroque: Theatre, Metamorphosis, and Design,* ed. Roy Eriksen, 26–51. Oslo: Novus Press, 1997.

Maniates, Maria Rika. *Mannerism in Italian Music and Culture, 1530–1630.* Manchester: Manchester University Press, 1979.

Mazzolini, Marco. "Tasso e Gesualdo ovvero del suono dei pensieri." *Studi Tassiani* 38 (1990): 7–40.

Melchiori, Giorgio. *Shakespeare's Dramatic Meditations: An Experiment in Criticism.* New York: Oxford University Press, 1976.

Milton, John. *Paradise Lost.* Ed. Alastair Fowler. London: Longman Group, 1976.

Mirollo, James. *Mannerism and Renaissance Poetry: Concept, Mode, Inner Design.* New Haven and London: Yale University Press, 1984.

Monteverdi, Claudio. *Madrigali guerrieri ed amorosi VIII.* Ed. F. Malipiero. Milan: Treves, 1929.

————. *Quinto libro de madrigali.* Venice: Amadino, 1606.

————. *Il Quinto libro de' Madrigali.* Ed. F. Malipiero. Milan: Treves, 1929.

Moses, Gavriel. "Tasso to Monteverdi: Intertextual Poetics." In *Studies in the Italian Renaissance: Essays in Memory of Arnolfo B. Ferruolo,* ed. Gian Paolo Biasin, Albert N. Mancini, and Nicholas J. Perella, 245–59. Naples: Società editrice napoletana, 1986.

Mulder, John R. *The Temple of the Mind: Education and Literary Taste in Seventeenth-Century England.* New York: Pegasus, 1969.

Murley, Clyde. "The Structure and Proportion of Catullus LXIV." *Transactions of the American Philological Association* 68 (1937): 305–17.

Nashe, Thomas. *The Unfortunate Traveller.* Harmondsworth: Penguin, 1972.

Nosow, Robert. "Le proporzioni temporali in due mess e di Dufay. *Se la face ay pale e Ecce ancilla Domini."* *Rivista italiana di musicologia* 28 (1993): 13–24.

Onians, John. "Alberti and Filarete." *Journal of the Warburg and Courtauld Institutes* 35 (1971): 97–114.

————. *Bearers of Meaning: The Classical Orders in Antiquity, the Middle Ages, and the Renaissance.* Princeton: Princeton University Press, 1988.

————. "On How to Listen to High Renaissance Art." *Art Bulletin* 7, no. 4 (1984): 411–37.

Otis, Brooks. *Ovid as an Epic Poet.* Cambridge: Cambridge University Press, 1966.

————. *Virgil: A Study of Civilized Poetry.* Oxford: Clarendon, 1964.

Ovidius, Naso. *Fasti.* Ed. James George Frazer. Cambridge, Mass.: Harvard University Press; London: Heinemann, 1967.

Palme, Per. "Ut Architectura Poesis." In *Idea and Form: Studies in the History of Art [to Gregor Paulsson],* ed. Nils Gösta Sandblad, 95–107. Figura n.s. Stockholm: Almquist and Wicksell, 1959.

Panofsky, Erwin. "Die Perspektive als 'Symbolische Form.' " In *Vorträge der Bibliothek Warburg, 1924–25,* ed. Fritz Saxl, 258–330. Leipzig: Teubner, 1927.

Patterson, Annabel M. *Hermogenes and the Renaissance: The Seven Ideas of Style.* Princeton: Princeton University Press, 1972.

Payne, Alina. *The Architectural Treatise in the Italian Renaissance: Architectural Invention, Ornament, and Literary Culture.* New York: Cambridge University Press, 1999.

Perelli, Antonella. "La 'divina' Clorinda." *Studi Tassiani* 39 (1991): 45–76.

Petrarca, Francesco. *Il Canzoniere.* Ed. Mario Marcazzan. Basiano: Bietti, 1966.

Pirotta, Nino. "Scelte poetiche di Monteverdi." *Nuova Rivista Musicale Italiana* 2, no. 1 (1968), 10–42.

Plato. *Commentary on Plato's Symposium.* Trans. S. R. Jayne. Columbia: University of Missouri, 1944.

————. *Timaeus.* Trans. R. G. Bury. 1929. Reprint, London: Heinemann, 1966.

Poulton, Diana. *John Dowland.* Berkeley and Los Angeles: University of California Press, 1982.

Prandi, Stefano. "Fortuna parallela del Tasso e Del Casa." *Studi Tassiani* 39 (1991): 119–23.

Praz, Mario. *Mnemosyne: The Parallel Between Literature and the Visual Arts.* Princeton: Princeton University Press, 1970.

Propertius, Sextus. *Select Elegies.* Ed. J. P. Postgate. London: Macmillan, 1962.

Puttenham, George. *The Arte of English Poesie* (1589). Ed. Gladys D. Willcock and Alice Walker. Cambridge: Cambridge University Press, 1970.

Quarnström, Gunnar. *The Enchanted Palace: Some Structural Aspects of "Paradise Lost."* Stockholm: Almquist and Wickell, 1967.

Quintilian. *Institutio oratoria.* Trans. H. E. Butler. 4 vols. London: Heinemann, 1963.

Rastelli, Dario. "Tasso e Monteverdi: Il Combattimento di Tancredi e Clorinda." In *Monteverdi e il suo tempo,* ed. Raffaello Monterosso, 557–69. Verona: Valdonega, 1969.

Rhu, Lawrence. *The Genesis of Tasso's Narrative Theory.* Detroit: Wayne State University Press, 1993.

Riccò, Laura. *Vasari scrittore. La prima edizione del libro delle "Vite."* Rome: Bulzoni editore, 1979.

Richardson, L., Jr. "Catullus 67: Interpretation and Form." *AJP* 88 (1967): 423–33.

Ricks, Christopher. *Milton's Grand Style.* New York: Oxford University Press, 1972.

Ricoeur, Paul. *Time and Narrative.* Trans. Kathleen McLaughlin and David Pellauer. Chicago: University of Chicago Press, 1984.

Riffaterre, Michael. "Describing Poetic Structures: Two Approaches to Baudelaire's 'Les Chats.'" In *Structuralism,* ed. Jacques Ehrmann. Garden City, N.Y.: Doubleday, 1970.

Robortello, Francesco, ed. *In librum Aristotelis de arte poetica explicationes.* Florence, 1548.

Ronga, Luigi. "Tasso e Monteverdi." In *Arte e gusto della musica dall' "Ars Nova" a Debussy,* ed. Luigi Ronga, 19–32. Milan and Naples: Ricciardi, 1956.

Rose, Mark. *Shakespearean Design.* Cambridge, Mass.: Harvard University Press, 1972.

Røstvig, Maren-Sofie. "Canto Structure in Tasso and Spenser." *Spenser Studies: A Renaissance Poetry Annual* 1 (1980): 177–200.

———. *Configurations: A Topomorphical Approach to Renaissance Poetry.* Oslo: Scandinavian University Press, 1994.

———. "The Hidden Sense." In *The Hidden Sense and Other Essays,* 3–112. Oslo: Oslo University Press, 1963.

———. "The Topomorphical Approach." In *The Spenser Encyclopedia,* ed. A. C. Hamilton et al. Toronto: Toronto University Press; London: Routledge, 1990.

———. "The Shepheardes Calender: A Structural Analysis." *Renaissance and Modern Studies* 13 (1969): 49–75.

———. "A Frame of Words. On the Craftsmanship of Samuel Daniel," *English Studies* 60 (1979): 122–37.

Rowland, Ingrid D. *The Culture of the High Renaissance: Ancients and Moderns in Sixteenty-Century Rome.* Cambridge: Cambridge University Press, 1998.

———. "Raphael, Angelo Colocci, and the Genesis of the Architectural Orders." *Art Bulletin* 76 (March 1994): 81–104.

Rubin, Patricia Lee. *Giorgio Vasari: Art and History.* New Haven and London: Yale University Press, 1995.

———. "'What Men Saw': Vasari's Life of Leonardo da Vinci and the Image of the Renaissance Artist." *Art History,* 13, no. 1 (1990): 34–46.

Ruscelli, Girolamo. *Del modo di comporre in versi nella lingua italiana* (1558). Venice, Occhi, 1815.

Sandhaug, Christina. "The Poetics of the Sidney Circle." Master's thesis, University of Tromsø, 1999.

Satowski, L. *Giorgio Vasari: Architect and Courtier.* Princeton: Princeton University Press, 1994.

Scaglione, Aldo. *The Theory of Composition.* Chapel Hill: University of North Carolina Press, 1972.

Scaliger, Julius Caesar. *Poetices libri septem.* Ed. August Buck. 1561. Reprint, Stuttgart and Bad Cannstatt: Friederich Frommann Verlag, 1964.

Scamozzi, Vincenzo. *L'Idea dell'architettura universale.* Venice: Lavtore, 1615.

Schiaffini, Alfredo. "Poesis e poeta in Dante." In *Studia philologica et literaria in honorem Leo Spitzer.* Bern: Francke, 1958.

Shakespeare, William. *The Second Part of King Henry the Fourth.* Ed. Mathias A. Schaaber. New Variorum. Philadelphia: J. B. Lippincott, 1940.

Shearman, John. *Mannerism.* Harmondsworth: Penguin, 1966.

Shute, John. *The First and Chief Groundes of Architecture.* Ed. Laurence Weaver. London: Country Life, 1912.

Sidney, Sir Philip. *An Apology for Poetry.* Ed. Geoffrey Shepherd. 1965. Reprint, Manchester: Manchester University Press, 1973.

Smith, Christine. *Architecture in the Culture of Early Humanism: Ethics, Aesthetics, and Eloquence, 1400–1470.* New York: Oxford University Press, 1992.

———. "Leon Battista Alberti e l'ornamento: rivestimenti parietali e pavimentazioni." In *Leon Battista Alberti,* ed. Joseph Rykwert and Robert Tavernor, 196–215. Milan: Electa, 1994.

Soellner, Rolf. *Shakespeare's Patterns of Self-Recognition.* Columbus: Ohio University Press, 1972.

Sozzi, B. T. "Introduzione ai Discorsi dell'arte poetica del Tasso." *Studi Tassiani* 26 (1977): 5–38.

———. "La poetica del Tasso." *Studi Tassiani* 5 (1955): 3–58.

Steadman, John. *Epic and Tragic Structure in Paradise Lost.* Chicago: University of Chicago Press, 1976.

Summers, David. *Michelangelo and the Language of Art.* Princeton: Princeton University Press, 1981.

Summerson, John. *The Classical Language of Architecture.* 1963. Reprint, London: Thames and Hudson, 1991.

Tasso, Torquato. *Il Carrafà o vero de la epica poesia.* Vol. 3 of *Trattati di poetica e di retorica del 500,* ed. Bernard Weinberg, 309–44. Bari: Laterza, 1970–72.

———. *La Cavaletta ovvero della poesia toscana.* Ed. Bruno Maier. In *Opere.* 5 vols. Milano: Rizzoli, 1963–65.

———. *Discorsi.* Ed. Francesco Flora. Bari: Laterza, 1960.

———. *Discourses on the Heroic Poem.* Trans. Mariella Cavalchini and Irene Samuel. New York: Oxford University Press, 1973.

———. *La Gerusalemme liberata.* Ed. Lanfranco Caretti. Torino: Giulio Einaudi, 1971.

———. "Lezione del Signor Torquato Tasso. Sopra il Sonetto LIX, 'Questa vita mortal, ch'n una, o'n due, ec.' di M. Giovanni Della Casa." In *Opere di Monsignor Giovanni Della Casa.* Venice: Angiolo Pasinello, 1728–29.

———. *Poesie.* Ed. Francesco Flora. Milan: Unione Tipografico Editore Torinese, 1952.

———. *Prose.* Ed. Francesco Flora. Milan and Rome: Rizzoli, 1935.

Thirsk, Joan. *Economic Policy and Projects.* Oxford: Clarendon Press, 1978.

Tobin, Richard. "Leon Battista Alberti: Ancient Sources and Structure in the *Treatises on Art.*" Ph.D. diss., Bryn Mawr College, 1979.

Varchi, Benedetto. "Lettura di Messer Benedetto Varchi Sopra il Sonetto della Gelosia di Monsignor Dalla Casa" (1545). In vol. 1 of *Opere di Monsignore Giovanni Della Casa,* 318–38.

———. "Lezione sul sonetto 'Non ha l'ottimo artista alcun concetto.' " In vol. 2 of *Scritti d'arte del cinquecento,* ed. Paola Barocchi, 1322–41. Milan and Naples: Ricciardi, 1960.

Varese, Claudio. *Torquato Tasso: Epos, Parola, Scena.* Messina and Florence: G. D'Anna, 1976.

Vasari, Giorgio. *Lives of the Most Eminent Painters, Sculptors, and Architects.* Trans. Gaston Duc de Vere and ed. Kenneth Clark. New York: Harry N. Abrams, 1987.

———. *Vita di Michelangelo.* Ed. Licia e Carlo L. Ragghianti. Milan and Rome: Rizzoli, 1978.

———. *La Vita di Michelangelo nelle redazioni del 1550 e 1568.* Paola Barocchi. Milan and Naples: Ricciardi, 1962.

———. *Le vite de' più eccellenti pittori, scultori et architettori.* 2 vols. Florence: Giunti, 1568.

———. *Le Vite de' più eccellenti pittori, scultori e architettori nelle redazioni del 1550 e 1568.* Ed. Rosanna Bettanni with commentary by Paula Barocchi. Florence: Sansoni, 1966–84. Florence: Studio per edizioni scelte, 1987.

———. *Le vite de' più eccellenti pittori, scultori et architettori scritte da Giorgio Vasari pittore aretino con nuove annotazioni e commenti.* 9 vols. Ed. G. Milanesi. Florence: Sansoni, 1878–85.

———. *Le vite de' più eccellenti pittori, scultori et architetti, pittori, et scultori italiani, da Cimabue insino a' tempi nostri nell'edizione per i tipi di Lorenzo Torrentino Firenze 1550.* Ed. L. Bellosi and A. Rossi. Turin: Einaudi, 1986.

Vida (Vives), Luis. *D. Augustini . . . De Civitate Dei libri XXII.* Basileae, 1570.

Vittorini, Pietro. *Commentarii in tres libros Aristotelis de arte dicendi.* Florence, 1579.

Weinberg, B., ed. *Trattati di poetica e retorica del Cinquecento.* Bari: Laterza, 1970–72.

Wind, Edgar. *Pagan Mysteries in the Renaissance.* Harmondsworth: Penguin, 1966.

Wise, T. P. *Cinna the Poet and Other Roman Essays.* Leicester: Leicester University Press, 1974.

Wittkower, Rudolf. *Architecture in the Age of Humanism.* 1949. Reprint, London: Academy Editions, 1988.

Worthington, Ian. *A Historical Commentary on Dinarchus: Rhetoric and Conspiracy in Later Fourth-Century Athens.* Chicago: University of Chicago Press, 1992.

Wotton, Henry. *The Elements of Architecture.* London: John Bill, 1624.

Zander, C. M. *Versus Italici antiqui.* Lund, 1880.

Zuccari, Federico. *L'Idea de' pittori, scultori e architetti.* Rome, 1607.

Page numbers in *italics* refer to illustrations.